$ 29-95

VISUAL BASIC® FOR MS-DOS®

Ramon Zamora
Don Inman
Bob Albrecht

P T R Prentice Hall
Englewood Cliffs, New Jersey 07632

Library of Congress Cataloging-in-Publication Data

Zamora, Ramon.
Visual basic for MS-DOS / Ramon Zamora, Don Inman, Bob Albrecht.
p. cm.
Includes index.
ISBN 0-13-948662-3
1. BASIC (Computer program language) 2. Microsoft Visual Basic for MS-DOS. I. Inman, Don. II. Albrecht, Bob.
III. Title.
QA76.73.B3Z36 1993
005.26'2—dc20 93-4524
CIP

Editorial/production supervision and interior design: *Northeastern Graphic Services, Inc.*
Cover design: *Lundgren Graphics, Ltd.*
Buyer: *Mary Elizabeth McCartney*
Acquisitions editor: *Paul W. Becker*

A Simon & Schuster Company
Englewood Cliffs, New Jersey 07632

The publisher offers discounts on this book when ordered in bulk quantities. For more information, contact:

Corporate Sales Department
PTR Prentice Hall
113 Sylvan Avenue
Englewood Cliffs, NJ 07632

Phone: 201-592-2863
Fax: 201-592-2249

Printed in the United States of America
10 9 8 7 6 5 4 3 2 1

ISBN 0-13-948662-3

Prentice-Hall International (UK) Limited, *London*
Prentice-Hall of Australia Pty., Limited, *Sydney*
Prentice-Hall Canada Inc., *Toronto*
Prentice-Hall Hispanoamericana, S.A., *Mexico*
Prentice-Hall of India Private Limited, *New Delhi*
Prentice-Hall of Japan, Inc., *Tokyo*
Simon & Schuster Asia Pte., Ltd., *Singapore*
Editora Prentice-Hall do Brasil, Ltda., *Rio de Janeiro*

Contents

Preface

This book provides hands-on experience with a powerful new programming language, *Visual Basic for MS-DOS*. If you are interested in learning how to build visually appealing computer applications that run in the Microsoft Disk Operating System (DOS) environment, this book is for you. This book's explicit, step-by-step tutorial style shows you how to successfully design and implement your first Visual Basic for MS-DOS programs.

If you have no prior programming experience, you can still use this book. Each Visual Basic application is described in detail, and every line of required program code is listed and explained. The book's many screen images show you exactly what to look for as you work your way through the interesting example applications. If you already know something about programming in a Basic language, you will discover that this book is the perfect introduction to the key features of Visual Basic. In no time, you will master the example programs and move on to design and build your own applications.

With the introduction of Microsoft Windows in 1985, computer users have been looking for simple programming tools that create Graphical User Interface (GUI) applications on IBM and compatible computers. Visual Basic for MS-DOS is a new development language that lets a general computer user create fully functional GUI applications. In addition, Visual Basic has been designed so that the code you write on MS-DOS computers can be easily moved to the Windows environment.

With this book and a copy of Visual Basic for MS-DOS, you will be creating professional-looking programs immediately. Visual Basic lets you draw the components of a program's user interface on the screen directly. These objects, which you draw and arrange into the user interface, are called control objects. Visual Basic control objects are preprogrammed to automatically detect and respond to a number of predefined, user-triggered events, such as the click of a mouse. To complete a Visual Basic application, you only have to write simple blocks of code that you assign to the program's visual control objects. The result is sophisticated-looking, GUI-style programs that require only a minimum amount of code to make them work.

Languages like Visual Basic for MS-DOS and for Visual Basic for Windows open the doors to an entirely new world of computer adventures, for beginners and professionals alike. These powerful languages let you quickly turn your ideas for products, games, and applications into on-screen realities—programs that you create and can change to meet your needs. This book, with its interesting examples and applications, is an ideal companion for your first experiences with a visual programming language such as Visual Basic for MS-DOS.

Trademark Acknowledgments

The following are trademarks of Microsoft Corporation:

Microsoft QBasic
Microsoft QuickBasic
Microsoft Windows
Microsoft Windows logo
Microsoft Excel
Microsoft Visual Basic for MS-DOS
Microsoft Visual Basic for Windows

1 Introduction to Visual Basic for MS-DOS

Since the introduction of Microsoft Windows in 1985, there has been a growing need for powerful programming tools to create Graphical User Interface (GUI) applications on IBM and compatible computers. Visual Basic for MS-DOS is a new development tool that lets a general computer user create fully functional GUI applications.

Microsoft Corporation designed this latest version of Visual Basic to work on MS-DOS, the operating system standard on the majority of today's personal computers. In developing the language, Microsoft made sure that applications created on the MS-DOS platform could be easily moved to Windows. The result: Visual Basic for MS-DOS is a unique event-oriented computer language that greatly simplifies the development of GUI applications running in both MS-DOS and Windows environments.

Visual Basic for MS-DOS comes in two versions. The Standard Edition, targeted for the general computer user, provides a full set of design and programming tools to help you build functional, personal applications. The Professional Edition, targeted for developers, provides additional tools for the product developer who wants to build and distribute full-featured programs. All of the example applications in this book can be designed, created, and run using the Standard Edition of Visual Basic for MS-DOS.

What Is Visual Basic?

Visual Basic is an event-oriented language, as contrasted with many of today's object-oriented programming (OOP) languages. In Visual Basic, each type of GUI object can respond to a predefined set of events. Procedures written in Visual Basic are fundamentally responses to the set of events that can be triggered by the program's user.

Visual Basic's designers have carefully positioned this visual language as a bridge product between today's structured languages and future OOP-like implementations. Its event-orientation paves the way for users with some programming experience to eventually become comfortable with upcoming OOP products. Visual Basic, as developed for both MS-DOS and

Windows platforms, seems positioned to become the middle stone of a planned evolution towards more sophisticated OOP environments.

Who Is This Book For?

This book focuses on the beginning to intermediate Visual Basic user. In this book, you will explore and learn to use the key features of this new language in fun and entertaining ways. When you complete this book, you will be ready to move on to more sophisticated programming projects.

Visual Basic's simplified event handling structures make it easy for you to utilize any experience you might have with other computer languages, such as QuickBasic and QBasic. In very little time, you will be creating Visual Basic applications, complete with GUI elements and features.

Readers with no prior programming experience can still use this book. This book's hands-on tutorials lead you through simple, step-by-step activities that show you how to design and build each example application. Numerous screen images support and amplify the tutorial materials. This book does not attempt to cover all of the features of Visual Basic for MS-DOS. The goal of this book is to help you learn Visual Basic's key features while you also learn to design and develop your first set of GUI applications.

What Is In This Book?

This book contains 12 chapters and a set of appendices. Chapter 1, this introductory chapter, provides you with an overview of Visual Basic for MS-DOS, and tells you how this book is organized. This chapter also introduces you to a few concepts and fundamentals of Visual Basic as you begin to use the language.

Chapter 2 provides you with an introduction to key Visual Basic tools and concepts. In this chapter, you learn to specify and create your first, simple Visual Basic application. You learn to place control objects on the Visual Basic form and to adjust the properties of the control objects and the form. You create your first event procedures and learn how to attach those event procedures to the control objects that you created. You conclude this chapter by running the application and saving the program to disk.

At the beginning of Chapters 2 through 12, you will find a reference table of key concepts and terminology, QuickBasic and QBasic keywords, new

Visual Basic keywords, and the names of event procedures developed within each of the chapters. Table entries also list the page numbers where the items are first introduced within each chapter.

In Chapter 3, you continue with an in-depth exploration of key Visual Basic elements that deal with event-oriented programming. You learn to use command buttons, the code window, and develop several customized event procedures. A complete hands-on tutorial introduces you to objects, events, and the further development of event procedures. You build a unique customized flash card application that could help someone study Japanese or another subject.

Chapter 4 walks you through a modification of the application developed in Chapter 3. You add features to the application, extend the code, and are encouraged to continue to add your own enhancements to the application. In the process of modifying the application for this chapter, you also explore some of Visual Basic's debugging tools and features.

Chapter 5 shows you how to build a custom calculation application and an application that can be used as a game. The calculation application shows you how to capture a user's input, perform calculations, and display results on a Visual Basic form. The game application explores some of the event-oriented features of Visual Basic as applied to the dynamic placement and movement of controls while an application is running.

Chapters 6 and 7 build upon the elements of Visual Basic covered in the first five chapters to develop a single, more complex application. In Chapter 6, you develop the framework of a Chemistry application that utilizes multiple forms, extensive data tables, and control arrays. The application development continues in Chapter 7, where you add a third form and additional data tables. By the time you complete the activities in these two chapters, you will have a firm grasp of how to use Visual Basic in more complex applications.

One powerful feature of Visual Basic involves its ability to create and display graphics. In Chapter 8, you explore Visual Basic's graphics capabilities. You learn to call up displays of colorful graphics images by using control objects on a Visual Basic form. In this chapter, you also explore Visual Basic's sound and music features.

Chapter 9 discusses the use of files within Visual Basic. You modify an earlier application that used large data tables so that the data are read from files. You also examine one of Visual Basic's toolkits that help you start to build your own set of file handling tools.

In Chapter 10, you modify an earlier application by adding menu controls to the application. You learn how to create and install Visual Basic menu control objects on a form and how to activate those objects with your own event procedures.

Error handling within Visual Basic relies on a simple set of built-in error control features. Chapter 11 explains how Visual Basic supports your development of error handling event procedures that detect and identify runtime error conditions.

Chapter 12 displays example application screens for a set of four suggested projects that you might pursue. This final chapter also outlines the additional features and capabilities found in the Visual Basic Professional Edition.

Finally, you will find a set of helpful appendices. These appendices provide information regarding MS-DOS/Windows compatibility issues, listings of Visual Basic keywords used in this book, identification of all applications and event procedures found in this book, and other useful information and resources.

Getting Started with Visual Basic

To use Visual Basic for MS-DOS, you must install the Visual Basic program and its files on your hard disk. The Visual Basic installation process is fully automated and simple to do. To install the program, locate the set of disks that are in your Visual Basic package. When you have the disks in hand, do the following:

1. Boot up your computer, and do what you need to do to get to the DOS prompt for the root directory on your hard disk (`C:\>`).
2. When you are at the root directory prompt (`C:\>`), put the disk labeled "Disk 1 - Setup" in drive A.
3. Type the following to start the installation procedure:

   Type `a: setup` and press **Enter.**
4. Follow the instructions that appear on the screen. Unless you have reason to do otherwise, accept the default options presented by the installation procedure.

When the installation completes, Visual Basic for MS-DOS will be installed in the directory `C:\VBDOS` on your hard disk. To let your system know where the Visual Basic program files are located, run the `NEW-VARS.BAT` file that has been installed in the VBDOS directory. This batch file updates your system PATH, INCLUDE, and LIB environment variables. If you need more information about MS-DOS environment variables, refer to your MS-DOS documentation.

Run Visual Basic

If you have run the `NEW-VARS.BAT` file, you can now run the Visual Basic program by typing the following at the DOS prompt (`C:\>`):

Type `vbdos` and press **Enter.**

If you have not run `NEW-VARS.BAT` to update the MS-DOS environment variables, you can still run Visual Basic by switching to the VBDOS directory, typing `vbdos`, and pressing **Enter.** If you are using the MS-DOS shell program, you can also run Visual Basic directly from the shell. Simply locate the `VBDOS.EXE` file in the VBDOS directory, and select and run that file.

The Visual Basic Programming Environment

When you run Visual Basic, the first screen you see looks like the one shown in Figure 1-1.

This section of the product is the Visual Basic *programming environment.* In this environment, you write the code and create the event procedures

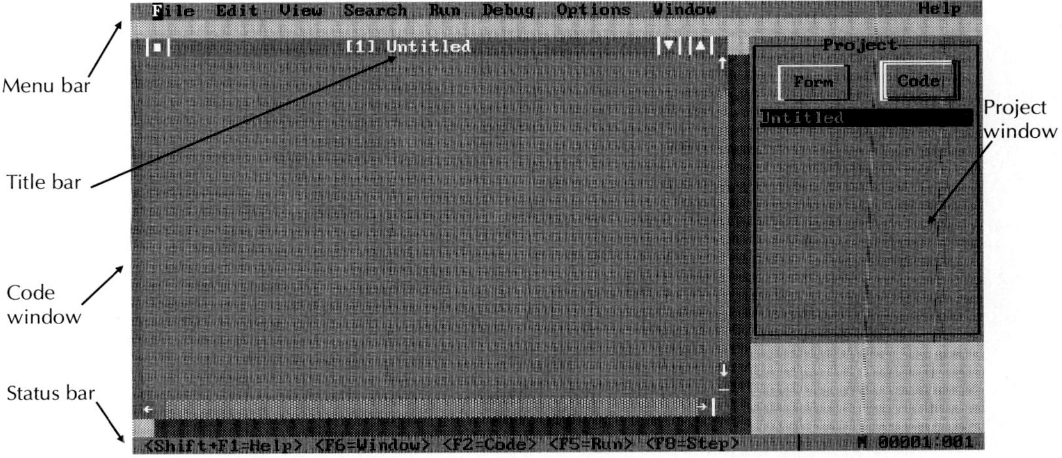

Figure 1-1 Visual Basic Programming Environment

that make your applications perform their specified tasks. The key parts of the programming environment include:

- The *Menu bar,* which appears across the top of the screen. This bar lists the available set of menus for this environment. You activate menu commands by pulling down a menu on this bar and choosing one of the commands that appear. If you are using a mouse, clicking an item on the bar pulls down that item's menu. If you do not have a mouse, you pull down menus by first pressing the **Alt** key to tell Visual Basic you want to use the Menu bar. You then press the highlighted letter of the menu item you want to use. The menu will pull down and display its list of commands.

> ☑ For the activities in this book, the authors have made the assumption that your computer has an attached pointing device, such as a mouse. In general, no keyboard-equivalent instructions have been included. All of the activities in this book can be performed from the keyboard, but you will find everything easier to do with a mouse. If you do not have a mouse, you are encouraged to either purchase one or borrow one from a friend while you are learning about Visual Basic.

- The *Code window,* which is the large rectangular area on the left side of the screen. There can be more than one Code window open at any time. Each Code window provides a space for creating, displaying, and editing portions of the application code.
- The *Title bar,* which goes across the top center of a Code window. The Title bar displays the window number (1) and the name of the code module (Untitled). For the active Code window, a control box appears on the left side of the window Title bar, while minimize and maximize buttons appear on the right side. The active Code window also displays scroll bars along the right and bottom window edges.
- The *Status bar,* which is the bar across the bottom of the screen. The Status bar displays shortcut keys and helpful information about the current window or command. This bar also shows the current line and column numbers of the cursor position.
- The *Project window,* which is the smaller rectangular area on the right side of the screen. This window provides a listing of the names of all

forms and code modules that go to make up an application. When you start Visual Basic, you automatically start a new project. The initial project file, `Untitled`, is listed in the Project window. This file name matches the name that appears in the Title bar of the Code window. The Project window has two command buttons: **Form** and **Code.** When active, the **Form** button can be used to display the Form dialog box, which, in turn, lets you edit forms. The **Code** button displays the **Code** dialog box, which lets you view and edit project code modules.

The Visual Basic Help Features

An important item on the Menu bar is the Help menu. If you pull down that menu, you will see a collection of Help commands and features to assist you as you use Visual Basic for MS-DOS. The Help features include:

- An alphabetized index of all the help topics in the product
- A table of contents that lets you branch to specific help topics and discussions
- A keyboard guide that summarizes help topics for keyboard-equivalent commands throughout the product
- Specific help information for any item that you have selected on the screen
- Help information on how to use the help system
- A visual, interactive tutorial that can help you learn how to use the Visual Basic system

You can use the Help features at any time, within any part of the product.

The Visual Basic Form Designer

The second major domain within Visual Basic is shown in Figure 1-2. This section of the product is called the *Form Designer.* You use the Visual Basic Form Designer to design and customize the forms for your applications. Using the Form Designer, you can add a variety of control objects to

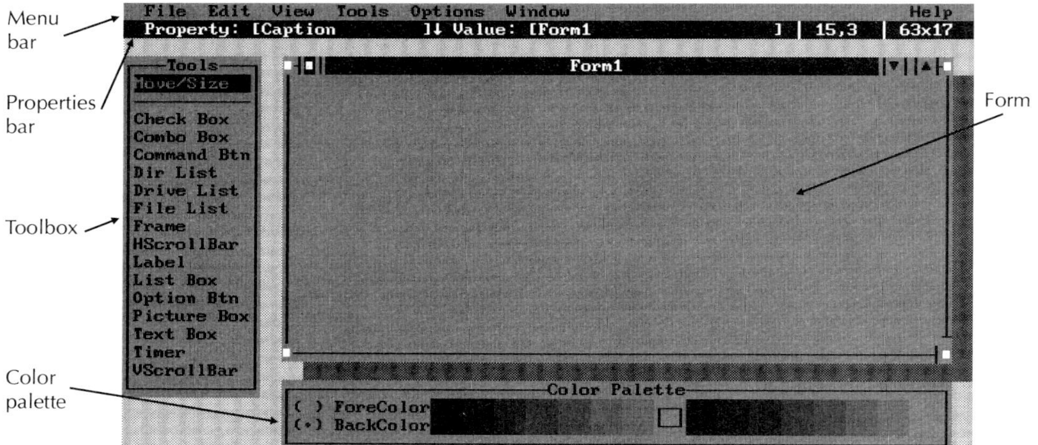

Figure 1-2 Visual Basic Form Designer

any form, and modify those objects to fit the needs of your application. The key features of the Form Designer include:

- The *Menu bar,* which appears across the top of the screen. This bar lists the set of menus items that are available within this environment.
- The *Properties bar,* which appears immediately below the Menu bar. This bar displays and lets you modify the properties of a form or control object. Clicking the downward-pointing arrow on the bar causes a pull-down menu of properties to appear.
- The *Toolbox,* which appears as a rectangular list of tool names on the left side of the screen. When you click a tool name in the Toolbox, you cause that control object to appear on the form. The tool names in the Toolbox can also be accessed from the Tools menu on the Menu bar.
- The *Form,* which is the large window on the right that covers most of the screen. This window and the control objects you place upon it, appear as part of your application's user interface.
- The *Color Palette,* which is the colorful rectangular box along the bottom of the screen. You use this palette to set the foreground and background colors of forms and control objects. The current color selection is marked with a black box.

Get Ready...Get Set...Go!

This brief introduction to Visual Basic for MS-DOS sets the stage for your to begin your explorations using this exciting language. If you have Visual Basic up and running, you can proceed to the next chapter, where you will learn to design and build your first Visual Basic application. As you work your way through this book, enjoy your many adventures with Visual Basic for MS-DOS.

2 Building Visual Basic Applications

At the beginning of each chapter is a list of concepts and terminology, QBasic/QuickBasic keywords, new Visual Basic keywords, and application event procedures that can be found in that chapter. The number in parentheses indicates the page in the chapter where a topic or item first appears.

A Visual Basic program, called an *application,* is a collection of visual elements and code that you design, test, and run to perform specific tasks. A Visual Basic application's visual elements include such items as forms, controls, and special objects (the Clipboard, the Printer, and the Screen). All Visual Basic visual elements are *objects.*

Concepts and Terminology

QBasic/QuickBasic Keywords

New Visual Basic Keywords

Visual Basic Event Procedures

Figure 2-1 shows an example of a Visual Basic application screen that you will build in this chapter. The screen displays three objects: the form or window used in this application, and two command buttons that you will place on the form.

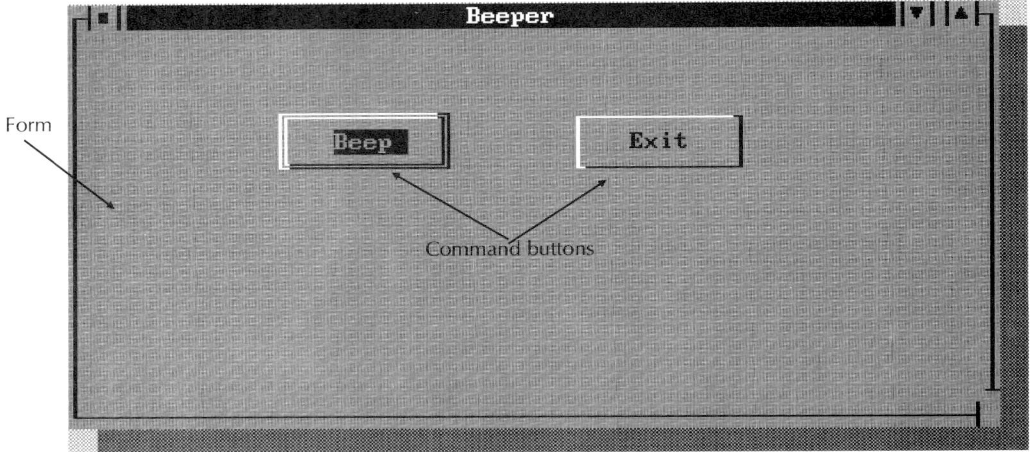

Figure 2-1 Structure of a Visual Basic application.

Objects and Event Procedures

In Visual Basic, objects communicate with each other (and with the system) by detecting and responding to events. *Events* are actions triggered by either the user or the system. Each Visual Basic object has a predefined set of events that it can recognize and to which it can possibly respond.

If you want an object to respond to an event (a mouse click, a key press, or a system action), you write a set of instructions to the computer, called an *event procedure,* and attach or associate that block of code to the object. When the object detects an event for which it has a defined event procedure, it invokes the procedure and performs the actions you have specified.

Figure 2-2 depicts what might happen when the user triggers an event (mouse click) that is detected by a control object (command button). In this case, the command button is assumed to have an attached event procedure that determines its response to the user's action. If the command button did not have this event procedure, the event would be detected but no response would occur.

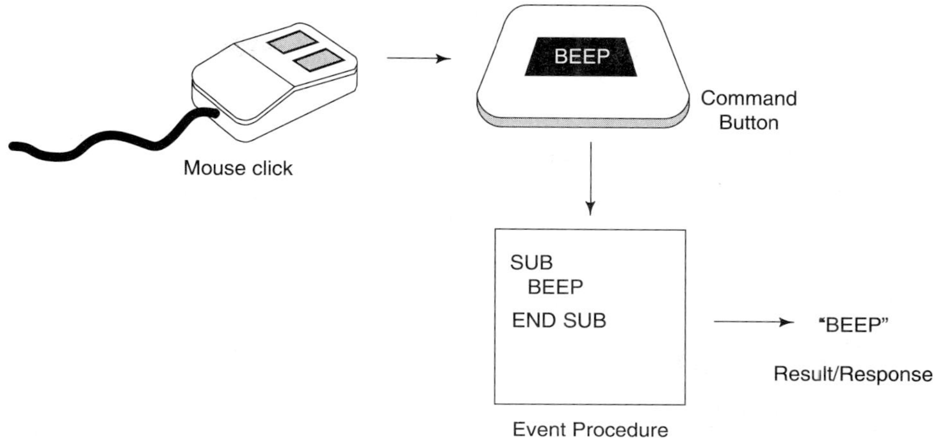

Figure 2-2 Example event/object interaction.

Forms and Controls

Forms and controls are the two key objects used to build Visual Basic applications. Forms are the visual containers for an application's controls. They become the base objects upon which you build an application's interface. Forms can appear on the screen in one of two ways—as a window or as a dialog box. Figure 2-3 shows examples of a Visual Basic form window and a Visual Basic dialog box.

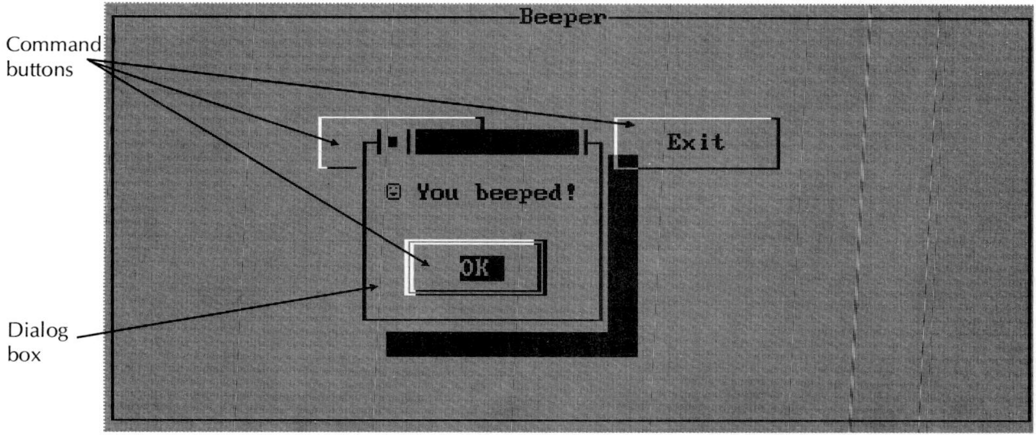

Figure 2-3 Form window and dialog box.

Controls are the objects you place on a form (buttons, scroll bars, menus, and list, option, text, and picture boxes) that determine what an application's interface looks like to the user. Visual Basic contains 16 unique types of control objects. You place controls on forms and attach event procedures to these controls, to create responses to events triggered by the user and the system. In Figure 2-3, you see several examples of Visual Basic controls as they appear on the form window and the dialog box.

Properties and Methods

Forms, controls, and other objects can appear and behave in a variety of ways. In Visual Basic, the appearance and behavior of forms, controls, and other objects can be determined by setting a group of characteristics called *properties*. Properties can determine the name of an object, its size, position, and color, and how it responds to particular events. Each object in Visual Basic possesses a group of properties that you can set and control.

In Visual Basic, objects are bundles of data and code that determine what the object can do and how it responds to events. Properties are one part of an object's data set. Another component of an object's set of data is the set of events to which it can respond.

An object's code elements includes event procedures that you write and preprogrammed code components called *methods*. An object uses the built-in methods to manipulate internal data sets, detect events, search for attached event procedures, and perform actions on the object itself. As with properties, each Visual Basic object has a set of methods that you can call upon in your Visual Basic applications.

Basic Modules

When building applications, you may discover the need for a code module that is not explicitly event-driven and that should not be attached to a particular object. Such a block of code is called a *Basic module*.

As an example, you might be numerically converting sets of input x-y coordinate values that the user types into text box locations on each of several forms. The fact that the user might be activating these conversions from one or more forms does not impact the calculation results. In this situation, the block of code that calculates the conversion results could be placed into a Basic module. Then each object that requires the conversion code can call upon the Basic module when needed.

You will learn more about the use of Basic modules later in this book. For now, just know that Visual Basic provides you with the ability to create and use both event procedures and generalized Basic modules within any application.

Summary of Terms and Concepts

Up to this point, several key Visual Basic terms and concepts have been introduced. The terms and concepts that have been discussed are as follows:

Application. A Visual Basic program. The collection of visual elements and code designed to perform a specific task.

Object. All the Visual Basic visual elements. Includes forms, controls, and special objects, such as the Clipboard, the Screen, and the Printer.

Event. Actions triggered by the user or the system. An event can be a keypress, a mouse click, or an action by the system.

Event procedure. A set of instructions to the computer that are attached to an object. When an object detects an event, the attached event procedure determines what actions the object performs.

Form. The visual containers for an application's controls. A form can appear as either a window or as a dialog box.

Controls. The objects placed on a form that determine what an application's interface looks like to the user. Visual Basic has 16 types of control objects you can place on a form and to which you can attach event procedures.

Properties. The characteristics of an object that determine its name, size, position, color, and how the object responds to events. You can set and control the properties of each Visual Basic object.

Method. Preprogrammed code components that an object uses to manipulate internal data sets, detect events, search for attached event procedures, and perform actions on the object itself. Each Visual Basic object has a set of methods that you can call upon in your Visual Basic applications.

Basic module. A code module that is not event driven and that is not attached to a particular object.

Projects

The complete collection of files that Visual Basic uses to generate an application is called a *project.* A Visual Basic project provides an organizational structure for all the different types of files you produce as you build, run, and test an application.

Table 2-1 shows the various types of project files that can appear during the development of a Visual Basic application. In your initial explorations of the Visual Basic system, you will focus on form modules. Later, as you create executable versions of your Visual Basic applications, you will learn about the other types of Visual Basic project files. For now, simply be aware that Visual Basic uses the concept of a project as a way to help you organize the files you generate as you create a Visual Basic application.

Table 2-1 Visual Basic Project File Types

File Type	Extension
Form	.FRM
Code	.BAS
Library	.LIB
Project	.MAK
Executable	.EXE
Include	.BI
Quick library	.QLB
Text	.TXT

Steps in Building an Application

Using the Visual Basic system, you can build, run, and test an application by following this suggested eight-step process:

1. **Start Visual Basic.** When you start Visual Basic, the program automatically creates a new project. This Visual Basic project becomes the container and organizer of the files you produce as you design and develop your application.

2. **Create a new form.** Visual Basic forms are the visual containers for any controls you plan to use. Each form you develop becomes a building block in the application's user interface.

3. **Place controls on the form.** The types of controls you use and the arrangement of those controls define the ways in which the user will interact with the application. In effect, the selected controls determine the application's user interface.

4. **Set the property characteristics for all defined objects.** Property settings can be used to alter the appearance and behavior of forms, controls, and other special objects.

5. **Write and attach code to the defined objects.** Using the Visual Basic system, create event procedures for each object/event situation that will require a response or action from the program.

6. **Save the project.** Save the project files you have created before running and testing the application.

7. **Run and test the application.** Run the application, and verify that the event procedures and the user interface respond as expected. Identify discrepancies and alter event procedures or the interface to correct problems.

8. **Create a stand-alone version.** After you verify that the program runs as designed and planned (Step 7), you can create a stand-alone or executable version of the application. Visual Basic contains utility programs that assist you with this task.

You will use some of these steps in the next section as you create and test your first Visual Basic application—Beeper.

A Beeper Application

Start Visual Basic on your computer system. When you start Visual Basic, you see the opening screen shown in Figure 2-4. This screen shows you several elements of Visual Basic's *programming environment*. The key parts of the programming environment include:

- **The Menu bar.** Appears across the top of the screen. Lists the available set of menus items for this environment.

- **The Code window.** The large rectangular area on the left side of the screen. Provides a space for creating, displaying, and editing application code.

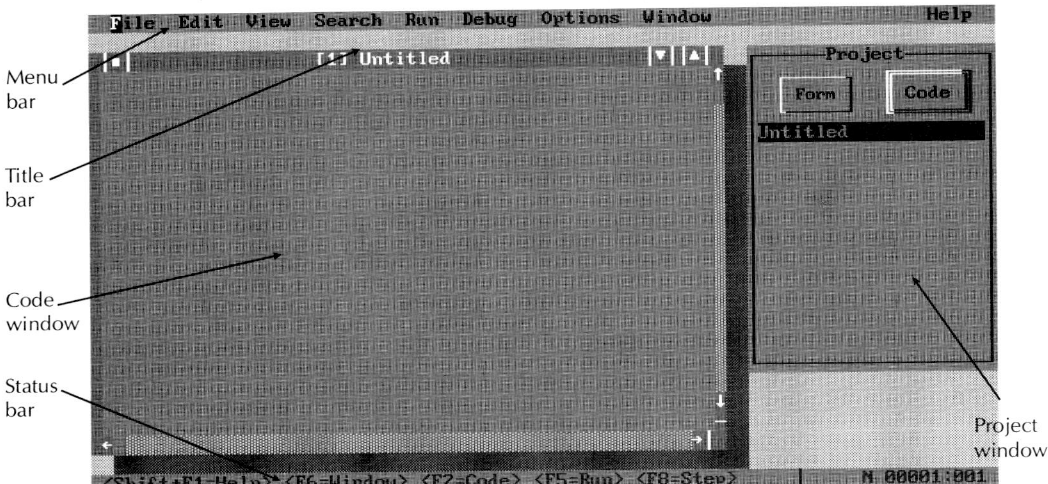

Figure 2-4 Visual Basic programming environment.

- **The Title bar.** The bar across the top center of the Code window. Displays the window number (1) and name of the code module (Untitled). There can be more than one Code window displayed at the same time.
- **The Status bar.** The bar across the bottom of the screen. Displays shortcut keys and helpful information about the current window or command. Also shows the current line and column numbers of the cursor position.
- **The Project window.** Rectangular area on the right side of the screen. Provides a listing of the names of all forms and code modules that go to make up an application. When you start Visual Basic, you automatically start a new project. The initial project file, `Untitled`, is listed in the Project window. This file name matches the name that appears in the Title bar of the Code window. The Project window has two command buttons: **Form** and **Code.** When active, the **Form** button can be used to display the **Form** dialog box, which, in turn, lets you edit forms. The **Code** button displays the **Code** dialog box, which lets you view and edit project code modules.

The Visual Basic Form Designer

To create the Beeper application, you will first use the Visual Basic *Form Designer*. To get to the Form Designer from the programming environment, do the following:

Choose the **New Form** command on the File menu.

Figure 2-5 shows the open File menu with the **New Form** command selected.

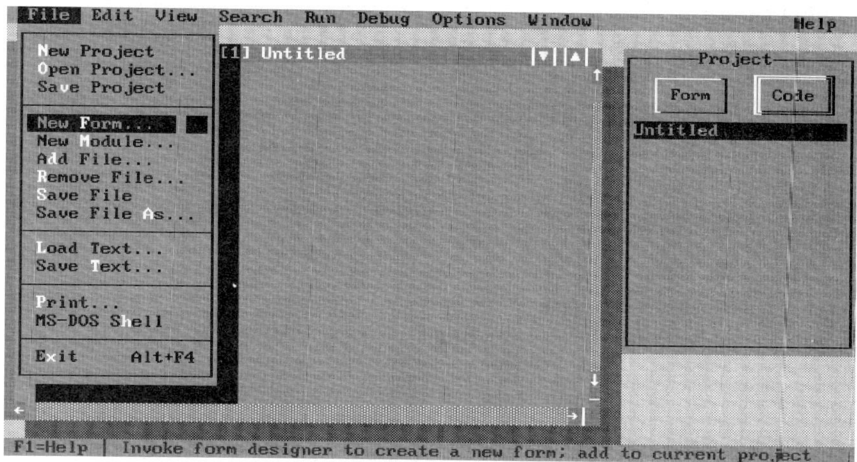

Figure 2-5 File menu with New Form command selected.

After you choose the **New Form** command, the **New Form** dialog box (Figure 2-6) appears. A default form name, `FORM1.FRM`, appears in the **File Name** text box.

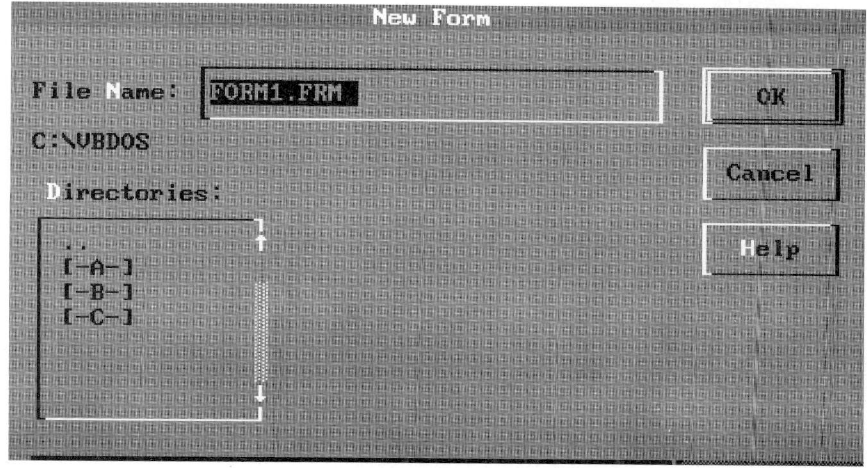

Figure 2-6 New Form dialog box.

In this dialog box, you enter the file name for the new form and specify the disk drive and directory where the file is to be saved. For every example in this book, we are assuming that all project files are being saved onto a formatted diskette in Drive A.

> ✔ Because of the way in which we started Visual Basic, our dialog box shows the current path name to be `C:\VBDOS`. On our system, this subdirectory contains Visual Basic system files and programs. In general, it is not a good idea to save Visual Basic project files in this subdirectory. Instead, either save your files to a formatted diskette or into a separate subdirectory that you create on your hard disk.

Figure 2-7 shows the **New Form** dialog box with the path and file name `A:BEEPER` entered into the **File Name** text box.

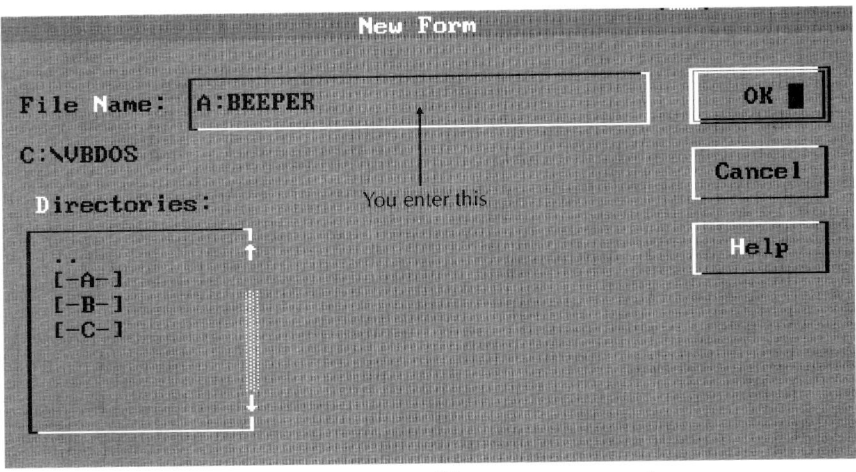

Figure 2-7 Path and New Form file name entered.

On your system, enter the following path and file name into the **New Form** dialog box:

Type `A:BEEPER`

Then do the following:

Click the **OK** button.

If there is a blank, formatted diskette in Drive A, the **New Form** dialog box disappears and you see the Visual Basic Form Designer on the screen (Figure 2-8). If you do not have a diskette in Drive A, Visual Basic will display a dialog box indicating that there is a problem.

> ☑ Based on your system's resources and capabilities, it may take anywhere from a few to several seconds before you see the Visual Basic Form Designer screen. Older, less powerful computers require more time to switch from the programming environment to the Form Designer.

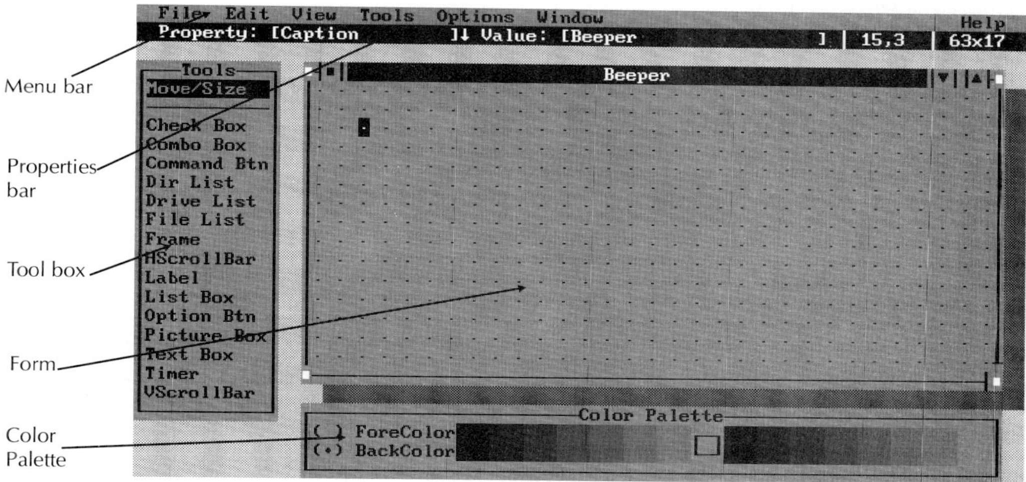

Figure 2-8 The Visual Basic Form Designer.

The key features of the Visual Basic Form Designer include:

- **The Menu bar.** Appears across the top of the screen. This bar lists the set of menus items that are available within this environment.
- **The Properties bar.** Appears immediately below the Menu bar. This bar displays and lets you modify the properties of a form or control object. Clicking the downward-pointing arrow on the bar causes a pull-down menu of properties to appear.
- **The Toolbox.** Appears as a rectangular list of tool names on the left side of the screen. When you click a tool name in the Toolbox, you

cause that control object to appear on the form. The tool names in the Toolbox can also be accessed from the Tools menu on the Menu bar.

- **The Form.** The large window on the right that covers most of the screen. This window and the control objects you place upon it appear as part of your application's user interface.
- **The Color Palette.** The colorful rectangular box along the bottom of the screen. You use this palette to set the foreground and background colors of forms and control objects. The current color selection is marked with a black box.

The form being displayed is labeled `Beeper`, the file name you entered in the **New Form** dialog box. No matter how you enter the file name, Visual Basic displays the name with an initial capital letter and the remaining letters in lowercase. You are now almost ready to use the Toolbox to draw controls on the form called `Beeper`.

Beeper Specification

Before you begin to use the Toolbox, review the following *specifications* for the Beeper application. The specifications outline the number and names of any forms to be designed, as well as the number, names, and types of controls to be used. The specifications also describe the triggering events and responses that must be coded into each control's event procedures.

Specification #2-1 (Form)

Beeper Application

Form	Event(s) to be detected	Response(s)
Beeper	None	None
Properties:	Default settings	

Notes/Comments: None

This application uses a single form (Beeper) and two command buttons (**Command1, Command2**). When the user clicks the **Command1 (Beep)**

Specification #2-1 (Command Buttons)

Beeper Application

Controls	Event(s) to be detected		Response(s)
Command1	Click		Make "beep" sound
Properties:	Location	13,3	
	Caption	`Beep`	
Command2	Click		Exit application
Properties:	Location	33,3	
	Caption	`Exit`	

Notes/Comments: None

button, the program should respond by making a "beep" sound. When the user clicks the **Command2 (Exit)** button, the program should exit the application. If the user clicks the form, nothing happens. The form will not respond to events.

The Properties values indicate object characteristics that you will be setting as you design and build the application.

Adding Controls to the Form

The Visual Basic Toolbox lists 15 of the 16 types of control objects that can be placed on a form. Table 2-2 provides a brief description of these 15 controls.

Table 2-2. Visual Basic Toolbox controls

Control Object Name	Function
Check box	Toggles the selection of an on and off (true/false, yes/no) option
Combo box	Allows a user to enter text or select from a list
Command button	Performs a specified action when chosen by the user
Directory list box	Enables the selection of a directory path

Table 2-2. Visual Basic Toolbox controls (*continued*)

Control Object Name	Function
Drive list box	Enables the selection of a disk drive
File list box	Enables the selection of file(s)
Frame	Provides a visual/functional way to group controls
Horizontal scroll bar	Displays position within a range of values; provides a visual way to navigate through a long list; has a horizontal orientation
Label	Displays text that the user cannot alter
List box	Allows the user to select from a list
Option button	Permits the selection of one item in a group of options
Picture box	Displays multiple text lines on a form; can also be used as a visual container for other controls
Text box	Provides an area for input or displayed text that can be edited
Timer	Specifies a time interval for timer events
Vertical scroll bar	Displays position within a range of values; provides a visual way to navigate through a long list; has a vertical orientation

> ☑ The sixteenth type of control object, Menu controls, are accessed by choosing the **Menu Design Window** command on the Window menu of the Form Designer. Choosing this command lets you design and specify a menu bar and menu commands that will appear as part of your application's interface. You will examine this type of control object later in this book.

For the Beeper application, you need two command buttons. To put the first command button on the form, do the following:

1. Move the mouse pointer to the command button (labeled `Command Btn`) tool in the Toolbox.
2. Double-click the left mouse button.

A command button, labeled `Command1`, appears in the center of the form (Figure 2-9). This control is surrounded by a *selection rectangle* with small rectangular boxes, called *sizing handles*, at each corner. You can use the sizing handles to alter the size of a control.

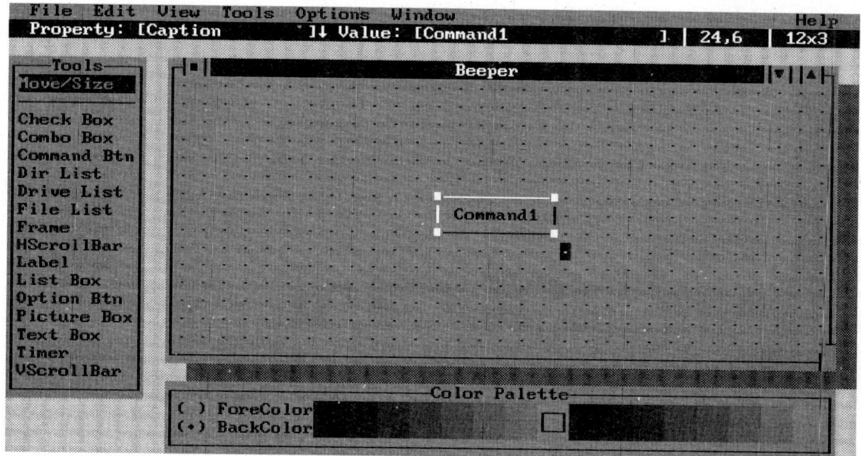

Figure 2-9 First command button on the form.

☑ If your form does not have the grid lines shown in Figure 2-9, toggle the grid on as follows:

Choose the **Grid Lines** command on the View menu.

Now move the button from the center of the screen to the upper left corner of the form, as follows:

1. Move the pointer to the **Command1** button.
2. Click the left mouse button and hold it down. The selection rectangle surrounding the button will highlight as long as you hold down the mouse button.
3. With the selection rectangle highlighted, move the mouse and drag the highlight up and to the left, into the upper left corner of the form.
4. When you have moved the highlight to the upper left corner of the form, release the mouse button. The **Command1** button now appears at the new location (Figure 2-10).

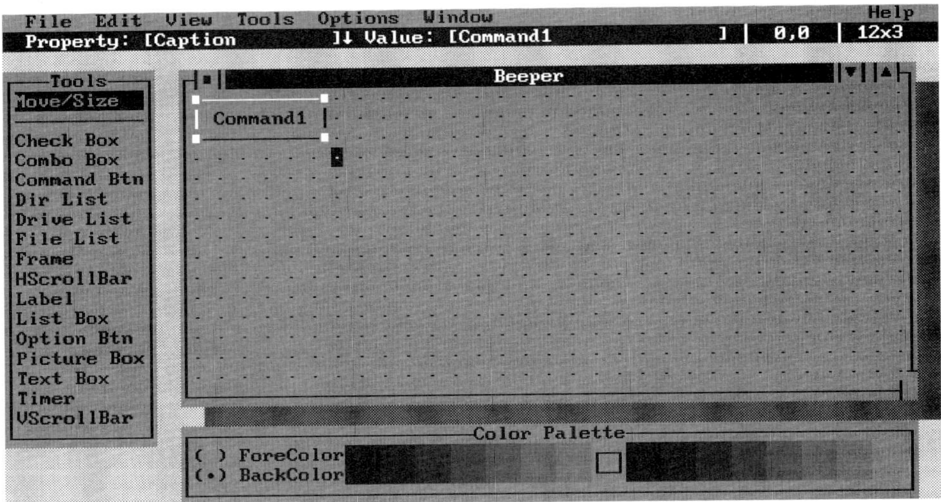

Figure 2-10 Command1 in upper left corner of the form.

Look at the Properties bar (the bar just below the Menu bar), as shown in Figure 2-11. This bar has four elements: a **Property** list box, a **Value** list box, a **Location** box, and a **Size** box.

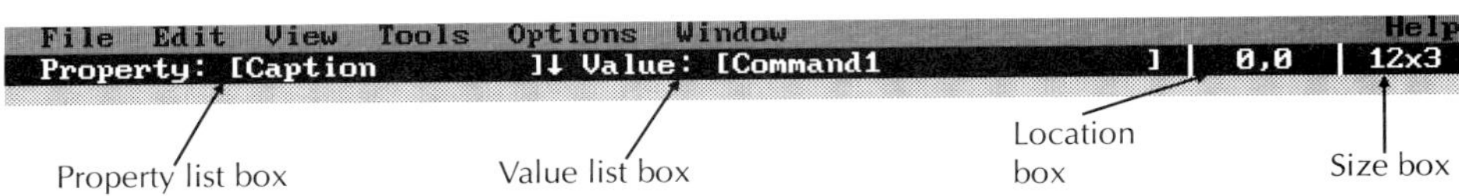

Figure 2-11 The Properties bar.

The **Location** and **Size** boxes provide information about the currently selected object. If **Command1** is still selected, the **Location** box displays the coordinates of the upper left corner of the button (0,0). The position 0,0 also represents the upper left corner of the form. The **Size** box indicates that **Command1** is 12 characters wide and 3 lines high (12×3).

Select and move the button to the upper right corner of the form. Figure 2-12 shows **Command1** moved into this position.

The **Location** box indicates that the upper left corner of **Command1** is at location 49,0. The corner of the button lies halfway between two grid points. There is space for two characters between any two horizontal grid points; each grid point is at the center of a character position.

Move **Command1** to the bottom right corner of the form. Figure 2-13 shows the form with **Command1** at that position.

Figure 2-12 Command1 in upper right corner of the form.

The **Location** box indicates that the upper right corner of the button is at position 49,12. Two vertical grid points mark off one line space on the form. Again, grid points are centered on character positions, forcing the top and bottom of each line to fall halfway between grid point locations.

Move **Command1** to the bottom left corner of the form. When you do so, your screen will look like Figure 2-14.

When **Command1** is in the bottom left corner of the form, the **Location** box shows the button to be at location 0,12.

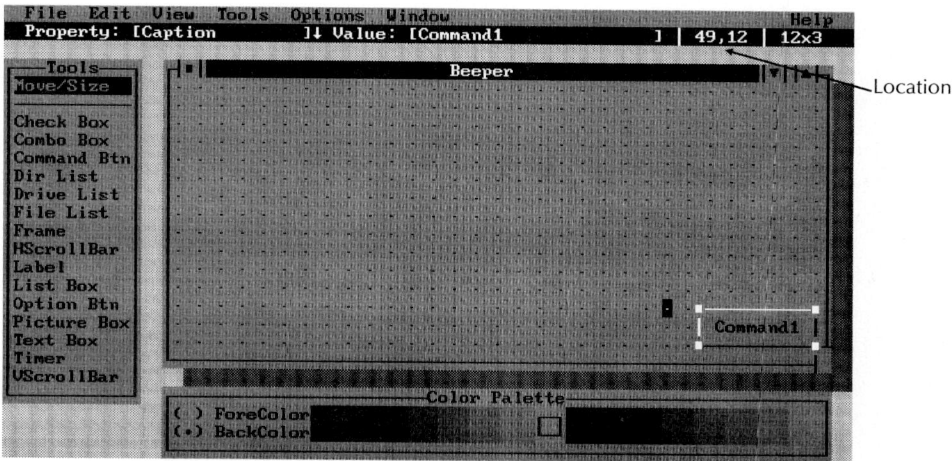

Figure 2-13 Command1 in bottom right corner of the form.

Figure 2-14 Command1 in bottom left corner of the form.

> ✔ As you move the highlight that represents a control object, notice that the Location box only updates when you release the mouse button. You may need to move an object several times to position it at an exact location on the form.

Select and move the button once again. Place the **Command1** button so that the **Location** box indicates that the upper left corner of the button is at location 13,3. This places the upper left button corner 14 characters in from the form's left edge, and 4 lines down from the form's Title bar. Figure 2-15 shows the **Command1** button at location 13,3.

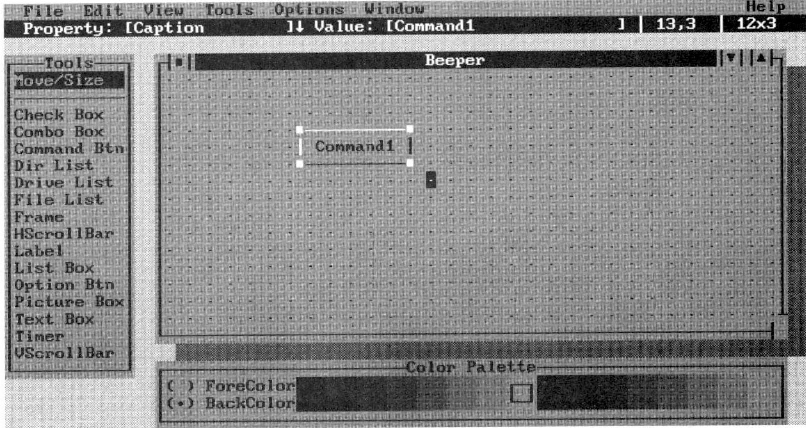

Figure 2-15 Command1 at location 13,3.

Adding a Second Control

To put the second command button on the form, do the following:

1. Move the mouse pointer to the command button (labeled `Command Btn`) tool in the Toolbox.
2. Double-click the left mouse button.

A second command button, labeled `Command2`, appears in the center of the form. Now move **Command2** up and to the right so that its upper left corner is located at position 33,3. Figure 2-16 shows the Beeper form with both command buttons in their final locations.

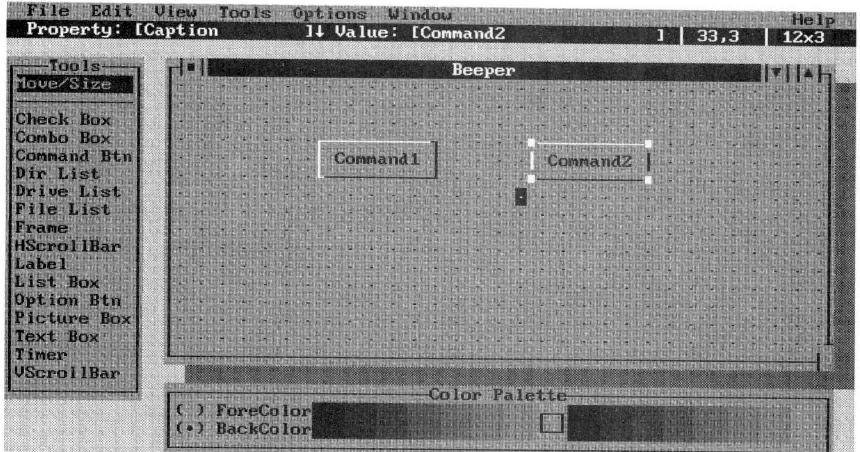

Figure 2-16 Form with both command buttons.

> ☑ To remove a control from a form, select the control and then press the **Delete** key. The selected control will disappear. Try it!
>
> 1. Move the mouse pointer to the command button (labeled `Command Btn`) tool in the Toolbox.
> 2. Double-click the left mouse button.
>
> A third command button, labeled `Command3`, appears in the center of the form (Figure 2-17).
>
> To remove this unwanted button, select it (click it) and then press the **Delete** key. The object will disappear. You can also remove a selected object by choosing the **Delete** command on the Edit menu.

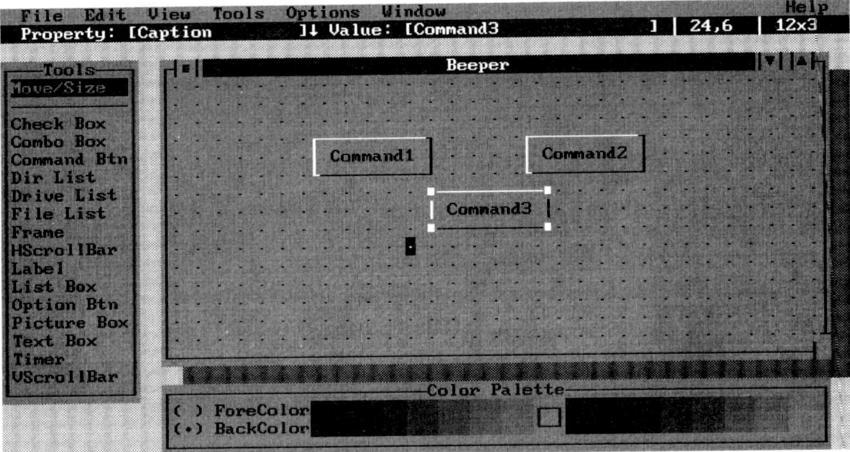

Figure 2-17 Form with unwanted command button.

Setting Properties

You can fine-tune the appearance and behavior of Visual Basic objects by using the **Property** and **Value** list boxes on the Properties bar (Figure 2-18). Every Visual Basic object has an attached set of property values that can be altered by using the Property bar. Visual Basic supports over 60 different properties, where each property applies to a specific set of objects. These properties let you fully customize your Visual Basic applications, and you can control and set these properties dynamically, while your programs are running.

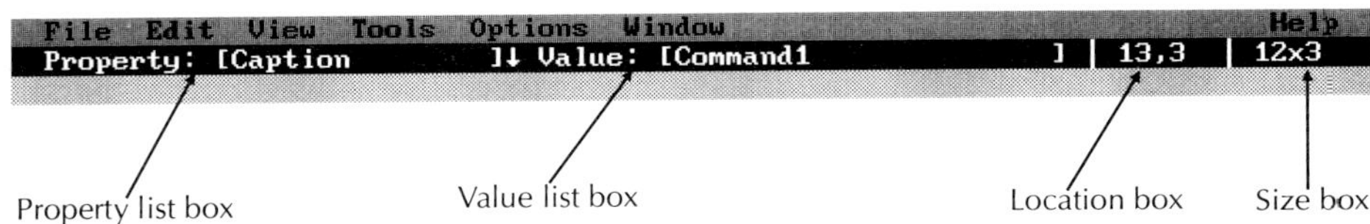

Figure 2-18 The Properties bar.

Follow along and use the Properties bar to change the caption (the displayed label) of the **Command1** button. Suppose you want **Command1** to be the button that when clicked, produces the "beep" sound. To make a better association between this button's function and its caption, change the caption as follows:

1. Click the **Command1** button to select it. A selection rectangle surrounds the button, and the value for the **Caption** property, `Command1`, shows in the **Value** list box area of the Properties bar (Figure 2-19).

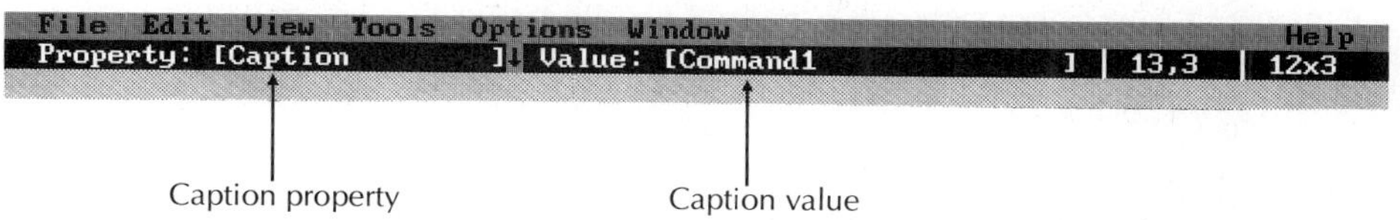

Figure 2-19 The Caption property.

> ✔ If the **Caption** property is not showing on the Properties bar, move the pointer to the down arrow icon that is at the right end of the **Property** list box region (the arrow that is to the left of the label `Value:`). Click this down arrow to display the list of properties for the selected object. Drag the highlight up or down the list until the Caption property is highlighted. When you release the mouse button with the Caption property highlighted, the **Property** list box changes to Caption; the **Value** list box displays the current caption for the selected object.
>
> Figure 2-20 shows the Properties bar with the contents of the **Property** list box displayed. You display this list by clicking the down arrow icon at the right end of the **Property** list box region on the Properties bar. When the **Value** list box has more than one value, a second down arrow icon appears at the right end of the **Value** list box region (to the left of the **Size** box).

2. With the **Command1** button selected and the caption value showing, select the caption value (`Command1`) in the **Value** list box. You select the caption value by clicking and dragging the pointer across the contents of the **Value** list box. When you perform this action, you see `Command1` highlighted on the Properties bar (Figure 2-21).

3. With the current caption value (`Command1`) highlighted, enter a new caption value for the selected object. Since this button will respond with a "beep" sound, enter the following caption:

   Type `Beep` and press **Enter.**

Figure 2-20 The Property list box displayed.

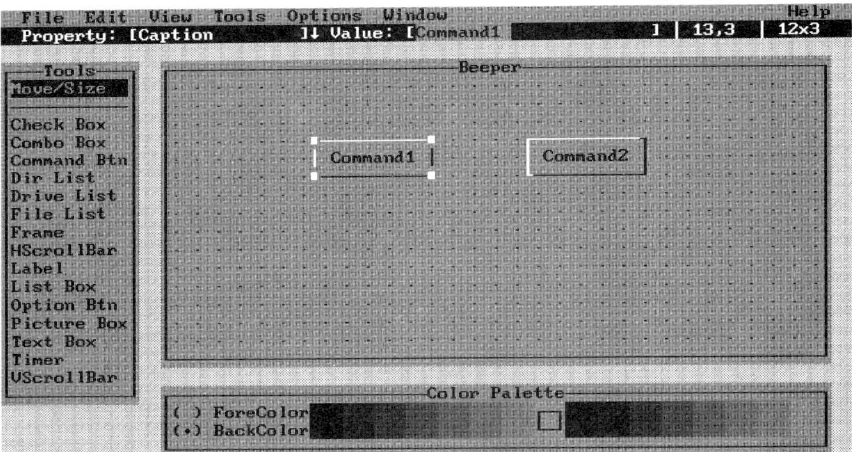

Figure 2-21 Caption value selected.

As you enter the new caption value, it replaces the current value on both the **Value** list box and the selected button.

Note that the caption value appears just the way you type the characters. If you type `beep`, the caption on the selected button will appear in lowercase letters. If you type `BEEP`, the button will be captioned `BEEP`.

Figure 2-22 shows the Beeper form with the first command button recaptioned as Beep.

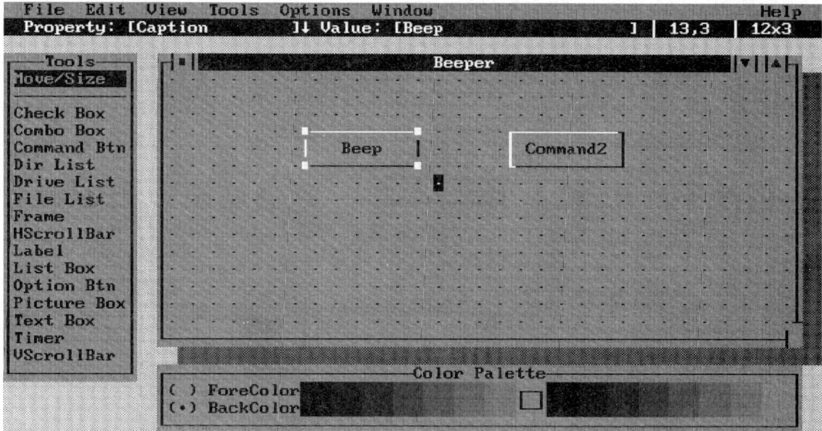

Figure 2-22 Beep button caption.

Now it is your turn. Following the same procedures that you used to change the caption of the first command button, change the caption of `Command2` to `Exit`.

1. Select the **Command2** button.
2. Select and highlight `Command2` in the **Value** list box.
3. Type `Exit` and press **Enter.**

As outlined in the Beeper specifications, this second command button is supposed to exit from the application when it is clicked. Figure 2-23 shows

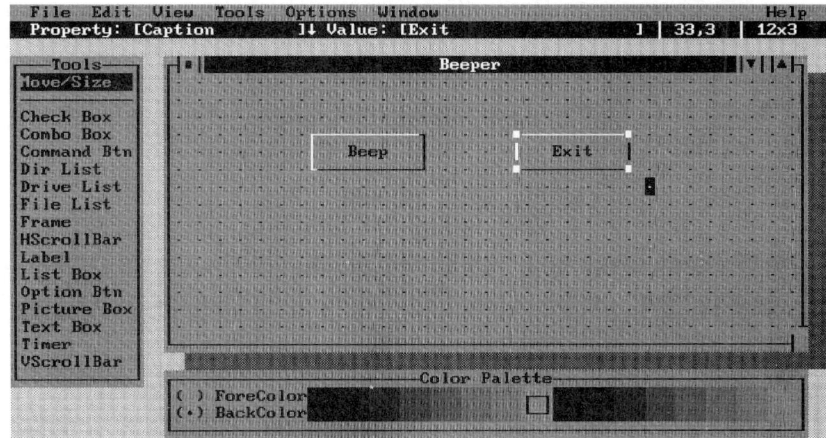

Figure 2-23 Both buttons with new captions.

what the screen looks like after the captions on both command buttons have been changed to new values.

Saving a Project

To save your current project, do the following:

1. Open the File menu and choose the **Save Project** command. The **Save Project** dialog box appears, as shown in Figure 2-24. A default project file name, PROJECT.MAK, shows in the **File Name** text box.

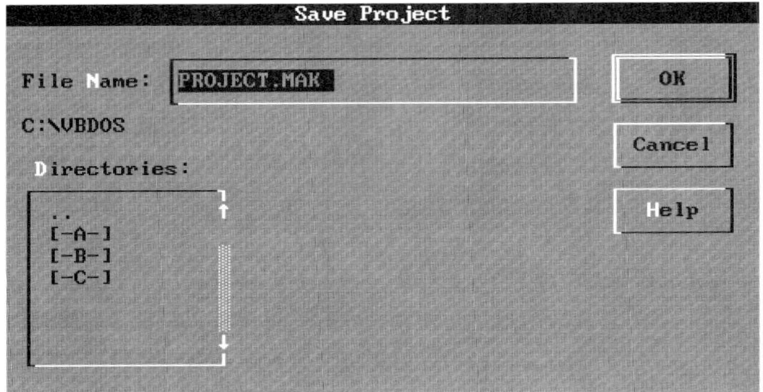

Figure 2-24 Save Project dialog box.

You use this dialog box to enter the file name for the project file and to specify the disk drive and directory where the files are to be saved. For every example in this book, we are assuming that all project files are being saved onto a formatted diskette in Drive A.

2. Enter the following path name and project file name into the text box on the dialog box:

   Type A:BEEPER

3. When you have entered the path name and project file name, do the following:

   Click the **OK** button.

Visual Basic saves two files during this save operation: BEEPER.MAK and BEEPER.FRM. BEEPER.MAK is the project file for the Beeper application. This file contains a list of all the other files being used by this project. In this case, `BEEPER.MAK` only contains one file name: `BEEPER.FRM`.

`BEEPER.FRM` is the form file that contains the Beeper form and the two command buttons **Beep** and **Exit.**

When the save operation completes, Visual Basic displays the Form Designer once again, as well as the completed form `Beeper`. The next step is to attach event procedures to the two command buttons on this form.

Coding an Event Procedure

An event procedure is a block of code you attach to an object. The attached code determines how an object responds to a specific detected event. Use the following steps to attach an event procedure and appropriate code to the **Beep** button on the `Beeper` form:

1. Open the Edit menu and choose the **Event Procedures** command. A dialog box appears (Figure 2-25), asking you to verify that you want to exit to the programming environment.

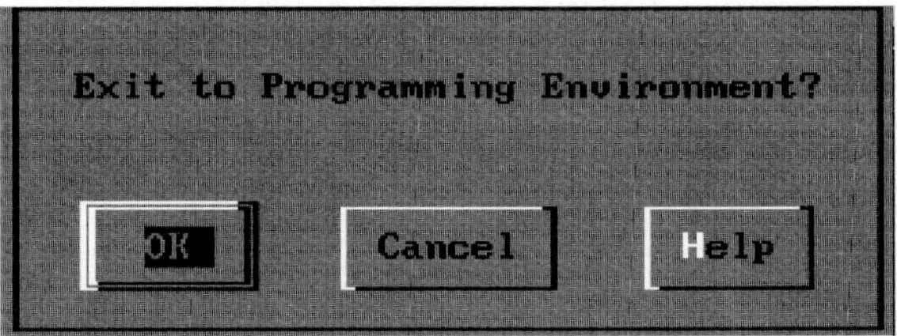

Figure 2-25 Exit to Programming Environment dialog box.

> ☑ Based on your system's resources and capabilities, it may take anywhere from a few to several seconds before you return to the programming environment. Older, less powerful computers require more time to switch from the Form Designer to the programming environment.

2. Click the **OK** button. Visual Basic closes the Form Designer window, opens the programming environment windows, and displays an **Event Procedures** dialog box (Figure 2-26).

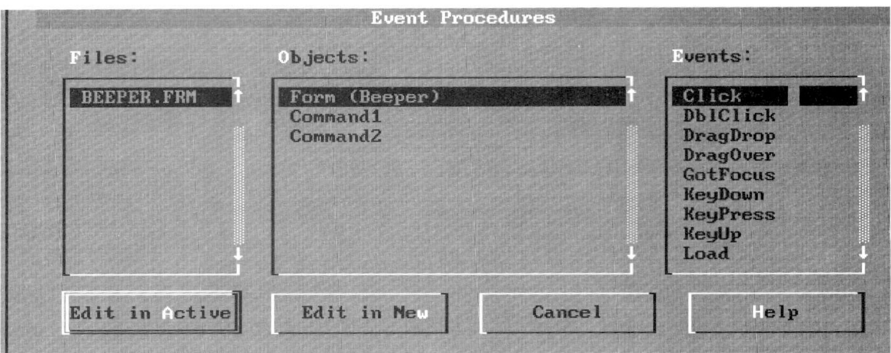

Figure 2-26 Event Procedures dialog box.

This dialog box has three lists: **Files, Objects,** and **Events.** The **Files** list has one file entry: BEEPER.FRM. This is the form file you saved when you saved the project files.

The Objects list shows three items: a form with the caption `Beeper`, and two command buttons (**Command1** and **Command2**). Note that in the list the command button captions (**Beep** and **Exit**) do not appear. What appears in the list are the *control names* for the buttons. Control name (**CtlName**) is a specific property of certain controls. In this case, the control name values default to the original caption values (**Command1** and **Command2**). If you wanted the control name values to be more descriptive, you would go back to the Form Designer and use the Properties bar to change the control names for these two buttons. For this exercise, you can easily remember that the **Command1** button is the **Beep** button and the **Command2** button is the **Exit** button.

The **Events** list displays the set of events that can be detected by the highlighted object in the **Objects** list. In Figure 2-26, the listed events are for the form object, Beeper.

Along the bottom of the dialog box is a set of buttons that lets you control the code creation and editing process (first two buttons), dismiss the dialog box (**Cancel**), and access the Visual Basic help feature (**Help**).

3. Click **Command1** in the **Objects** list to select that item. When you select this item, the **Events** list changes to those events that can be

detected by a command button. You can see that list in Figure 2-27, where the first event in the list, `Click`, is highlighted.

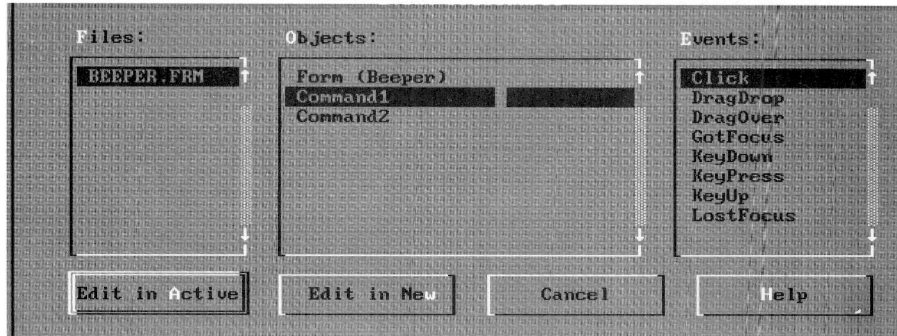

Figure 2-27 Event list for the Command1 object.

4. Click the **Edit in Active** button. When you click this button, Visual Basic dismisses the **Event Procedures** dialog box and displays the Code window shown in Figure 2-28.

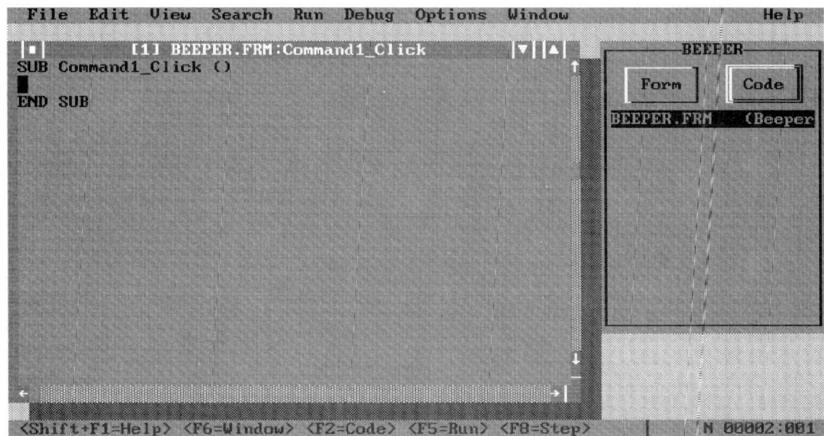

Figure 2-28 Event Procedures Code window.

At the top of the Code window you see the window title:

```
[1] BEEPER.FRM:Command1_Click
```

The window number appears in the set of brackets. In this case, the window name is a concatenation of the file name of the Beeper form

(BEEPER.FRM), a colon (:), and the event procedure name (Command1_Click). The event procedure name is a concatenation of the object's control name (Command1), an underline symbol (_), and the event (Click) that will trigger this procedure.

In the text area of the Code window, you see a template for the procedure to be written. The template displays the SUB and END SUB lines of the procedure, with a blank line where the code for the procedure will appear. The keyword SUB is short for *subprogram.* The cursor should be at the first character position of the blank line.

```
SUB Command1_Click ()

END SUB
```

The general syntax for an event procedure such as this one is:

SUB *object control name_event name (arguments)*
  local variables and constant definitions
  code statements

END SUB

The words SUB and END are Visual Basic keywords. When used in this fashion, they help define the beginning (SUB) and end (END SUB) of an event procedure. For this event procedure, there will be no arguments.

5. With the cursor at the first character position of the blank line in the event procedure, enter the following to indent the code two spaces:

   Press the **spacebar** twice.

6. Now enter this line of code:

   Type beep

If you now move the cursor up or down with the arrow keys, or click the mouse, the screen shows this block of code:

```
SUB Command1_Click ()
  BEEP
END SUB
```

Visual Basic recognized the keyword you entered into the second line of the procedure. Visual Basic acknowledges the entry of a valid keyword by changing the word into all capital letters. You entered `beep`; Visual Basic displays the entry as `BEEP`.

You have completed the code for the first event procedure, `Command1_Click`. This is the event procedure that will be activated when the **Beep** button is clicked on the Beeper form. Figure 2-29 shows the code for this event procedure, as seen in the Code window.

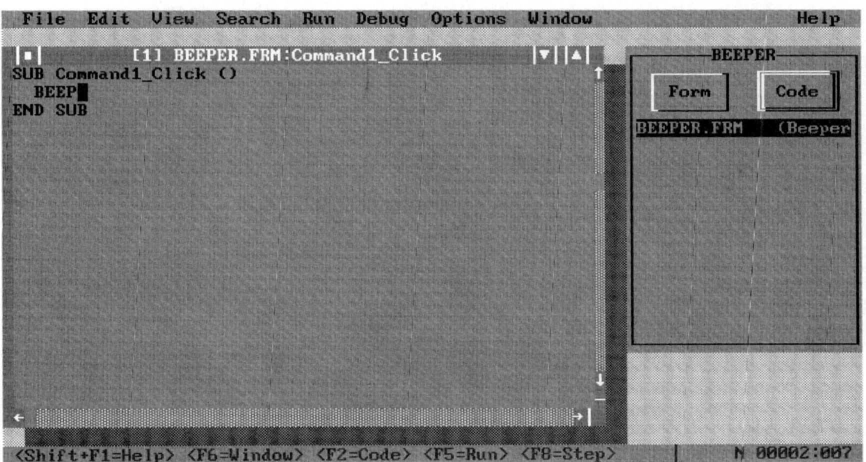

Figure 2-29 Event procedure Command1_click.

Attaching an Event Procedure to the Exit Button

To proceed and attach an event procedure and code to the **Exit** button, do the following:

1. Open the Edit menu and choose the **Event Procedures** command. The **Event Procedures** dialog box reappears.
2. Click **Command1** in the **Objects** list to select that item. Look at the **Events** list for this object. Notice that the `CLICK` event is displayed in all capital letters. This visual cue informs you that you already have an event procedure for the selected object, **Command1.**
3. Click **Command2** in the **Objects** list to select that item. The `Click` event in the **Events** list should be highlighted and should not appear in all capital letters.
4. Click the **Edit in New** button. Visual Basic dismisses the **Event Procedures** dialog box and displays the Code windows shown in Figure 2-30.

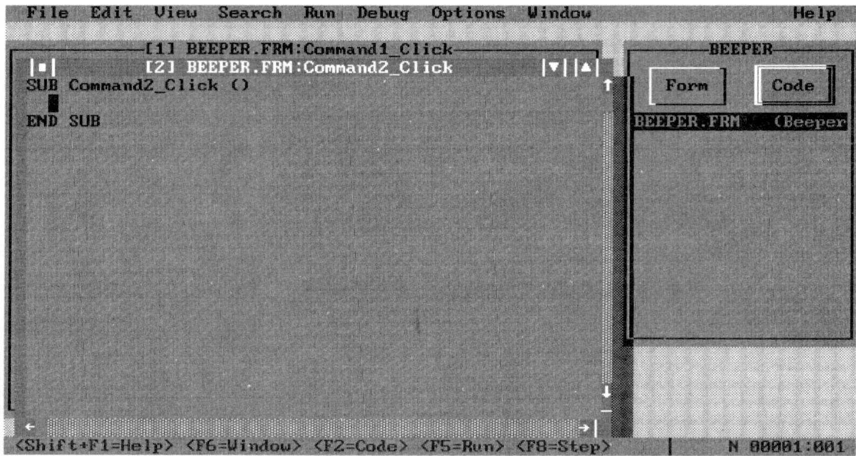

Figure 2-30 Code Windows for beeper procedures.

The new Code window, identified as window 2, sits on top of window 1, the event procedure for the **Beep** button. At the top of this Code window, you see the window title:

```
[2] BEEPER.FRM:Command2_Click
```

In the text area of the code window, you see a code template for the procedure to be written:

```
SUB Command2_Click ()

END SUB
```

5. With the cursor at the first character position of the blank line in the event procedure, enter the following to indent the code two spaces:

   Press the **spacebar** twice.

6. Now, enter this line of code:

   Type `end`

If you now move the cursor up or down with the arrow keys, or click the mouse, the screen shows this block of code:

```
SUB Command2_Click ()
  END
END SUB
```

Visual Basic again acknowledged the entry of a valid keyword by changing the word into all capitals letters. You entered `end`; Visual Basic displays the entry as `END` (Figure 2-31).

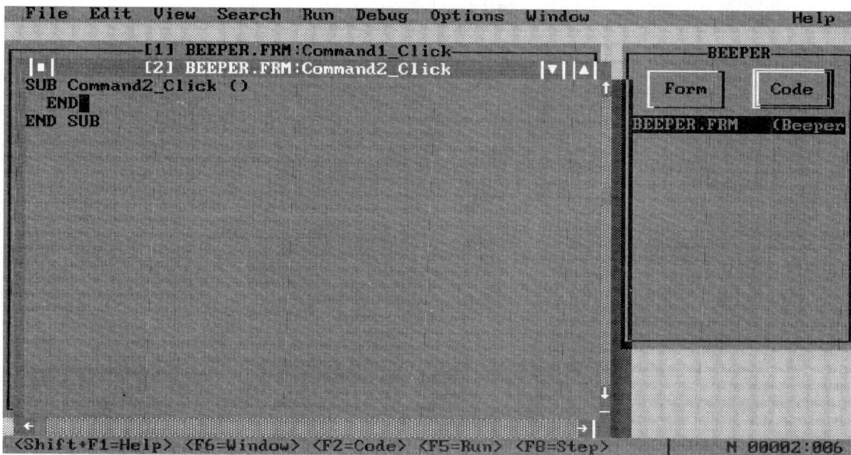

Figure 2-31 Event procedure Command2_Click.

You have completed the code for the second event procedure, `Command2_Click`. This is the event procedure that will be activated any time the **Exit** button is clicked on the Beeper form.

7. Open the File menu and choose the **Save Project** command. Visual Basic automatically remembers the file and path names for this project, and saves the updated form file to the disk. The Beeper form now contains two controls (**Beep** and **Exit**), and each of these controls has an attached event procedure. You are ready to run and test the Beeper application.

Running the Application

To run the Beeper application, see what the form looks like on the screen, and test out its controls and event procedures, do the following:

1. Open the Run menu and choose the **Start** command. If all is well, the Visual Basic programming environment (menu, status line, windows) will disappear. A window with the title `Beeper` appears

(Figure 2-32). On the window are the two command buttons (**Beep** and **Exit**). **Beep** is selected.

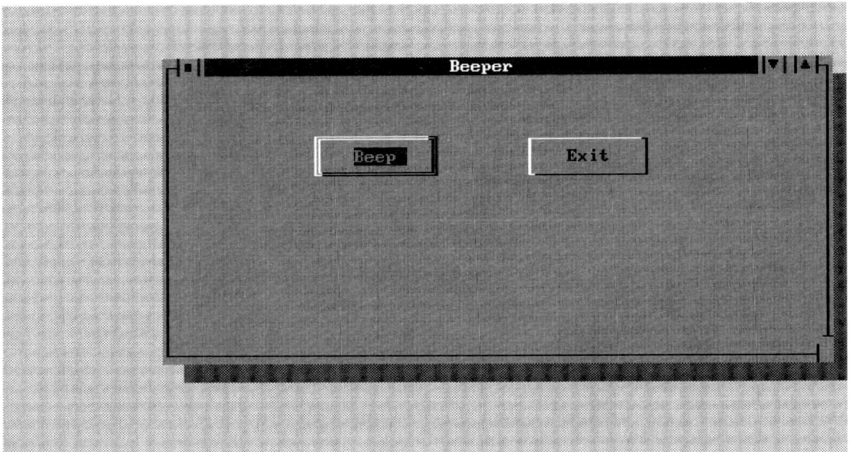

Figure 2-32 The Beeper application.

Try all of the controls on this window. Click the **Beep** button. Your computer should emit a "beep" sound each time you click that button. Press **Tab** to move the highlight back and forth between **Beep** and **Exit.** Click the Title bar and drag the window to a new location. Try using the **minimize** and **maximize** buttons (upper right corner of the window). Click on the **control box** (upper left corner).

> ✔ If you click the **minimize** button on the Beeper form, the form collapses into the Beeper icon, shown in Figure 2-33. You restore the form by double-clicking on the icon. You can also redisplay the form by clicking the icon once to open the control box menu and choosing the **Restore** command.

Figure 2-33 Beeper form minimized.

2. When you have exercised all of the controls and are satisfied that the application is working correctly, click the **Exit** button. You should see the following message:

```
Press any key to continue
```

3. Press the **Enter** key. The Beeper application screen disappears, and Visual Basic restores the programming environment.
4. Open the File menu and choose the **Exit** command. Visual Basic clears the screen and returns you to MS-DOS. If you did not save the project after you added a second event procedure to the **Exit** button, you will be prompted at this point to save your work. If you see a dialog box asking you if you want to save your project files, click the **Yes** button. Visual Basic should automatically remember the file and path names for this project, and will save any updated files to the disk.

Editing and Changing an Application

As you have now discovered, Visual Basic is relatively easy to use. The Beeper application example you have built is not complex, but the resultant program (form, controls, event procedure structure) gives you a hint of Visual Basic's sophistication and elegance.

To continue your explorations, consider the following modified specification for the Beeper application (new item in italics).

Specification #2-2 (Form)

Beeper Application

Form	Event(s) to be detected	Response(s)
Beeper	None	None
Properties:	Default settings	

Notes/Comments: None

Specification #2-2 (Command Buttons)

Beeper Application

Controls	Event(s) to be detected		Response(s)
Command1	Click		Make "beep" sound
			Display dialog box with message
Properties:	Location	13,3	
	Caption	`Beep`	
Command2	Click		Exit application
Properties:	Location	33,3	
	Caption	`Exit`	

Notes/Comments: None

The change to be made to Beeper involves displaying a *dialog box* and *message* each time the **Beep** button detects a Click event. To make this change, you edit the **Beep** button event procedure `Command1_Click` as follows:

1. Start Visual Basic.
2. Open the File menu and choose **Open Project.**
3. Using the **Open Project** dialog box, locate the project file for the Beeper application. The file name for this project is `BEEPER.MAK`.
4. When the file name `BEEPER.MAK` appears in the list box, select that file name and click the **OK** button. A Code window titled `BEEPER.FRM` appears on the programming environment screen.
5. After Visual Basic loads the project files, open the Edit menu and choose the **Event Procedures** command.
6. On the **Event Procedures** dialog box that appears, select the **Command1** item in the **Objects** list box.

7. Click the **Edit in Active** button. The event procedure Code window for the **Beep(Command1)** button appears. The code for this event procedure is displayed in the window.
8. Change the code for this event procedure to match what follows:

```
SUB Command1_Click ()
  Msg$ = CHR$(1) + " You beeped!" 'new line
  BEEP
  MSGBOX Msg$                     'new line
END SUB
```

9. When you have made these changes, open the Run menu and choose the **Start** command.
10. Click the **Beep** button. Figure 2-34 shows the dialog box that now appears when **Beep** is clicked. To dismiss the dialog box, click the **OK** button. To exit the application, click the **Exit** button.

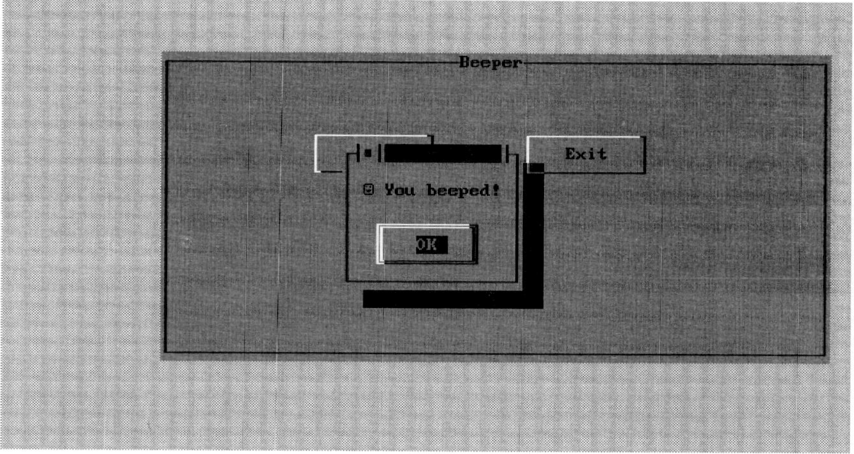

Figure 2-34 The modified beeper application.

In the event procedure that produces the dialog box and message, `Msg$` is a string variable that contains the "happy face" character, `CHR$(1)`, plus the text message " You beeped!" `MSGBOX` is a Visual Basic keyword that produces a standard dialog box and waits for the user to click a button. The contents of any string or string variable that appears after the `MSGBOX` keyword becomes the message displayed in the dialog box.

The `MSGBOX` statement, as written in the event procedure, produces a single **OK** button. A second parameter can be added to the `MSGBOX` argument list that tells Visual Basic to display up to three buttons and a variety of captions. This second parameter can also be used to automatically select the default button. A third parameter lets you specify the title on the dialog box.

> ☑ When you complete your explorations of this modified application and attempt to leave the Visual Basic system, you will be asked if you wish to save the altered files. Go ahead and save files. Visual Basic will overwrite the old Beeper project files with the modified versions. Those files with the modifications will then be used in the final part of this chapter.

Beyond the Beep

As a final experiment, we suggest you try one more exploration with the Beeper application. Here is another version of the original specification (new items in italics).

Specification #2-3 (Form)

Beeper Application

Form	Event(s) to be detected	Response(s)
Beeper	None	None
Properties:	Default settings	

Notes/Comments: None

This specification asks you to add a third command button (**Chime**) to the Beeper application. When the user clicks **Chime,** the event procedure activates the Visual Basic **SOUND** statement and produces three notes or tones. Figure 2-35 provides an example of what the Beeper form might look like with the additional **Chime** button in place.

Go ahead and modify the Beeper application according to the last set of specifications. Add the third command button, **Chime,** and attach an event procedure to the button that plays three tones or notes using the **SOUND** statement.

Specification #2-3 (Command Buttons)

Beeper Application

Controls	Event(s) to be detected		Response(s)
Command1	Click		Make "beep" sound
			Display dialog box with message
Properties:	Location	13,3	
	Caption	`Beep`	
Command2	Click		Exit application
Properties:	Location	33,3	
	Caption	`Exit`	
Command3	*Click*		*Sound three notes or tones*
Properties:	Location	23,7	
	Caption	*`Chime`*	

Notes/Comments: *Notes or tones that go with Chime can be produced using the Sound statement.*

Syntax: SOUND frequency, duration

frequency: *in hertz; values 37 to 32767*

duration: *in clock ticks; values 0 to 65535; 18.2 clock ticks* = 1 second

Summary

In the last part of this chapter, you encountered the following terms and concepts:

Project. The complete collection of files that generate a Visual Basic application. Refer back to Table 2-1 for the various types of files that can be found within a project.

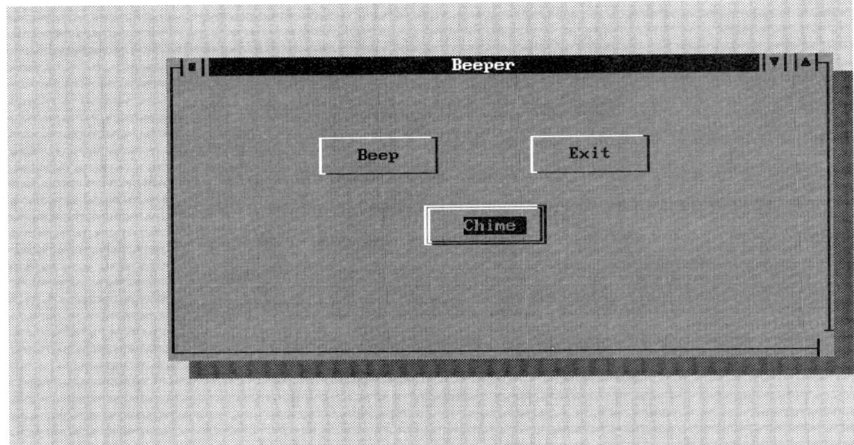

Figure 2-35 Beeper application with Chime button.

Selection rectangle. The outline that surrounds a selected object of the Form Designer. When present, a selection rectangle has sizing handles at each corner of the outline.

Sizing handles. Small box shapes that appear at the corners of a selection rectangle. You use the sizing handles to alter the size of a control object.

Control name. The name used to identify a control object. Visual Basic automatically assigns default control names when controls are created. You can change an object's control name by altering the **CtlName** property.

In addition, you learned how to design, develop, edit, save, and run a simple Visual Basic application, Beeper. You created two event procedures (Command1_Click, Command2_Click) and used the following QBasic/QuickBasic keywords: SUB, END SUB, END, BEEP, CHR$, and SOUND. You also used a new Visual Basic keyword, MSGBOX, to display a dialog box and a message to the user.

Congratulations! This concludes your initial exploration of the Visual Basic system. When you are ready, proceed to the next chapter, where you will design and develop a Visual Basic application that uses other types of control objects.

3 Creating Custom Applications

In this chapter, you will continue to explore the Visual Basic design and programming environments. You will use Visual Basic to create and customize an application called FlashCard. As you design and build FlashCard, you will use the Visual Basic Forms Designer to layout and design the form shown in Figure 3-1.

Concepts and Terminology

QBasic/QuickBasic Keywords

New Visual Basic Keywords

Visual Basic Event Procedures

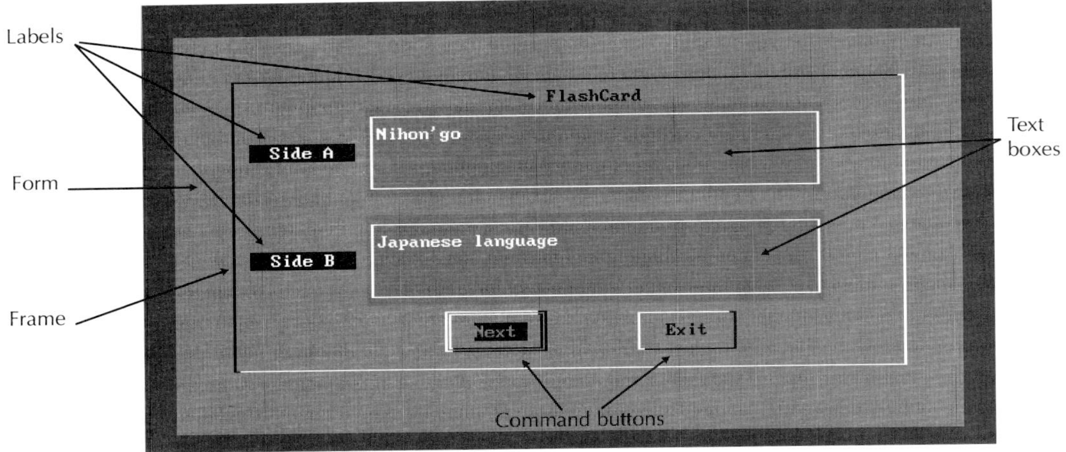

Figure 3-1 The FlashCard Application Form

Once you design the form, you will then add appropriate event procedures to handle both user interactions and the display of information.

FlashCard Application Specifications

Figure 3-1 shows what the FlashCard application interface will look like to the user. Before you build that interface, review the following specifications for the form and controls for the FlashCard application. These specifications outline all the key elements (interface and code) that will appear in the final FlashCard program. The specifications are broken out into separate sections for the form and the different types of controls (frame, labels, text boxes, and command buttons).

FlashCard Form Specification

The form called Flash will respond to one triggering event, the loading of the form (Load). The form's response to that event will be to execute code that declares program variables, sets desktop and form attributes, reads data into the program, and initializes the states of command buttons that appear on the form.

To duplicate the form shown in Figure 3-1, you will need to use the property settings listed in the specification. If you deviate from these settings, your version of the form may differ slightly from the images in this book.

Specification #3-1 (Form)

FlashCard Application

Form	Event(s) to be detected		Response(s)
Flash	Load		Declare variables
			Set Desktop/Form attributes
			Read data
			Initialize buttons
Properties:	Location	3,2	
	Size	74 × 22	
	BorderStyle	None	
	FormName	Flash	
	Colors	White (background)/black (foreground)	

Notes/Comments: This is the form for the application.

FlashCard Frame Specification

The Visual Basic *frame* object helps to organize or group control objects. Certain objects (such as option buttons), when placed on a frame, work together as a unit. Otherwise, frames can be used to give the overall form a more interesting presentation. Frame objects are created and modified just like other controls and can be modified by event procedures when the program is running.

When using frames and picture box controls, place these objects on the form before installing other controls. If you do so, then controls placed on frames and picture boxes become the *children* of these *parent* objects, and move when the parents are move.

Specification #3-1 (Frame)

FlashCard Application

Frame	Event(s) to be detected		Response(s)
Flash	None		None
Properties:	Location	5,2	
	Size	64 × 17	
	Caption	Blank	

Notes/Comments: Inner frame on the form; used as a design element.

FlashCard Label Specifications

In this application, you will use *label* controls for the first time. Visual Basic label controls can be used as static design and informational elements or dynamic message areas that respond to user interactions. For this application, the three label controls will be static informational elements (see page 53).

FlashCard Text Box Specifications

You will install two *text box* controls on the FlashCard form. These text boxes will reveal specific messages when the user clicks the **Next** command buttons (there will be two command buttons with the same caption—`Next`).

To keep the user from interacting with the text that will be displayed, these two controls will be disabled. The **Enabled** property determines whether or not a user can interact with a control. If this property is set to true (−1), the control is enabled for interactions. If you set the property to false (0), the control is disabled (see page 54).

FlashCard Command Button Specifications

The form Flash has three *command buttons*. Two buttons (*Command1* and *Command3*) will control the display of text in the text boxes. Both these

Specification #3-1 (Labels)

FlashCard Application

Controls	Event(s) to be detected		Response(s)
Label1	None		None
Properties:	Location	33,3	
	Size	13×1	
	Colors	White (background)/black (foreground)	
	Caption	`FlashCard`	
	Alignment	Center	
Label2	None		None
Properties:	Location	7,6	
	Size	10×1	
	Colors	Gray (background)/bright white (foreground)	
	Caption	`Side A`	
	Alignment	Center	
Label3	None		None
Properties:	Location	7,12	
	Size	10×1	
	Colors	Gray (background)/bright white (foreground)	
	Caption	`Side B`	
	Alignment	Center	

Notes/Comments: None

buttons are captioned `Next`, and *reside in the same location on the form* but function differently. A third button (**Command2**) will let the user exit the application.

Command1 and **Command3** will determine what text is being displayed in the two text boxes (**Text1** and **Text2**). The buttons are located on top of

Specification #3-1 (Text Boxes)

FlashCard Application

Controls	Event(s) to be detected		Response(s)
Text1	None		None
Properties:	Location	18,4	
	Size	43 × 5	
	Colors	Blue (background)/bright white (foreground)	
	Text	Blank	
	Enabled	False (0)	
Text2	None		None
Properties:	Location	18,10	
	Size	43 × 5	
	Colors	Blue (background)/bright white (foreground)	
	Text	Blank	
	Enabled	False (0)	

Notes/Comments: Enabled set to false (0) so that user cannot alter text that appears in text boxes.

☑ Although it seems easier to put only a single command button on the form, using two unique control objects better demonstrates how code is developed in an event-oriented programming system. Each control object (command button) and its associated event procedure "knows" exactly what to do when that object is active and detects a Click event. This type of isolation of objects and code helps you develop modular code procedures that are easier to manage and easier to debug.

Specification #3-1 (Command Buttons)

FlashCard Application

Controls	Event(s) to be detected		Response(s)
Command1	Click		Clear text boxes Display Side A data Hide this button Set focus and show **Command3**
Properties:	Location	25,15	
	Size	10 × 3	
	Caption	`Next`	
Command2	Click		Hide form Exit application
Properties:	Location	43,15	
	Size	10 × 3	
	Caption	`Exit`	
Command3	Click		Display Side B data Hide this button Set focus and show **Command1** Check data index reset it
Properties:	Location	25,15	
	Size	10 × 3	
	Caption	`Next`	

Notes/Comments: **Command1** and **Command3** have same caption and are located on top of each other. The program (event procedures) will manage which button is being displayed based on the state of the user interactions.

each other. To the user, there appears to be only one button. The program (event procedures) will manage which button is being displayed based on the state of the user interactions.

Figure 3-2 identifies the various control objects used in the design of the FlashCard application.

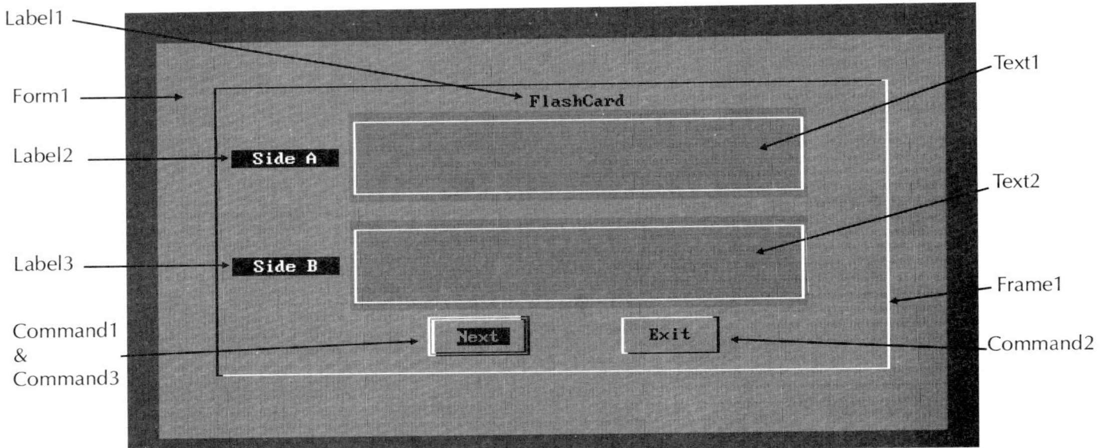

Figure 3-2 FlashCard application control objects.

Building the FlashCard Form

The FlashCard application uses a single form, called Flash. To build the application, you first create this form using the Visual Basic Form Designer. To begin this project, follow these steps:

1. Start Visual Basic. You see the Visual Basic programming environment screen with an Untitled Code window and the Project window. (If Visual Basic has an application loaded, choose the **New Project** command on the File menu to clear the system.)

2. Choose the **New Form** command on the File menu. The **New Form** dialog box appears.

3. Type `A:FLASH` to specify the path and file name of the file to be used. For the examples in this book, we assume that all project files are being saved onto a formatted diskette in Drive A.

Figure 3-3 shows the **New Form** dialog box with the path and file name `A:FLASH` entered.

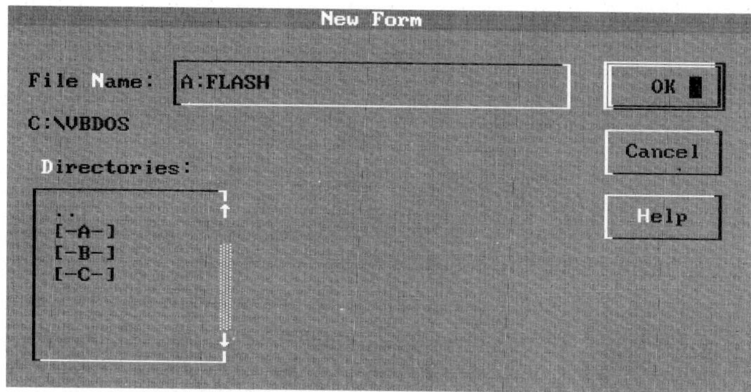

Figure 3-3 New Form dialog box.

4. Click the **OK** button to record your entry. The **New Form** dialog box disappears, and you see the Visual Basic Form Designer screen (Figure 3-4).

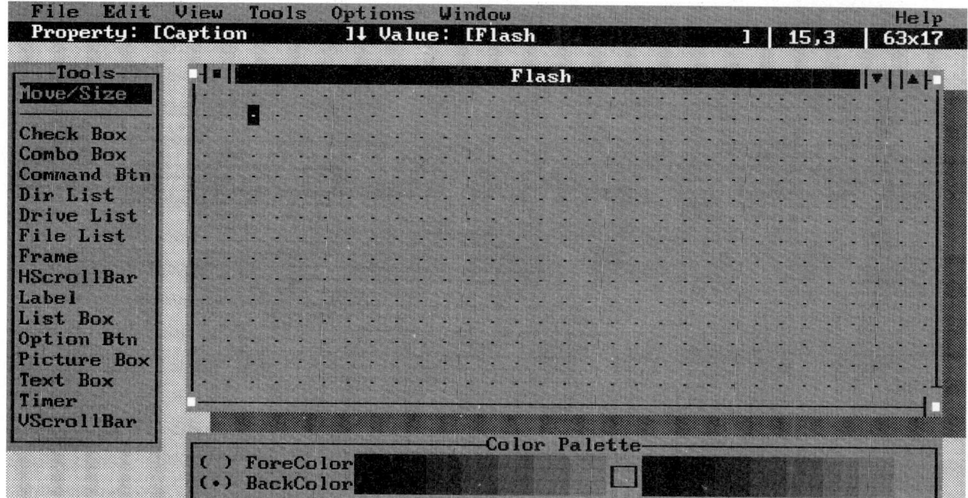

Figure 3-4 Visual Basic Form Designer.

Customizing the Form

The new form Flash appears on the Form Designer screen along with the Toolbox and the Color Palette. You will now proceed to customize the form on the screen to match the specifications outlined earlier in this chapter. To perform this task, proceed as follows:

1. Click the title bar on the form and drag it to location 3,2 (location of the upper left corner of the form). You may have to move the form several times to get it into the designated position. When Flash is placed correctly, the screen appears as shown in Figure 3-5. At this location, Flash overlays a portion of the Toolbox. The **Location** box on the Properties bar indicates the coordinates of the upper left corner of the form.

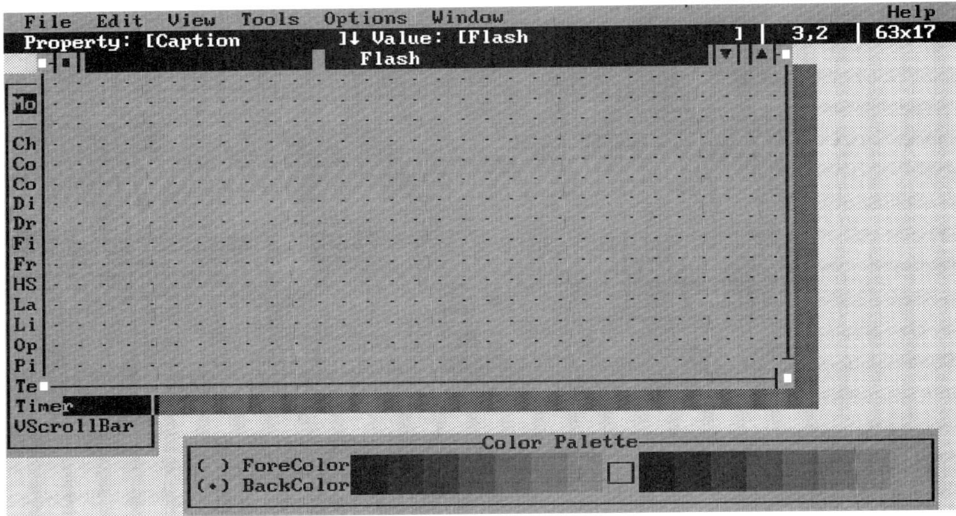

Figure 3-5 Form Flash at location 3,2.

2. Click the bottom right corner of the form and drag down and to the right to make the form larger (resize the form). Keep adjusting the size of the form until the size parameters in the Properties bar show Flash to be 74 characters by 22 lines (74 × 22). At this size (74 × 22) and location (3,2), Flash almost completely covers the Color Palette at the bottom of the screen (Figure 3-6).

3. Click the down arrow on the **Property** list box (Properties bar) to open the menu of properties for the form. In Figure 3-1, the form appears as a single rectangular object with no Title bar, control box, or resizing buttons. One property that partially determines what items appear on the form is **BorderStyle.**

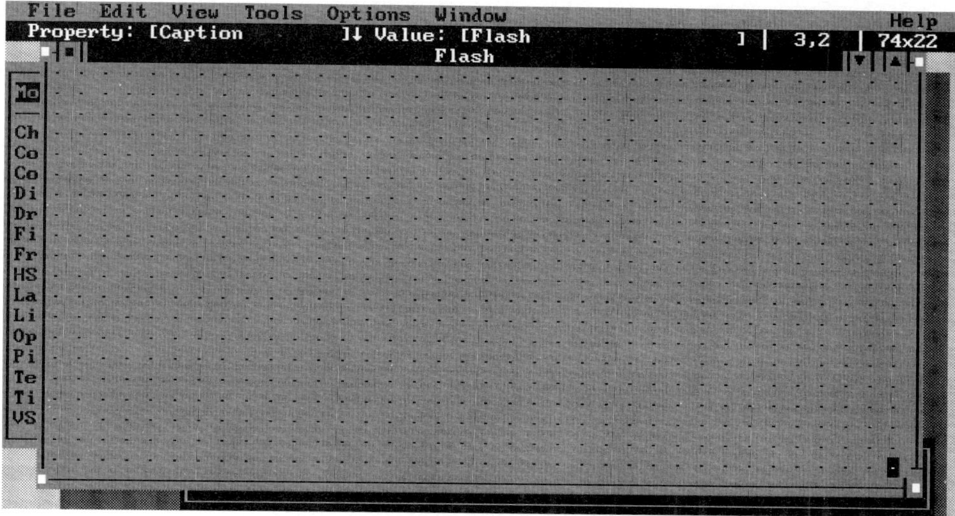

Figure 3-6 Flash moved and resized.

4. Choose **BorderStyle** on the open **Property** list box menu. The **Value** list box displays the current border style for this form: Sizable Single. Figure 3-7 shows the open **Property** list box with **BorderStyle** selected.

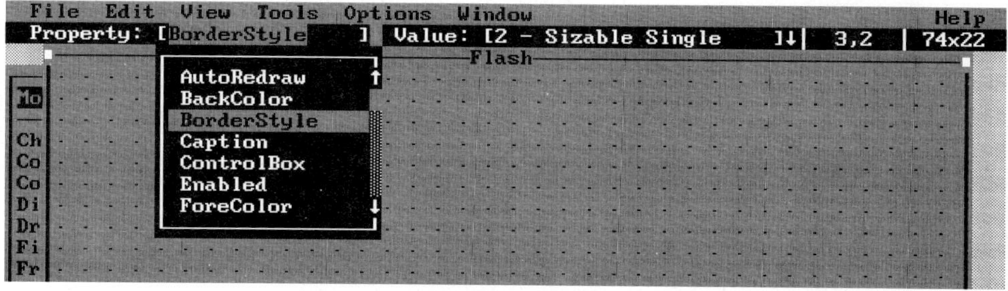

Figure 3-7 Property list box menu.

5. Click the down arrow on the **Value** field to display the menu of value settings available for the **BorderStyle** property (Figure 3-8).

   A list of seven (numbered 0–6) settings are available for this property. The current setting, **Sizable Single,** produces the form shown on the screen. "Sizable" options refer to forms that the user can resize. "Fixed" options produce forms that cannot be resized by the user. The settings **Single, Double,** and **Solid** determine to the type of

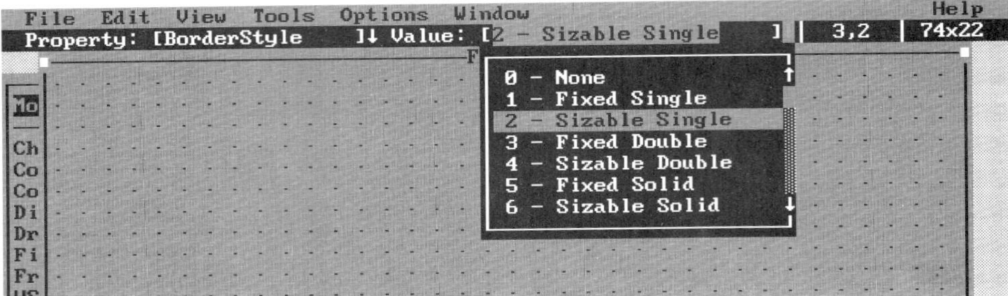

Figure 3-8 Value list box menu for BorderStyle property.

borders that appear on the form. For the FlashCard application, the form Flash uses the **None** setting. This setting produces a solid form with no borders, control box, Title bar, caption, or resizing features.

6. Choose **None** on the Values menu for the **BorderStyle** property. Figure 3-9 shows what Flash looks like when **BorderStyle** is set to a value of **None.**

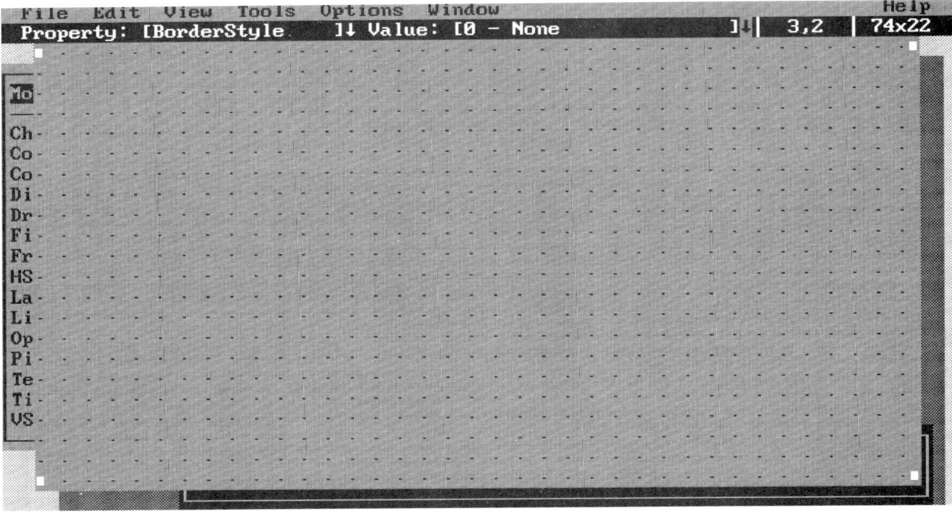

Figure 3-9 Flash with BorderStyle None.

Save the Project

Save your work before you proceed with adding controls and code to the form Flash. To save the FlashCard project, proceed as follows:

> ✔ If you use different property and control settings for your version of Flash, your screen images may not correspond to those shown in this book. We encourage you to experiment with alternate settings after you have successfully built the FlashCard application, as outlined in this tutorial.

1. Open the File menu and choose the **Save Project** command. You use this dialog box to enter the path and project file name for the save operation. For the examples in this book, we are assuming that all project files are being saved onto a formatted diskette in Drive A.
2. Enter the following path and project file name into the text box on the dialog box:

   Type `A:FLASH`

3. When you have entered the path and project file name, do the following:

   Click the **OK** button.

Visual Basic saves two files during this save operation: `FLASH.MAK` and `FLASH.FRM`. `FLASH.MAK` is the project file for the FlashCard application. This file contains a list of all the other files being used by this project. In this case, `FLASH.MAK` only contains one file name: `FLASH.FRM`.

`FLASH.FRM` is the form file you just created and customized.

When the save operation completes, Visual Basic once again displays the Form Designer and the customized form Flash. Your next step will be to add controls to this form.

Adding Controls to the Form

There are four sets of controls to be placed on the form Flash: a frame, labels, text boxes, and command buttons. In this tutorial, you will add each set of controls as a unit and customize them for this application.

Putting a Frame on the Form

FlashCard uses one frame control object to contain the rest of the controls on the form Flash. Since the form obscures the Toolbox, you will add the frame by using the Tools menu, as follows:

1. Open the Tools menu and choose the **Frame** command. A frame control, Frame1, appears at the center of the form.
2. Click and drag this object to location 5,2.
3. Resize this object to size 64 × 17.
4. Open the **Property** list box menu (Property bar) and choose **Caption.**
5. Delete the current contents of the **Value** list box (`Frame1`). The caption will disappear on the frame, leaving a solid rectangular box overlaying the form (Figure 3-10).

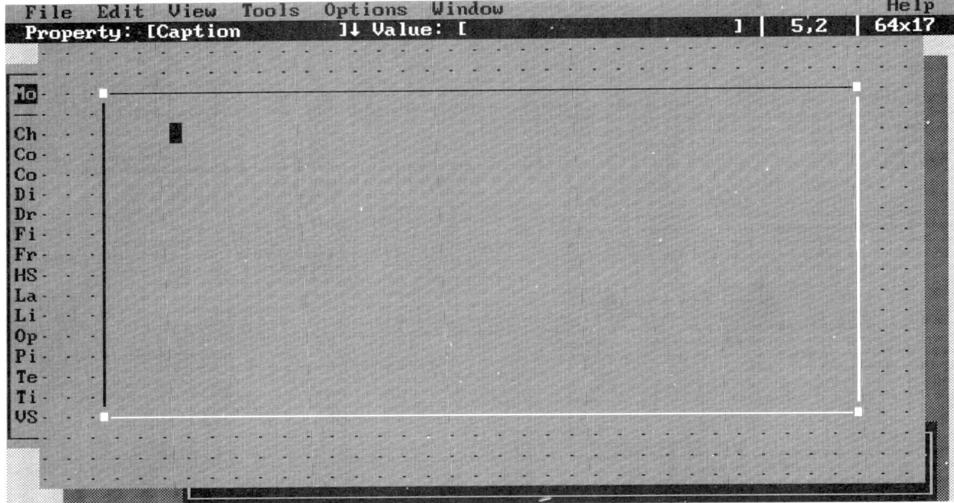

Figure 3-10 The FlashCard form with a frame.

6. Save the project. To periodically record and preserve your changes to the project, save the project using the **Save Project** command on the File menu.

> ☑ As you continue adding controls to the form, you may occasionally experience that controls seem to "disappear" if you accidentally click the frame object covering the form. If this situation occurs, press the **Tab** key repeatedly to "reveal" the objects that have "disappeared." Each time you press **Tab,** Visual Basic moves the focus to the next object, even if it is "hidden." Objects "hidden" behind other objects are thus "revealed" when Visual Basic gives them the focus.

Putting Labels on the Form

Flash has three labels. One label is used as a header at the top of the form, above the upper text box. This label's caption is the name of the application, `FlashCard`.

Two labels appear to the left of the text boxes. The captions for these labels are Side A and Side B, respectively. Since the form obscures the Toolbox, you will add the labels to the form by using the Tools menu. To put the first label on the form, follow these steps:

1. Open the Tools menu and choose the **Label** command. A label control object appears at the center of the form. This object's control name and caption is `Label1`.

2. Click and drag this object to location 33,3.

3. Resize this object to size 13 × 1.

4. Open the **Property** list box menu (Property bar) and choose **Alignment.**

5. Open the **Value** list box menu (Property bar) and change the value setting for the **Alignment** property to **Center.** This setting aligns the object's caption to the center of the object.

6. Open the **Property** list box menu and choose **Caption.**

7. Delete the current contents of the **Value** list box (`Label1`) and type this new caption for the label:

   Type `FlashCard` and press **Enter.**

   Figure 3-11 shows Flash with the first label, `FlashCard`, in place. The control name for this label is still Label1; `FlashCard` is the label's caption.

8. Save the project. To periodically record and preserve your changes to the project, save the project using the **Save Project** command on the File menu.

To put the other two labels, `Side A` and `Side B`, on the form, you follow the same procedure you used to create, position, and modify the `FlashCard` label.

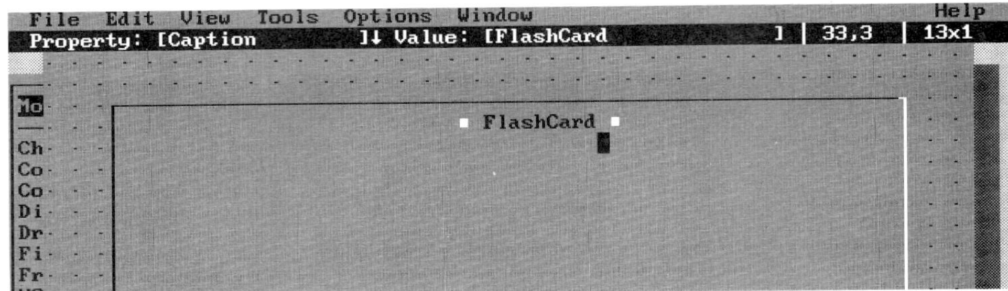

Figure 3-11 Label FlashCard in place.

Adding the Label: `Side A`

Follow these steps to put the label `Side A` on the form:

1. Open the Tools menu and choose the **Label** command. A label control object, `Label2`, appears at the center of the form.
2. Click and drag this object to location 7,6.
3. Resize this object to size 10 × 1.
4. Open the **Property** list box menu (Property bar) and choose **Alignment.**
5. Open the **Value** list box menu (Property bar) and change the value setting for the **Alignment** property to **Center.**
6. Open the **Property** list box menu and choose **Caption.**
7. Delete the current contents of the **Value** list box (`Label2`) and type this new caption for the label:

   Type `Side A` and press **Enter.**
8. Set the label's **BackColor** and **ForeColor** properties to `Gray` and `Bright White`, respectively.

   Figure 3-12 shows Flash with the two labels, `FlashCard` and `Side A`, in place.
9. Save the project.

Adding the Label: `Side B`

To put the `Side B` label on the form, follow the same steps you used to create the label `Side A`. Do this task on your own by referring back to the steps in the previous section.

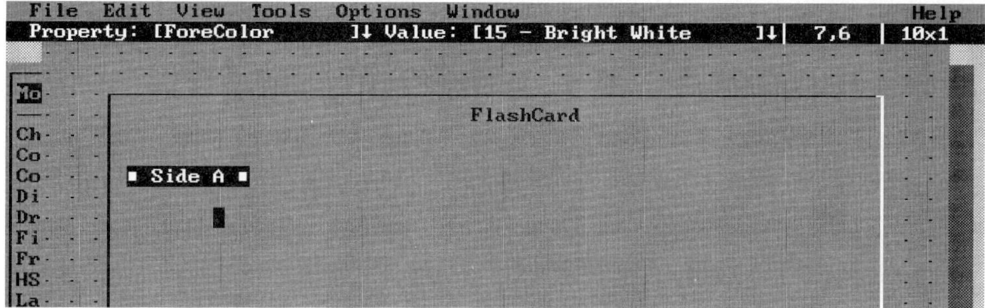

Figure 3-12 Label Side A in place.

The Side B label is the same as Side A, with these two exceptions:

- Side B is located at position 7,12.
- Side B's caption is `Side B`.

When you complete the task of creating, placing, and modifying the Side B label, your screen will look like the one shown in Figure 3-13.

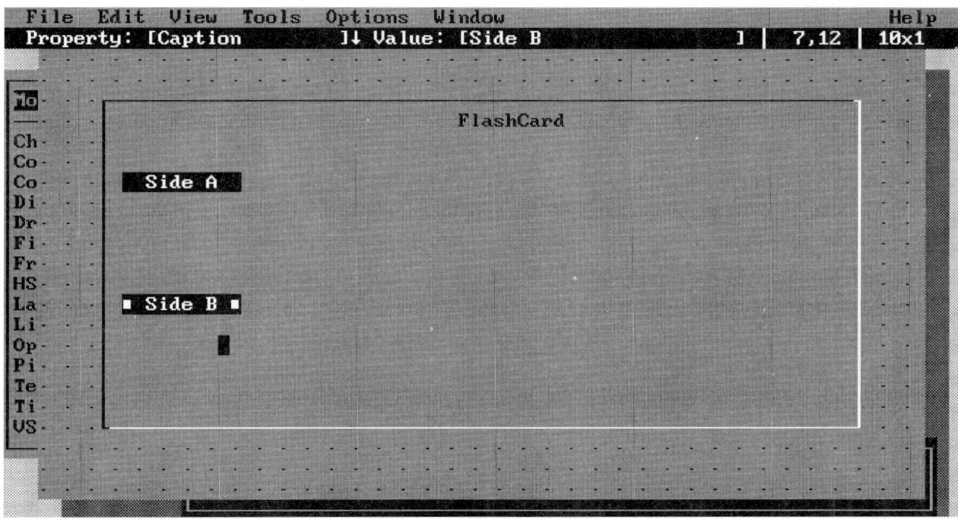

Figure 3-13 Flash with all labels in place.

Installing Text Boxes on the Form

The FlashCard application will use two text boxes to display messages to the user. The text boxes will be positioned in the center of the form and will be prominent elements.

To install text box objects on the form, you proceed as with any other control object: open the Tools menu, choose the object, position the object, and customize its features. To place the first text box on the form Flash, do the following:

1. Open the Tools menu and choose the **Text Box** command. A text box control object, **Text1,** appears at the center of the form.
2. Click and drag this object to location 18,4.
3. Resize this object to size 43 × 5.
4. Open the **Property** list box menu (Property bar) and choose **Enabled.**
5. Open the **Value** list box menu (Property bar) and change the value setting for the **Enabled** property to **False** (0). The **Enabled** property controls whether or not the user can change the text displayed in the text box. If the text box is disabled (**Enabled** property set to **False**), the user cannot alter the text. For the FlashCard application, the text boxes are disabled.
6. Open the **Property** list box menu and choose **Text.**
7. Delete the current contents of the **Value** list box (`Text1`) and press **Enter**. This sets the initial contents of the text box to an empty field.
8. Set the text box's **BackColor** and **ForeColor** properties to `Blue` and `Bright White`, respectively.

   Figure 3-14 shows the form with the first text box, **Text1,** in place.
9. Save the project.

Adding the Second Text Box

To put the second text box on the form, follow the same steps you used to create the first text box, **Text1.** Do this task on your own, referring back to the steps in the previous section as required.

The **Text2** text box is the same as **Text1,** with this exception:

- **Text2** is located at position 18,10.

When you complete the task of creating, placing, and modifying **Text2,** Flash will appear as shown in Figure 3-15.

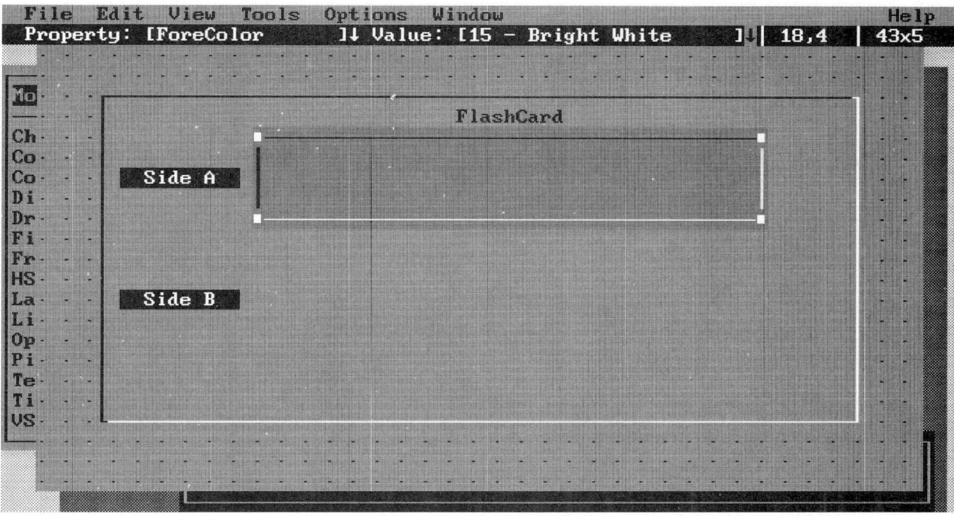

Figure 3-14 First text box in place.

Installing Command Buttons

This application employs three command buttons to control the actions on the screen. The buttons appear along the bottom of the form, below the lower text box. Two buttons, **Command1** and **Command3,**

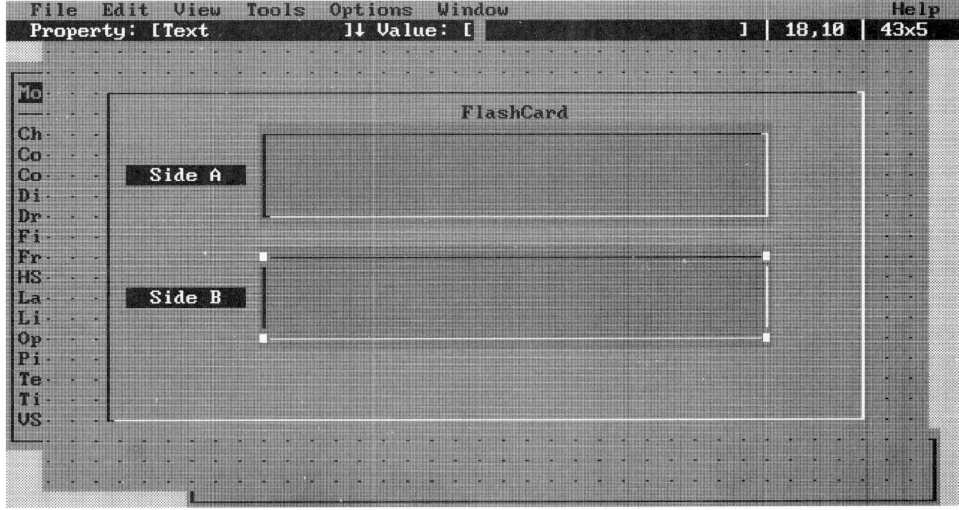

Figure 3-15 Flash with both text boxes in place.

have the same caption (Next) and reside in the same location on the form. To the user they will appear as a single button. To the program they will be two distinct objects that produce different responses based on the state of the program.

The **Command2** button will be captioned Exit and will be used to let the user exit the application.

To install the first command button, **Command1,** proceed as follows:

1. Open the Tools menu and choose the **Command Button** command. A command button, **Command1,** appears at the center of the form.

2. Click and drag this object to location 25,15.

3. Resize this object to size 10 × 3.

4. Open the **Property** list box menu (Property bar) and choose **Caption.**

5. Delete the current contents of the **Value** list box (Command1) and enter the following caption:

   Type Next and press **Enter.**

   Figure 3-16 shows the form with the command button, **Command1** (Next), in place.

6. Save the project.

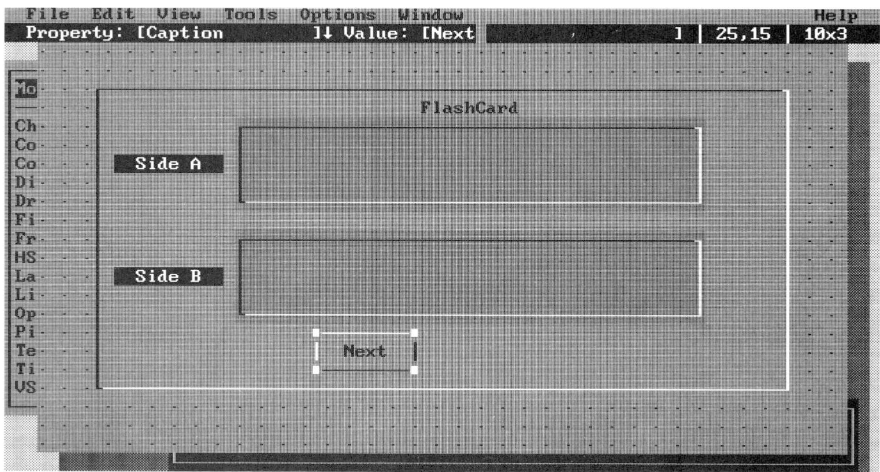

Figure 3-16 Command1 in place.

Adding the Second Command Button

To put the second command button on the form, follow the same steps you used to create **Command1.** Do this task on your own, referring back to the steps in the previous section as required.

Command2 is the same as **Command1,** with these exceptions:

- **Command2** is located at position 43,15.
- **Command2**'s caption is `Exit`.

When you finish creating **Command2,** Flash will appear as shown in Figure 3-17.

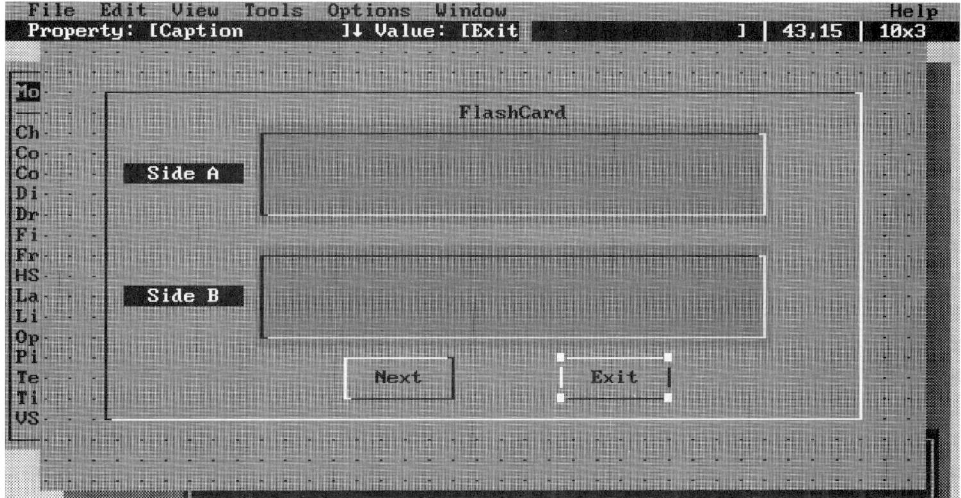

Figure 3-17 Flash with Next and Exit in place.

Adding the Third Command Button

To put the third command button, **Command3,** on the form, you follow the same steps you used to create **Command1.** Perform the following steps:

1. Open the Tools menu and choose the **Command Button** command. A command button, **Command3,** appears at the center of the form.
2. Click and drag this object to location 25,15.
3. Resize this object to size 10 × 3.
4. Open the **Property** list box menu (Property bar) and choose **Caption.**

5. Delete the current contents of the **Value** list box (`Command3`) and enter the following caption:

   Type `Next`

   Since **Command3** is in the same location as **Command1** and has the same caption, the screen shown in Figure 3-17 will look unchanged after you have created and positioned **Command3.**

6. Save the project.

This step completes the design stage of the project. You are now ready to verify the form design, develop the code, and add the data that will make the application perform its tasks.

> ☑ If you have "hidden" control objects on a form, press the **Tab** key repeatedly to "reveal" these objects. Each time you press **Tab,** Visual Basic moves the focus to the next object. Objects "hidden" behind other objects are "revealed" when Visual Basic gives them the focus. To see how this feature works, set the Property bar to **CtlName** (control name) and press **Tab** until `Command1` displays in the **Value** field. When this control name appears, the selected object (one with the focus) is the first command button you created. At this point, **Command3** is "hidden" behind **Command1.** Continue pressing **Tab** until `Command3` appears in the value field. When `Command3` displays, the third button is selected and "revealed." **Command1** is now "hidden" behind **Command3** once again.

Verify the Form Design

You can verify how the form design looks by running the application before you actually write any code. To do so, follow these steps:

1. If you have not already done so, save the project.

2. Open the File menu and choose the **Exit** option. Visual Basic closes the Form Designer windows and opens the programming environment windows. The empty Code window, `FLASH.FRM`, appears on the left side of the screen.

3. Open the Run menu and choose the **Start** command. The screen changes to a display of the FlashCard application (Figure 3-18). How

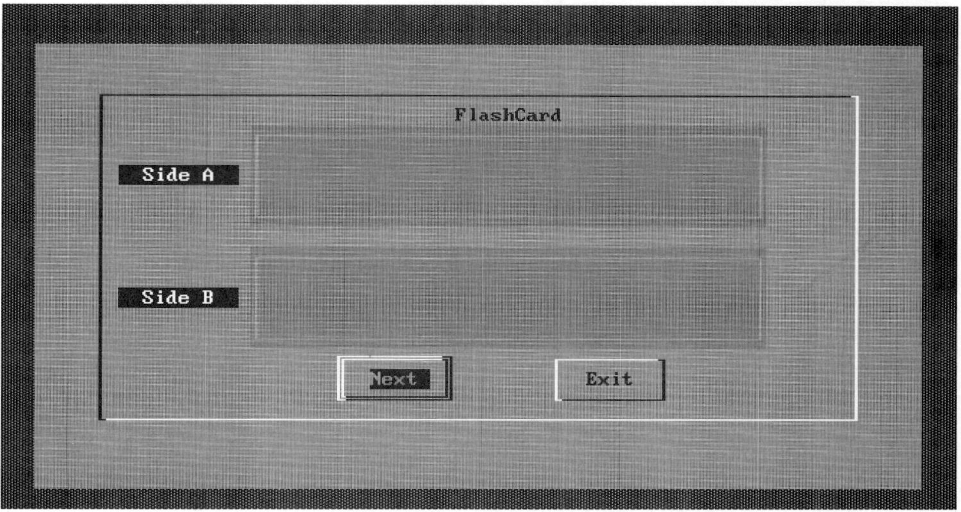

Figure 3-18 FlashCard application screen.

does your screen match up with the one shown in the figure? Do you need to make adjustments or changes? Try clicking the buttons. What happens? These objects should highlight when clicked, but nothing happens. As yet, they contain no code to respond to a Click event.

4. To exit from this screen, hold down **Ctrl** and press the **Break** key. Visual Basic restores the programming environment windows.

   If you wish to make adjustments to your design, click the **Form** button on the Project window, and then click **OK** on the dialog box that appears. The **Form** button lets you switch from the programming environment to the Form Designer screen.

5. If you do make changes to your design, save the project to record the changes.

Developing Code for FlashCard

If you have not already done so, save the project. If you are not already there, proceed to the Visual Basic programming environment to begin to develop the project's event procedures. In the programming environment, the empty code window, `FLASH.FRM`, appears on the left side of the screen.

One module within every project will be designated as the *main module,* the starting point where processing begins. For the FlashCard application, the form Flash and its associated code elements (declarations, data statements, and event procedures) will be the main module. Part of the code for Flash, a set of declarations and data statements, will be entered directly onto the `FLASH.FRM` code window.

In Visual Basic, you cannot put any executable statements on the form's code window. All executable statements must appear in event procedures or external code modules.

1. With the cursor in the upper left corner of the code window, enter the following set of Visual Basic declarations and data statements:

```
'FlashCard Application
'Form-Level Code: Setup
   COMMON SHARED NmbrCards AS INTEGER
   COMMON SHARED index AS INTEGER
   DIM SHARED SideA$(1 TO 5)
   DIM SHARED SideB$(1 TO 5)
   CONST TRUE = -1
   CONST FALSE = 0
'Data for FlashCard
   DATA 5
   DATA Nihon'go, Japanese language
   DATA Ohayo gozaimasu, Good morning
   DATA Kon'nichi wa, Hello or Good day
   DATA Kon'ban wa, Good evening
   DATA Sayonara, Goodbye
```

As a matter of style, remark statements (statements that begin with the single quotation mark character) are used to annotate each section of the code and to place comments to the right of some lines of code. The use of the single quotation mark is shorthand for the Visual Basic REM keyword.

Declarations and data statements have been indented using the **Tab** key. When you enter these Visual Basic statements in this manner, your code window will look like the one shown in Figure 3-19.

Two variables, `NmbrCards` and `index`, are declared to be `COMMON SHARED` variables of type `INTEGER`. You use the declaration **COMMON SHARED** to define global variables that can be used by subprocedures

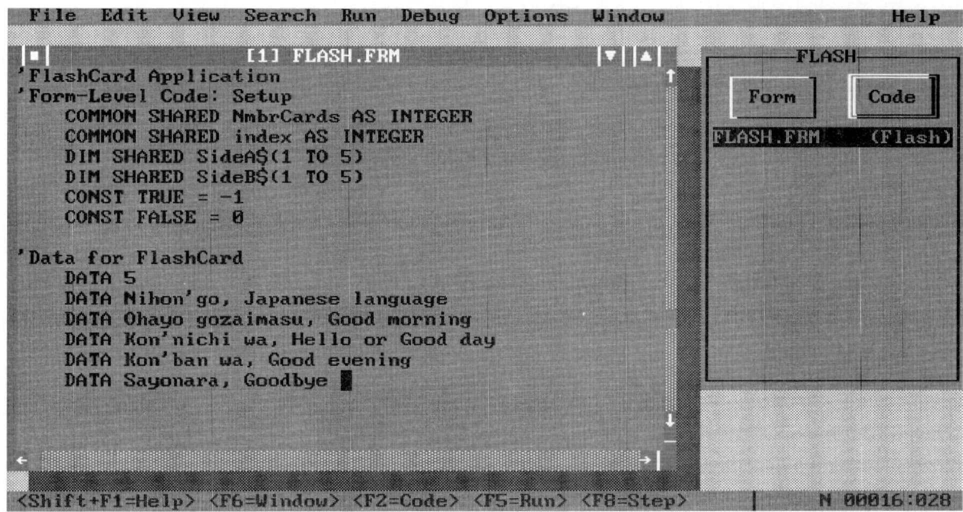

Figure 3-19 Declarations and data in Code window.

and functions directly. **COMMON SHARED** variables are shared between different modules within the same application. When you declare variables in this way, you do not have to pass them as parameters or declare them in the subprocedures where they are used.

Two string variable arrays, `SideA$` and `SideB$`, are dimensioned (`DIM`) and also declared to be shared variables. When dealing with variable arrays within a single module, using `DIM SHARED` makes those variables available to the subprocedures within that module. In this case, these arrays will be used to hold the text items to be displayed in the text boxes on the form.

`CONST` statements are also used to define two shared global constants, `TRUE` and `FALSE`. These constants appear in nearly all of this application's event procedures. Using constants helps make the procedures more readable, since words (TRUE, FALSE) are used in place of numbers (−1, 0). An accepted coding convention is to assign −1 to be the value for "true." Actually, the "true" condition can be satisfied by using any nonzero value.

The `DATA` statement section shows the data that will be read and used by the FlashCard program. The first data element, the number 5, indicates how many pairs of Japanese/English phrases appear in the subsequent `DATA` statements. This number will be read into the variable **NmbrCards.**

The remaining DATA statements contain pairs of matched Japanese/English phrases. The FlashCard application can be generalized to use any sets of matched data items—words/definitions, riddles/answers, and so forth. You determine the application's content by whatever data items you place in the DATA statements.

2. Save the project. You have completed the coding for the main module. The next step is to add the code for the event procedures that will direct the program's actions and responses.

> ☑ If you want Visual Basic to check the syntax of the code you enter, open the Options menu and choose the **Syntax Checking** command. Visual Basic's **Syntax Checking** command verifies the syntax of each line of code you enter, formats the line, and translates the code into executable form (if the syntax is correct). If this command is not active, Visual Basic reports syntax (and run-time) errors when you run the program.

Coding the Form_Load Procedure

To code the Form_Load procedure, perform the following steps:

1. Open the Edit menu and choose the **Event Procedures** command.
2. Visual Basic displays an **Event Procedures** dialog box (Figure 3-20).

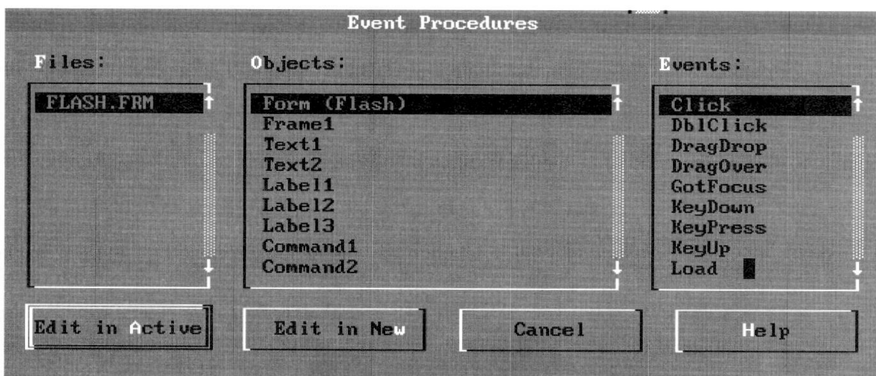

Figure 3-20 Event Procedure Form_Load window.

This dialog box has three lists: **Files, Objects,** and **Events.** The **Files** list has one file entry: FLASH.FRM. This is the form file for the FlashCard application.

The **Objects** list displays a list of items: a form with the caption Flash, a frame control (**Frame1**), two text boxes (**Text1, Text2**), three labels (**Label1, Label2,** and **Label3**), and two command buttons (**Command1** and **Command2**). The third command button (**Command3**) is at the bottom of the list but is not visible until you scroll the **Objects** list up the screen. Note that in the list the command button captions (Next and Exit) are not shown. You only see the *control names* for the buttons.

The **Events** list displays the set of events that can be detected by the highlighted object in the **Objects** list. In Figure 3-20, the listed events are for the form Flash. The highlight in the **Events** list is on Click.

The last item showing in the **Events** list for the form Flash is the event Load. The **Load** event occurs when a form is first loaded. You can use this event to trigger a procedure that initializes data, sets a form's properties, and performs whatever housekeeping tasks need to be done when you start an application.

For FlashCard, the **Form_Load** event procedure will be used to set desktop and form attributes, read text data into the string arrays, establish an index variable indicating which set of text items are being displayed, and initialize the buttons being displayed.

3. Move the highlight in the **Events** list to Load.

4. Click the **Edit in Active** button. When you click this button, Visual Basic dismisses the **Event Procedures** dialog box and displays the Code window shown in Figure 3-21.

   At the top of the Code window, you see the window title:

   ```
   [1] FLASH.FRM:Form_Load
   ```

   The window name is a concatenation of the file name of the form (FLASH.FRM), a colon symbol (:), and the event procedure name (Form_Load). The event procedure name is a concatenation of the object's control name (Form), an underline symbol (_), and the event (Load) that will trigger this procedure.

   In the text area of the Code window, you see a template for the procedure to be written into:

   ```
   SUB Form_Load ()

   END SUB
   ```

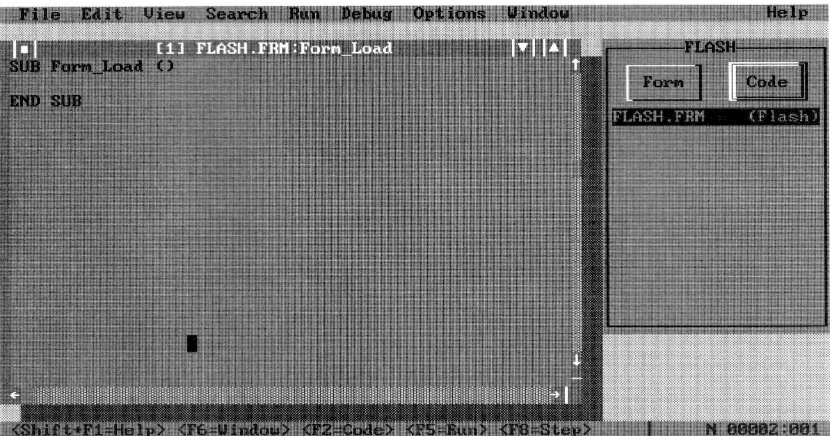

Figure 3-21 Event Procedures dialog box.

The general syntax for an event procedure such as this one is:

SUB *object control name_event name (arguments)*
local variables and constant definitions
code statements
END SUB

The words SUB and END are Visual Basic keywords. When used in this fashion, they help define the beginning (SUB) and end (END SUB) of an event procedure. For this event procedure, there will be no arguments.

5. Enter the following code (shown in bold) into this event procedure template:

```
SUB Form_Load ()
 'Set Declarations
 DEFINT A-Z

 'Set Desktop/Form Attributes
 CLS
 SCREEN.ControlPanel(7) = 32 'DESKTOP_PATTERN
 SCREEN.ControlPanel(5) = 8  'DESKTOP_BACKCOLOR
 SCREEN.ControlPanel(3) = 0  'ACTIVE_WINDOW_SHADOW
 SCREEN.ControlPanel(8) = 15  'DISABLED_ITEM_COLOR
 'Get Data
 READ NmbrCards
```

```
    FOR index = 1 TO NmbrCards
        READ SideA$(index), SideB$(index)
    NEXT index
    index = 1

    'Hide second Next button
    Command3.Visible = FALSE

    'Show first Next button
    Command1.Visible = TRUE
END SUB
```

In this context, CLS operates as a Visual Basic method that clears any text entries from the text boxes on the form. CLS can be preceded by a control name so that it operates on a particular control (*CtlName*.CLS). When used in a form module without a preceding control name, CLS applies to the whole form and does not affect background images or controls. When used in a non-form module with no forms showing, CLS can be used to clear various parts of the screen.

The set of **SCREEN.ControlPanel** statements alter parts of the desktop display (pattern, background color, and active window shadow) and the color of any disabled items. Compare the image in Figure 3-18 with the image shown in Figure 3-22. Figure 3-22 shows what the FlashCard application screen looks like with these **SCREEN.ControlPanel** settings applied.

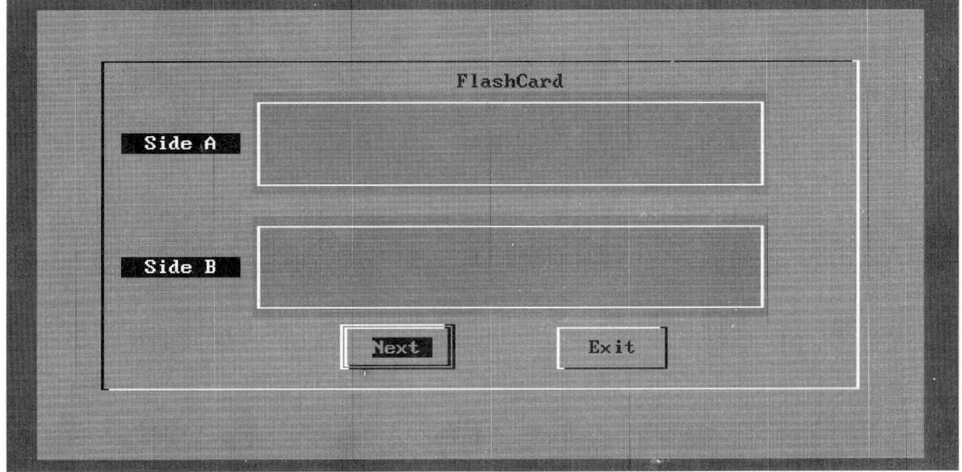

Figure 3-22 FlashCard with ControlPanel settings applied.

With these settings, the desktop pattern is set to a "space" or blank character (ASCII code 32). The color of the desktop is set to gray (8). The shadow surrounding the active window is turned off (0). The foreground color of all disabled items (the two text boxes) is set to bright white (15).

Table 3-1 lists all of the available SCREEN.ControlPanel array subscripts and constants. The ControlPanel array lets you set or interrogate the status of 17 useful run-time display settings. When you put a **SCREEN.ControlPanel** statement into a procedure, you can use either a subscript or a constant to designate which ControlPanel array item is being accessed. For a complete description of the ControlPanel properties, refer to Visual Basic on-line Help feature concerning this property.

The next section of code reads the number of cards into the variable NmbrCards and then reads the pairs of data into the string arrays SideA$ and SideB$. When the read operation is complete, the global variable, index, is set to a value of one.

The remaining code hides the third command button (**Command3**) and insures that the first command button (**Command1**) is

Table 3-1. SCREEN ControlProperty properties and constants.

Subscript	Constant
0	ACCESSKEY_FORECOLOR
1	ACTIVE_BORDER_BACKCOLOR
2	ACTIVE_BORDER_FORECOLOR
3	ACTIVE_WINDOW_SHADOW
4	COMBUTTON_FORECOLOR
5	DESKTOP_BACKCOLOR
6	DESKTOP_FORECOLOR
7	DESKTOP_PATTERN
8	DISABLED_ITEM_FORECOLOR
9	MENU_BACKCOLOR
10	MENU_FORECOLOR
11	MENU_SELECTED_BACKCOLOR
12	MENU_SELECTED_FORECOLOR
13	SCROLLBAR_BACKCOLOR
14	SCROLLBAR_FORECOLOR
15	THREE_D
16	TITLEBAR_BACKCOLOR
17	TITLEBAR_FORECOLOR

visible. This technique is used to make sure that the user interacts with the proper button when the program first starts.

6. When you enter this block of code, save the project.

Coding the Command Button Procedures

To code the command button procedures, follow these steps:

1. Open the Edit menu and choose the **Event Procedures** command.
2. Visual Basic displays an **Event Procedures** dialog box.
3. Move the highlight in the **Objects** list to `Command1`.
4. Move the highlight in the **Events** list to `Click`.
5. Click the **Edit in Active** button. When you click this button, Visual Basic dismisses the **Event Procedures** dialog box and displays a new Code window.

   At the top of the Code window, you see the window title:

   ```
   [1] FLASH.FRM:Command1_Click
   ```

   In the text area of the Code window, you see a template for the procedure to be written into:

   ```
   SUB Command1_Click ()

   END SUB
   ```

6. Enter the following code (shown in bold) into this event procedure template:

   ```
   SUB Command1_Click ()
        'Clear the contents of the text boxes
        Text1.Text = ""
        Text2.Text = ""

        'Set the Side A text box contents
        Text1.Text = SideA$(index)

        'Hide current Next button
        Command1.Visible = FALSE

        'Show second Next button
        Command3.Visible = TRUE
        Command3.SETFOCUS

   END SUB
   ```

The two assignment statements at the start of the procedure clears the contents of the text boxes, **Text1** and **Text2.** The syntax for this type of property change operation is as follows:

CtlName.Property = New_value

The control names for the text boxes are **Text1** and **Text2.** To clear the contents of the text boxes, you change the **Text** property to a new string value. In the event procedure, the **Text** property of both boxes is set to the empty string ("").

After the text boxes are cleared, the program then sets **Text1** to the contents of the **SideA$** array based on the current value of the global variable index. This action causes the contents of **SideA$(index)** to display in the **Text1** area on the form.

The procedure then uses the **Visible** property to hide the current button (**Command1**). A click on this button triggered the event that caused the current procedure (**Command1_Click**) to activate. The other `Next` button (**Command3**) is made visible, and the focus (highlight) is placed on that button using the **SETFOCUS** method.

7. When you enter this block of code, save the project.

Coding the Exit Button Event Procedure

To code the event procedure for the **Exit** button (**Command2**), perform these steps:

1. Open the Edit menu and choose the **Event Procedures** command.
2. Visual Basic displays an **Event Procedures** dialog box.
3. Move the highlight in the **Objects** list to `Command2`.
4. Move the highlight in the **Events** list to `Click`.
5. Click the **Edit in Active** button. When you click this button, Visual Basic dismisses the **Event Procedures** dialog box and displays a new Code window.

   At the top of the Code window, you see the window title:

   ```
   [1] FLASH.FRM:Command2_Click
   ```

   In the text area of the Code window, you see a template for the procedure to be written into:

```
SUB Command2_Click ()

END SUB
```

6. Enter the following code (shown in bold) into this event procedure template:

```
SUB Command2_Click ()
      SCREEN.HIDE
      END
END SUB
```

This event procedure uses the Visual Basic keyword SCREEN and the HIDE method to remove the form from the screen when the user clicks the **Exit** button. This action acknowledges, to the user, that **Exit** has been clicked. Without this type of confirmation, the form stays on the screen and the user may not notice the message Visual Basic displays, telling the user to press a key to continue.

7. When you enter this block of code, save the project.

Coding the Command3 Event Procedure

To code the event procedure for the second **Next** button (**Command3**), perform these steps:

1. Open the Edit menu and choose the **Event Procedures** command.
2. Visual Basic displays an **Event Procedures** dialog box.
3. Move the highlight in the **Objects** list to `Command3`. This object name is at the bottom of the list and is not visible until you scroll the list to the end.
4. Move the highlight in the **Events** list to `Click`.
5. Click the **Edit in Active** button. When you click this button, Visual Basic dismisses the **Event Procedures** dialog box and displays a new Code window.

   At the top of the Code window, you see the window title:

   ```
   [1] FLASH.FRM:Command3_Click
   ```

   In the text area of the Code window, you see a template for the procedure to be written into:

   ```
   SUB Command3_Click ()

   END SUB
   ```

6. Enter the following code (shown in bold) into this event procedure template:

```
SUB Command3_Click ()
     'Set the Side B text box contents
     Text2.Text = SideB$(index)

     'Hide current Next button
     Command3.Visible = FALSE

     'Show first Next button
     Command1.Visible = TRUE
     Command1.SETFOCUS

     'Check for end of data
     index = index + 1
     IF index = NmbrCards + 1 THEN index = 1
END SUB
```

   This procedure sets the contents of **Text2.** The text that appears on the form is taken from the SideB$ array, based on the current value of the variable index. The procedure then hides the current button (**Command3**) and causes the first button (**Command1**) to become visible and to highlight (be the focus) on the form.
   As a final step, the procedure increments the value of `index` and checks to see if `index` exceeds the number of data cards. If `index` is larger than NmbrCards, `index` is set back to a value of one.

7. When you enter this block of code, save the project.

This concludes the steps required to develop code for the FlashCard application. You are ready to run the program and verify that the code you have entered works correctly.

Run FlashCard

To run the program, open the Run menu and choose the **Start** command. If there are no syntax or run-time errors in the code, the form Flash will appear on the screen, with no entries in the text box areas.

When you click the **Next** button, the first Japanese word or phrase appears in the **Text1** box (Figure 3-23).

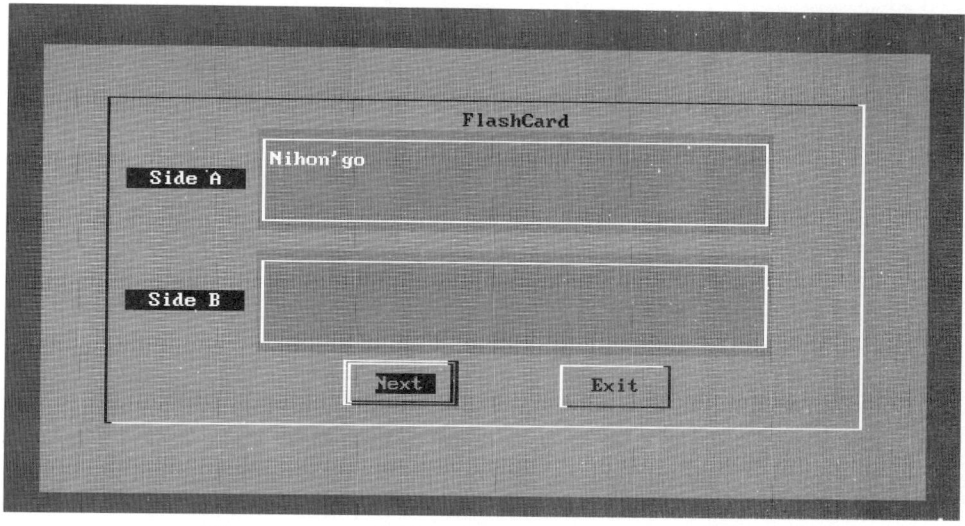

Figure 3-23 FlashCard after Next is clicked.

If you click **Next** again, the corresponding English word or phrase appears in the **Text2** area (Figure 3-24).

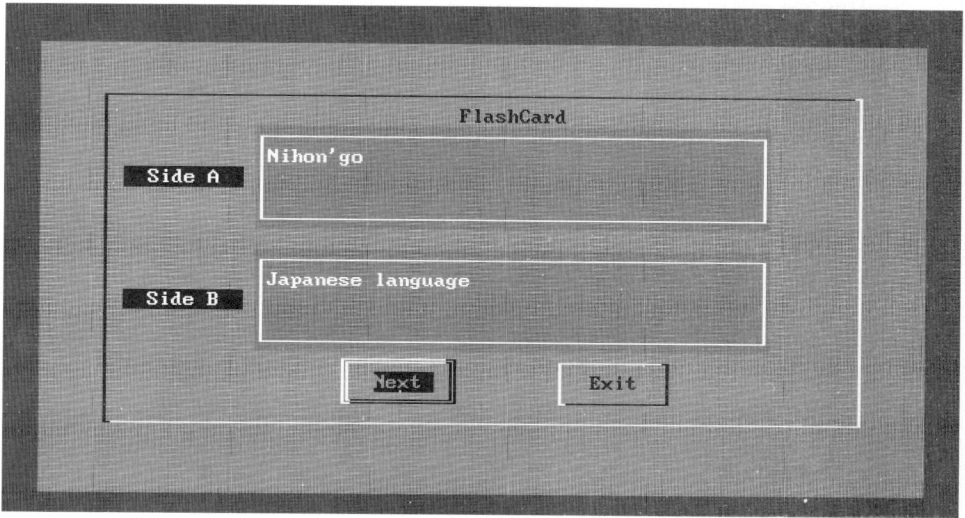

Figure 3-24 FlashCard with Japanese/English text.

If you continue to click **Next,** the text boxes will clear and a new Japanese entry will appear, followed by a new English entry. This process will continue until all five pairs of Japanese/English entries have been displayed. Then the application resets the index into the data arrays and display the pairs again from the beginning.

To exit the application, you click the **Exit** button. When you do so, the FlashCard form disappears and you see a message telling you to press any key to continue. When you press a key, you return to the Visual Basic programming environment.

Summary

In this chapter, you designed, developed, and ran a Visual Basic application called FlashCard. You created four event procedures (**Form_Load, Command1_Click, Command2_Click, Command3_Click**). In those procedures, you used the following QBasic/QuickBasic keywords: REM, COMMON, SHARED, AS, INTEGER, DIM, CONST, DATA, SUB, END SUB, DEFINT, CLS, READ, FOR-NEXT, END, and IF-THEN. You also used the new Visual Basic keywords SCREEN, HIDE, and SETFOCUS. In addition, you explored the Visual Basic concepts and terminology dealing with objects, event procedures, and object properties. For a complete list of these items, refer to the opening page of this chapter.

In the next chapter, you will modify and enhance the FlashCard application. You will also explore the Visual Basic debugging tools and features. When you are ready, proceed to Chapter 4, "Modifying a Custom Application."

4 Modifying a Custom Application

In the previous chapter, you created a custom application called FlashCard. In this chapter, you will modify FlashCard, expanding its features and capabilities. You will add check box controls and alter the FlashCard code so that it handles two completely different data sets of any length. You will also explore the use of form-level subprocedures, as well as some of the Visual Basic debugging tools. Your first task will involve adding two check box controls to the FlashCard form, as shown in Figure 4-1.

Concepts and Terminology

QBasic/QuickBasic Keywords

Visual Basic Event Procedures

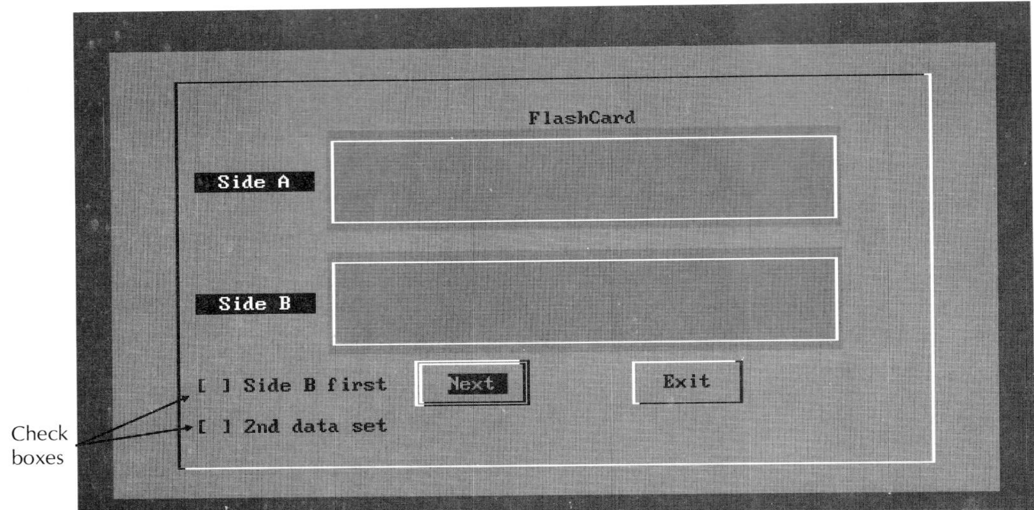

Figure 4-1 FlashCard with Check Box Controls

You will quickly discover that making alterations to an existing Visual Basic application is easy. To make a modified version of FlashCard, you can borrow most of the structure and code of the original application. You will have to add only a small amount of new code to transform the original application into a more functional and useful program.

Making a Copy of the Form

Before you start Visual Basic, make a copy of the form Flash, as follows. At the DOS prompt, enter the following command:

Type copy `a:\flash.frm a:\flash2.frm` and press **Enter.**

This command will create a copy of the form `FLASH.FRM` under the file name `FLASH2.FRM`. You will use `FLASH2.FRM` in this chapter to create a modified version of FlashCard. In this way, your original version of Flash-Card will remain intact.

New FlashCard Specifications

You will be adding two check box controls to the FlashCard form. You will modify the application's existing code to handle three new situations that let the user:

- Switch between two completely different sets of data.
- Decide which data element (Side A, Side B) is revealed first.
- Install two data sets of any length.

The only new controls are the two check boxes you will place on the form. The specifications for these two controls are as follow.

Specification #4-1 (Check Boxes)

FlashCard Application

Controls	Event(s) to be detected		Response(s)
Check1	None		None
Properties:	Location	7,15	
	Size	17 × 3	
	Caption	`Side B first`	
Check2	None		None
Properties:	Location	7,17	
	Size	17 × 3	
	Caption	`2nd data set`	

Notes/Comments: None

A check box control consists of a pair of square brackets ([]) followed by a caption off to the right. Check boxes allow the user to toggle (on/off) the character displayed within the brackets. When a check box is on, a letter `X` appears between the brackets. If there is no `X` in the brackets, the check box is off. The user toggles a check box by clicking anywhere on the control (brackets or caption).

When clicked, a check box automatically toggles a property of the control called **Value.** You do not have to create an event procedure to handle this property change. If the control is on, a click turns the control off and sets the **Value** property to zero; if the control is off, a click toggles it on and sets **Value** to one. You determine the state of a box object by looking at its **Value** property (0 = off, 1 = on, 2 = unavailable). This determination can be made from within other event procedures.

Modifying the Form

To begin modifications to the FlashCard form, do the following:

1. Start Visual Basic. The system displays a new project with an Untitled Code window.
2. Open the File menu and choose the **Add File** command. An **Add File** dialog appears (Figure 4-2).
3. Put your project diskette into drive A (the diskette on which you have been saving your Visual Basic project files). Double click on `[-A-]` in the **Directories** list box. This action directs Visual Basic to change the path to the A drive (`A:\`).
4. In the **File Type** option group at the bottom of the dialog box, click the **Form** option `[*.FRM]`. When that option is selected, the **Files** list box displays the list of form files on the diskette in drive A.
5. Select `FLASH2.FRM` file name in the **Files** list and click the **Edit in Active** button. Visual Basic loads the selected form, its controls, and code. The file you just loaded is identical to `FLASH.FRM`, the form you created in the previous chapter. If you were to run the application at this point, you would see the same form and data as you did in Chapter 3.
6. Click the **Form** button on the Project window. Visual Basic transfers you to the Form Designer.

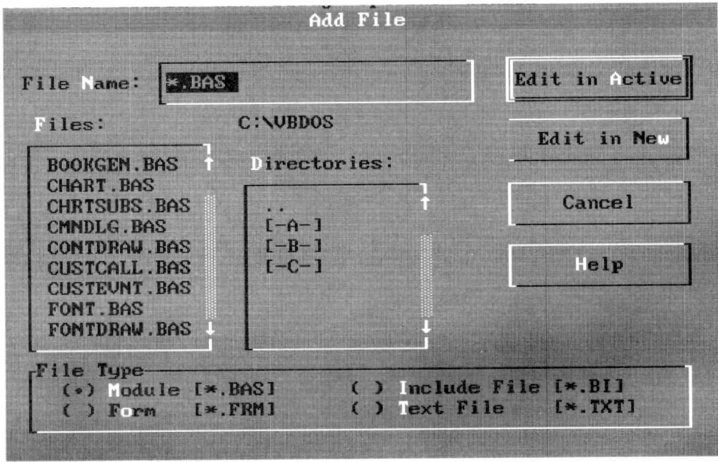

Figure 4-2 Add File dialog box.

Changing the FormName

When you copied FLASH.FRM to FLASH2.FRM, you altered the file name of the project file. Changing the file name, however, does not alter the **FormName** property. That property still carries the value `Flash`.

Click the down arrow on the **Property** list box and choose the **FormName** property. `Flash` appears in the **Value** list box area. Change the **FormName** value from `Flash` to `Flash2`, to match the name being used for the project file (`FLASH2.FRM`). This change does not affect the way the application works, but is done to reinforce the fact that you are working with a new project (`FLASH2`).

Adding a Check Box to the Form

The initial check box control will be captioned `Side B first`. This check box will be used to let the user control which text item gets displayed first.

To install the check box **Check1,** proceed as follows:

1. Open the Tools menu and choose the **Check Box** command. A check box, Check1, appears at the center of the form.

2. Click and drag this object to location 7,15.

3. Resize this object to size 17 × 3.

4. If this object's **Caption** value is not displayed on the Property bar, open the **Property** list box menu and choose **Caption.**

5. Delete the current contents of the value field (`Check1`) and enter the following caption:

   Type `Side B first` and press **Enter.**

   Figure 4-3 shows the new form Flash2 with the initial check box, **Check1** (`Side B first`), in place.

6. Open the File menu and choose the **Save Project** command. Save the project using the file name `FLASH2.MAK`. Save the project in the same directory or on the same floppy where you have `FLASH2.FRM`.

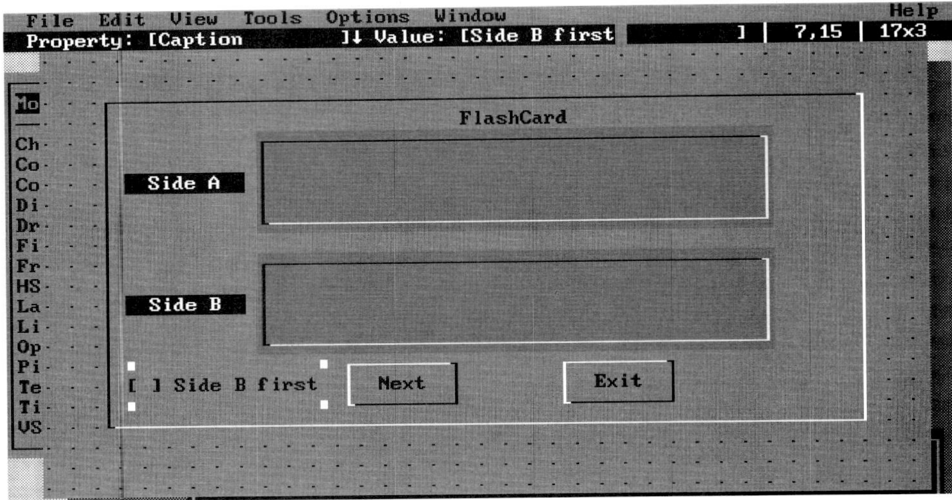

Figure 4-3 Check1 in place.

Adding the Second Check Box

To put the second check box on the form, follow the same steps you used to create **Check1.** Do this task on you own, referring back to the steps in the previous section, as required.

Check2 is the same as **Check1,** with these exceptions:

- **Check2** is located at position 7,17.
- **Check2**'s caption is `2nd data set`.

When **Check2** is in place, Flash2 will appear, as shown in Figure 4-4.

Adjusting the Frame

As you can see in Figure 4-4, a portion of the bottom left edge of the frame is being covered by the second check box. To fix this problem, you will adjust the frame object. The adjustments will involve expanding the frame vertically (up and down) to fill more of the form. To make these adjustments, do the following:

1. Click the frame (on any area of the frame not covered by another control). All the other controls may "disappear" when the frame is selected.
2. Alter the location of the frame so that its upper left corner is at 5,1.

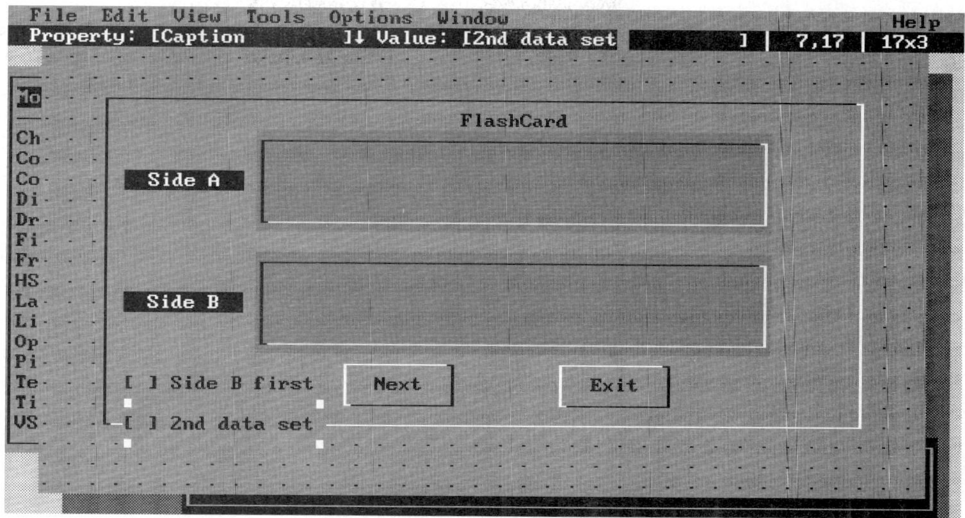

Figure 4-4 Flash2 with check boxes in place.

> ☑ Controls that seem to "disappear" when you click the frame object can be restored by pressing the **Tab** key repeatedly. Each time you press **Tab,** Visual Basic moves the focus to the next object, even if it is "hidden." Objects "hidden" behind other objects are thus "revealed" when Visual Basic gives them the focus.

3. Change the size of the frame so that it is sized 64 × 20.
4. When the frame is correctly positioned and sized, press **Tab** until all controls "reappear."

   Figure 4-5 shows the form Flash2, with the frame moved and resized. The second check box no longer obscures part of the bottom edge of the frame.
5. Save the project.

Checking the Design

You can check the design of this new form by running the application. Leave the Form Designer, and go to the programming environment, as follows:

Open the File menu and choose the **Exit** command.

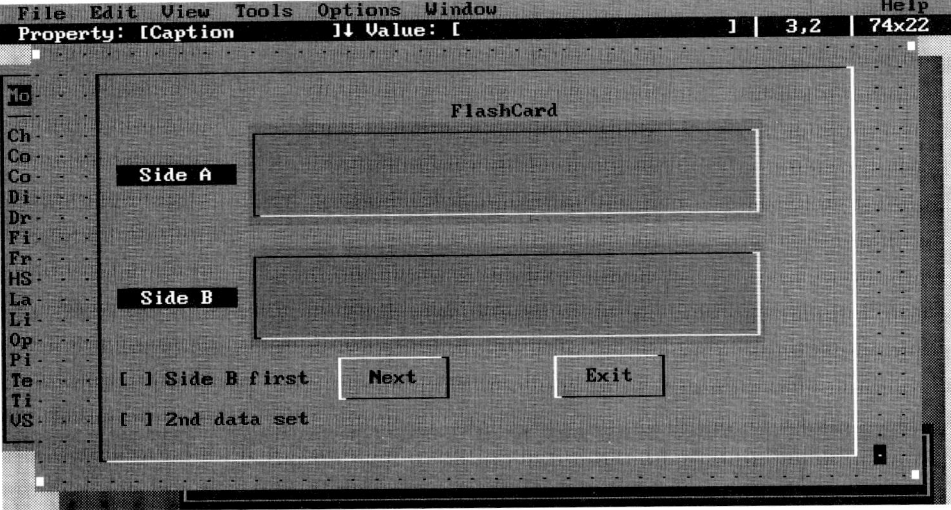

Figure 4-5 Flash2 with the frame adjusted.

If you have not saved the project files, Visual Basic will give you an opportunity to save your work. Do so; save the project before you exit the Form Designer.

When you reach the programming environment, open the Run menu and choose the **Start** command. The form shown previously (Figure 4-1) appears on the screen. The two new check box controls appear on the form.

Try clicking the check boxes. When the application starts running, the check boxes are toggled off. When you click one of these boxes, you toggle it on and an X appears between the square brackets on the left side of the control. If you click a box that is already on, the X disappears and the control is toggled off.

The **Next** and **Exit** buttons are also active. Since the code of the original FlashCard application was transferred into this new version, you can click **Next** and the program works as before. To exit the application, click **Exit.**

When you finish experimenting with the new check boxes and exercising the application, do the following:

Click **Exit** and then press **Enter** on the keyboard.

Visual Basic returns you to the programming environment. If you need to make changes to your form, do so by returning to the Form Designer. When you finish making changes, save the project files and return to the programming environment. If you need to do so, run the application again to verify your changes to the design.

When you finish checking the application's design elements, you are ready to alter the code in this application to utilize the two new check box controls.

Altering the Application's Code

Most of the code changes you will make involve slight alterations of existing code and the addition of some new code. The application needs to "watch" the state of the two new check boxes and display data based on the current settings of the boxes.

If the first check box is toggled on, the application will display Side B data on the first click of the **Next** button and then display Side A data on the subsequent click of **Next.** This allows users to test their knowledge of the data items in both directions (in this case Japanese/English, English/Japanese).

The second check box, when on, will cause the application to display an alternate data set. The **DATA** statements on the form module will be expanded to include these new data items.

In addition to these changes related to the check boxes, the application will also be generalized to handle data sets of any length.

Changing the Form Module Code

If it is not already displayed, bring the code for the form module (`FLASH2.FRM`) into the active window. Since `FLASH2.FRM` is a copy of `FLASH.FRM`, the current code is the same set of main module variable declarations and **DATA** statements found in `FLASH.FRM`.

If you need to retrieve this block of code, do the following:

1. Click the **Code** button on the Project window. The **Code** dialog box appears.
2. With the highlight on `FLASH2.FRM` in the item-to-be-edited list, click the **Edit in Active** button. Visual Basic will make the active Code window `FLASH2.FRM`, and the set of declarations and **DATA** statements should appear.
3. Enter the following changes and new code elements (items shown in bold) into the form module. The items not in bold are unchanged in this application. Items in bold have either been changed or added.

For example, the declarations that deal with setting up the SideA$ and SideB$ arrays have been changed from **DIM** to **COMMON** declarations. The size of these two arrays will be set dynamically in the **Form_Load** event procedure (using **REDIM** statements), based on the value of NmbrCards that will be read from the **DATA** area. Visual Basic does not allow executable statements in this opening code block, so the **REDIM** statements have to be placed in the first executable code block (**Form_Load**).

> ✔ Declaring variables to be **COMMON SHARED** makes them available globally to all subprocedures within an application. Placing the **SHARED** declaration in a subprocedure lets the program share module variables with that single subprocedure. The SHARED keyword by itself cannot be used in module-level code, and can only appear within a subprocedure.

```
'FlashCard Application
'Form-Level Code: Setup
     COMMON SHARED NmbrCards AS INTEGER
     COMMON SHARED index AS INTEGER
     COMMON SHARED SideA$()
     COMMON SHARED SideB$()
     CONST TRUE = -1
     CONST FALSE = 0

'Data for FlashCard
     DATA 6
     'Data set #1
     DATA Nihon'go, Japanese language
     DATA Ohayo gozaimasu, Good morning
     DATA Kon'nichi wa, Hello or Good day
     DATA Kon'ban wa, Good evening
     DATA Sayonara, Goodbye
     DATA Oyasumi nasai, Good night
     'Data set #2
     DATA tako, octopus
     DATA anago, sea eel
     DATA maguro, tuna
     DATA saba, mackerel
     DATA kaki, oyster
     DATA uni, sea urchin roe
```

The **DATA** statements have been altered to allow for six pairs of items in each data set, and a second set of data items have been added. The second data set are Japanese/English words you would encounter when you order sushi.

4. Save the project.

Changing the Form_Load Event Procedure

Bring up the code for the **Form_Load** event procedure and make changes, as follows:

1. Click the **Code** button on the Project window. The **Code** dialog box appears.
2. Move the highlight to the `Form_Load` item and click the **Edit in Active** button. Visual Basic will make the active Code window **FLASH2.FRM:Form_Load,** and the code for this event procedure will appear.
3. Enter the following changes and new code elements (items shown in bold) into this event procedure:

```
SUB Form_Load ()
   'Set Declarations
   DEFINT A-Z

   'Set Desktop/Form Attributes
   CLS
   SCREEN.ControlPanel(7)  = 32 'DESKTOP_PATTERN
   SCREEN.ControlPanel(5)  = 8  'DESKTOP_BACKCOLOR
   SCREEN.ControlPanel(3)  = 0  'ACTIVE_WINDOW_SHADOW
   'SCREEN.ControlPanel(8) = 15 'DISABLED_ITEM_COLOR

   'Get Data
   READ NmbrCards
   'Dimension arrays
   REDIM SideA$(0 TO 1, 1 TO NmbrCards)
   REDIM SideB$(0 TO 1, 1 TO NmbrCards)
   'Read data set #1
   FOR index = 1 TO NmbrCards
      READ SideA$(0, index), SideB$(0, index)
   NEXT index
   'Read data set #2
```

```
   FOR index = 1 TO NmbrCards
      READ SideA$(1, index), SideB$(1, index)
   NEXT index
   index = 1

   'Hide second Next button
   Command3.Visible = FALSE

   'Show first Next button
   Command1.Visible = TRUE
END SUB
```

Two **REDIM** statements have been added to this event procedure. Using NmbrCards, these statements dynamically redimension SideA$ and SideB$ into two-dimensional arrays. Each array is dimensioned to hold the two data sets (Japanese/English words and phrases, and sushi terms). The original FOR-NEXT loop has been adjusted to read in the first data set. A second FOR-NEXT loop has been added to read in the second data set. This block of code could be generalized to handle any number of data sets that are all the same size.

4. Save the project.

Changing the Command1_Click Event Procedure

Bring up the code for the **Command1_Click** event procedure and make changes, as follows:

1. Click the **Code** button on the Project window. The **Code** dialog box appears.
2. Move the highlight to the `Command1_Click` item and click the **Edit in Active** button. Visual Basic will make the active Code window **FLASH2.FRM:Command1_Click,** and the code for this event procedure will appear.
3. Enter the following changes and new code elements (items shown in bold) into this event procedure:

```
SUB Command1_Click ()
   'Clear the contents of the text boxes
   Text1.Text = ""
```

```
    Text2.Text = ""

    'Set contents of a text box
    'Determine the data set to be used
    Dset = 0
    IF Check2.Value = 1 THEN Dset = 1
    'Determine which side to show first
    IF Check1.Value = 0 THEN
       Text1.Text = SideA$(Dset, index)
    ELSE
       Text2.Text = SideB$(Dset, index)
    END IF

    'Hide current Next button
    Command1.Visible = FALSE

    'Show second Next button
    Command3.Visible = TRUE
    Command3.SETFOCUS
END SUB
```

The key change to this event procedure involves code that determines which data set is to be displayed. A local variable, `Dset`, is assigned a value of zero, which points to the first set of data. Then an **IF-THEN** statement is used to check the state of the second check box, **Check2.** If that check box is on (`Check2.Value =1`), then `Dset` is assigned a value of one, which points to the second data set.

The IF-THEN-ELSE structure in this procedure checks the state of the first check box, **Check1.** If the check box is on, Side B is displayed; if the box is off (`Check1.Value = 0`), then Side A is displayed. As you might imagine, a similar version of this block of code will be used in the **Command3** event procedure.

4. Save the project.

Changing the Command3_Click Event Procedure

Bring up the code for the **Command3_Click** event procedure and make changes, as follows:

1. Click the **Code** button on the Project window. The **Code** dialog box appears.

2. Move the highlight to the `Command3_Click` item and click the **Edit in Active** button. Visual Basic will make the active Code window **FLASH2.FRM:Command3_Click,** and the code for this event procedure will appear.

3. Enter the following changes and new code elements (items shown in bold) into this event procedure:

```
SUB Command3_Click ()
  'Set contents of a text box
  'Determine the data set to be used
  Dset = 0
  IF Check2.Value = 1 THEN Dset = 1
  'Determine which side to show first
  IF Check1.Value = 0 THEN
    Text2.Text = SideB$(Dset, index)
  ELSE
    Text1.Text = SideA$(Dset, index)
  END IF

  'Hide current Next button
  Command3.Visible = FALSE

  'Show first Next button
  Command1.Visible = TRUE
  Command1.SETFOCUS

  'Check for end of data
  index = index + 1
  IF index = NmbrCards + 1 THEN index = 1
END SUB
```

The code changes in this procedure mirror the changes made in the **Command1_Click** procedure. A local variable, `Dset`, points to the appropriate data set based on the state of the **Check2** control. The IF-THEN-ELSE structure checks the state of control **Check1** and displays the required text item. Note that the key change in this block of code over the one used in **Command1_Click** is the inversion of which text box receives text for display. Where **Command1_Click** displays Side A, this procedure needs to display Side B, and vice-versa.

4. Save the project. You are now ready to test your changes to the code.

Running the FlashCard Application

Once you have made all of the suggested code changes, save the project files and do the following:

1. Open the Run menu and choose the **Start** command.
2. If you have no errors in your code, Visual Basic will clear the screen and display the Flash2 form on the screen (Figure 4-6). This screen will look the same as the one you saw when you checked the application's design. The difference is in the code you have added or changed.

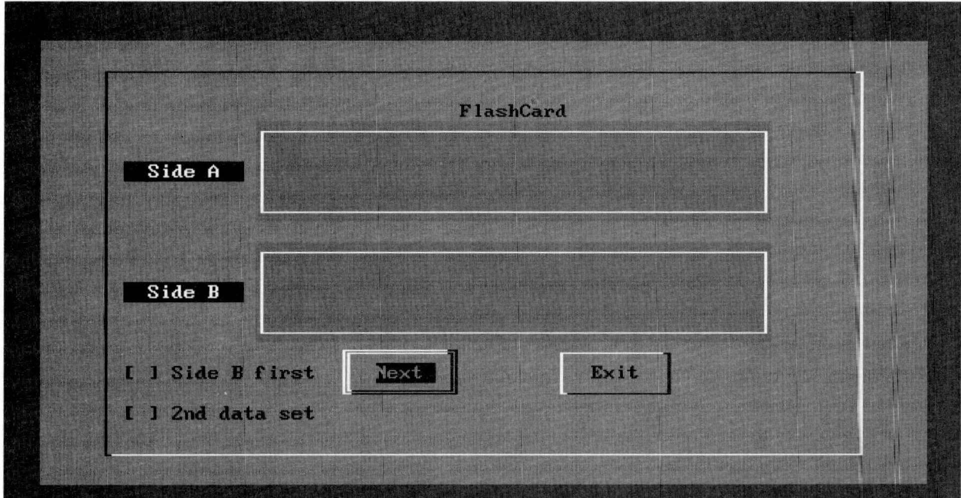

Figure 4-6 Flash2 form.

3. Experiment with the application. Toggle the check boxes and watch what happens to the display. When the first check box is on (**Check1**), does Side B display before Side A? When the second check box (**Check2**) is on, do you see the second data set (sushi words)? If both check boxes are on, do you see Side B of the sushi terms before you see Side A? If both boxes are off, does the application behave like the original FlashCard, but with one additional term in the data set (`Oyasumi nasai, Good night`)?

   If you encounter errors, Visual Basic will halt the program and give you a brief message about the type of error that has been encountered. You can then use the Visual Basic Help feature to get more information about the error. You can also print the project code using the Visual Basic **Print** command on the File menu.

In addition to the Help system and Print features, Visual Basic also provides a set of debugging tools that can assist you in isolating error conditions and situations.

Using Visual Basic Debugging Tools

Figure 4-7 shows the list of commands on the Visual Basic Debug menu. The top part of the menu contains the commands that control the setting and deletion of **Watch** variables and expressions and **Watchpoints.** A **Watch** variable or expression is used to continuously watch a variable or expression during program execution. The Watch result is displayed and updated in the Debug window.

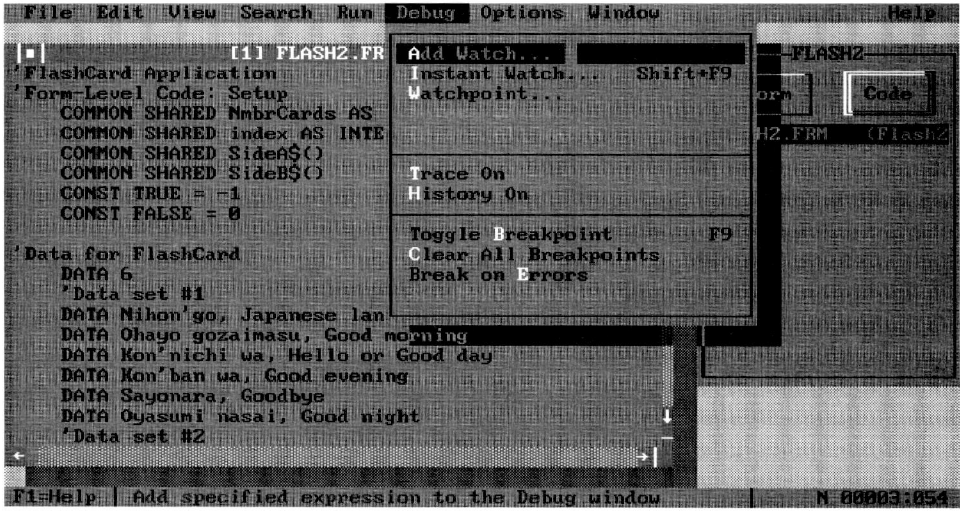

Figure 4-7 Visual Basic Debug menu.

A **Watchpoint** can be used to suspend program execution when a watched expression becomes true. A Watchpoint behaves like a dynamic breakpoint that is conditioned by a particular condition.

An **Instant Watch** shows the contents of a variable or expression when a program is suspended. Like Watches, both Watchpoint and Instant Watch results are displayed and updated in the Debug window. You can use the **Delete Watch** and **Delete All Watch** commands to delete individual Watches or all Watches, respectively.

The **Trace** command directs Visual Basic to show you each line of code as it is executed. The **Trace** command also lets you browse the last 20 lines of code that were executed once a program stops running.

The **History** command runs the program until it stops and lets you browse the last 20 lines of code that were executed.

The bottom four commands control the setting and removal of breakpoints in the program. By putting the cursor on a line of code and selecting the **Toggle Breakpoint** command, you tell Visual Basic that you want to suspend program execution at that line of code. The **Break on Errors** command stops program execution in the first line of the most recent error handling routine. To use this command, you need to have an error handling routine in your application. A discussion of error handling routines will be covered later in this book. The **Set Next Statement** command directs Visual Basic to begin execution with a particular statement.

Taken together, this set of debugging commands provides you with a robust set of tools for locating program errors.

Setting a Watchpoint

To see how you use one of the Visual Basic debugging tools, bring up the code for the **Command1_Click** event procedure as follows:

1. While in the programming environment, click the **Code** button on the Project window. The **Code** dialog box appears.
2. Move the highlight to the Command1_Click item and click the **Edit in Active** button. Visual Basic will display the code for the **FLASH2.FRM:Command1_Click** event procedure.
3. With the **Command1_Click** procedure code on the screen, open the Debug menu and choose the **Watchpoint** command. A **Watchpoint** dialog box appears (Figure 4-8).
4. Enter the following expression:

   Type `Dset > 0`

5. Click **OK** to dismiss the dialog box and record your **Watchpoint** expression. The Visual Basic Debug window will appear (Figure 4-9).

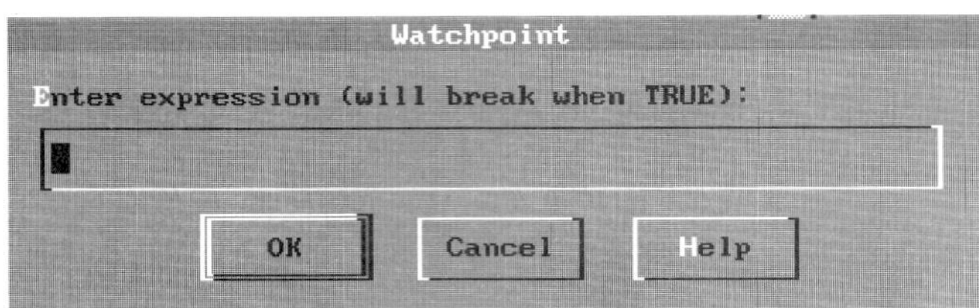

Figure 4-8 Watchpoint dialog box.

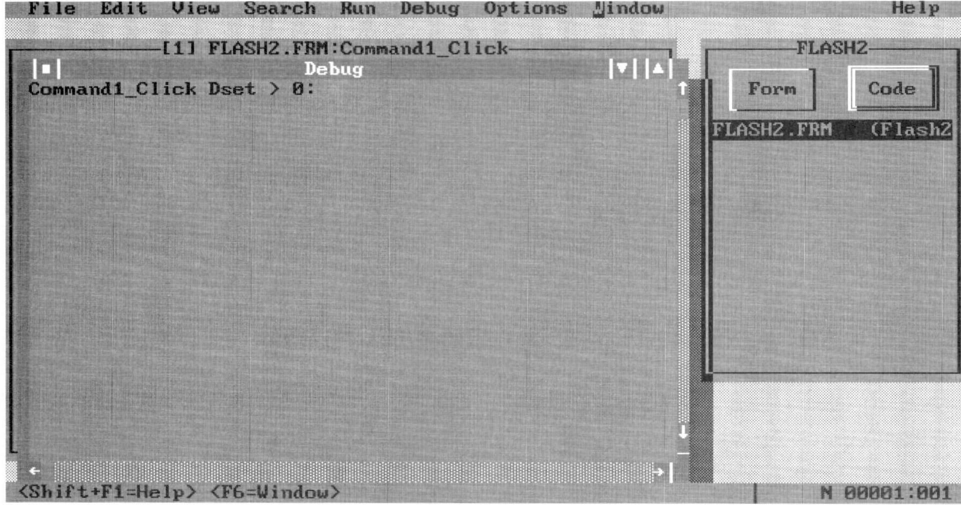

Figure 4-9 Visual Basic Debug window.

The expression being watched is shown in the Debug window:

```
Command1_Click Dset > 0:
```

There is no result shown after the colon (:) at this time. Later, when you run the application and the expression becomes true, Visual Basic will suspend the program and display the result `<TRUE>` after the colon.

Executing with a Watchpoint

To see how the **Watchpoint** behaves during program execution, do the following:

1. Open the Run menu and choose the **Start** command. The new Flash-Card application will display.

According to the display, "anago" is the Japanese word for "Good morning." This problem corrects itself as you proceed to exercise the application. However, you can write (or copy) a small amount of code that will permanently correct the error. In doing so, you can also learn a bit about using Visual Basic subprocedures.

Adding a Subprocedure

You are about to create a form-level subprocedure called **FlashSet. FlashSet** will be called from the **Form_Load** event procedure and replace part of that procedures existing code. **FlashSet** will also be called from two new event procedures tied to the check boxes, **Check1** and **Check2.**

If you use the steps outlined as follows, you will only need to enter a minor amount of new code:

1. Open the File menu and choose the **Open Project** command.
2. When the **Open Project** dialog box appears, open the `FLASH2.MAK` project you saved earlier in this chapter. Visual Basic will place you in the programming environment.
3. Click **Code** on the project window, highlight `Form_Load`, and Click **Edit in Active.** The code for the **Form_Load** procedure will appear in the Code window.
4. Highlight the following block of code within this procedure:

```
index = 1

'Hide second Next button
Command3.Visible = FALSE

'Show first Next button
Command1.Visible = TRUE
```

5. With the block of code highlighted, open the Edit menu and choose the **Cut** command. The selected text disappears from the Code window and moves onto the Visual Basic Clipboard.
6. At the location where the code has been cut, enter the following immediately above the **END SUB** statement:

   Type `FlashSet`

FlashSet will be the name of a new subprocedure that you are about to define and create. The code in **Form_Load** now appears as follows:

```
SUB Form_Load ()
  'Set Declarations
  DEFINT A-Z

  'Set Desktop/Form Attributes
  CLS
  SCREEN.ControlPanel(7) = 32 'DESKTOP_PATTERN
  SCREEN.ControlPanel(5) = 8  'DESKTOP_BACKCOLOR
  SCREEN.ControlPanel(3) = 0  'ACTIVE_WINDOW_SHADOW
  SCREEN.ControlPanel(8) = 15 'DISABLED_ITEM_COLOR

  'Get Data
  READ NmbrCards
  'Dimension arrays
  REDIM SideA$(0 TO 1, 1 TO NmbrCards)
  REDIM SideB$(0 TO 1, 1 TO NmbrCards)
  'Read data set #1
  FOR index = 1 TO NmbrCards
     READ SideA$(0, index), SideB$(0, index)
  NEXT index
  'Read data set #2
  FOR index = 1 TO NmbrCards
     READ SideA$(1, index), SideB$(1, index)
  NEXT index

  FlashSet
END SUB
```

7. With the cursor still on the line with the procedure name **FlashSet,** open the Edit menu and choose the **New Sub** command. A **New Sub** dialog box appears. The name `FlashSet` appears in the text box.

8. Click **Edit in Active** to tell Visual Basic to create a new subprocedure called **FlashSet.** The Code window appears along with a code template for the **FlashSet** subprocedure.

```
SUB FlashSet ()

END SUB
```

9. Press **Enter** to open up a blank line below the first line of the sub-procedure. Then open the Edit menu and choose the **Paste** command. The code that was cut from the **Form_Load** procedure is pasted into **FlashSet.**

```
SUB FlashSet ()
  index = 1

  'Hide second Next button
  Command3.Visible = FALSE

  'Show first Next button
  Command1.Visible = TRUE
END SUB
```

10. Save the project at this point.

Borrowing Code

Just as you cut and pasted code from **Form_Load** into **FlashSet,** you can also use Visual Basic to copy code from other parts of the program. For example, when **FlashSet** is called from the check box event procedures (to be written), it would be handy to have **FlashSet** clear the text boxes. **Command1_Click** already contains a block of code that clears the text boxes. To retrieve that code, copy it, and paste it into **FlashSet,** do the following:

1. Click **Code** on the Project window. The **Code** dialog box appears.
2. Highlight `Command1_Click` and click **Edit in Active.** The code for this event procedure appears in the Code window.
3. Select the following block of code by clicking and dragging the pointer over these lines of code:

```
'Clear the contents of the text boxes
Text1.Text = ""
Text2.Text = ""
```

4. Open the Edit menu and choose the **Copy** command. The selected block of code is copied onto the Clipboard.
5. Click **Code** on the Project window.
6. Highlight `FlashSet` and click **Edit in Active.**

7. Position the cursor below the first line of **FlashSet** (SUB line), open the Edit menu, and choose **Paste.** The block of code from **Command1_Click** is pasted into **FlashSet.**

```
SUB FlashSet ()
  'Clear the contents of the text boxes
  Text1.Text = ""
  Text2.Text = ""

  'Reset index
  index = 1

  'Hide second Next button
  Command3.Visible = FALSE

  'Show first Next button
  Command1.Visible = TRUE
END SUB
```

   We have added a **REM** statement above the line that assigns index a value of one. If you wish, enter that **REM** statement into your version of **FlashSet.**

8. Save the project.

You have now created a Visual Basic form-level subprocedure called **FlashSet.** If you open the Code window for the form, FLASH2.FRM, you will discover that Visual Basic has automatically inserted a **DECLARE** statement in the declarations code section. The **DECLARE** statement is used to globally declare user-defined keywords that represent subprocedures or functions.

To complete this set of changes, you need to create two simple event procedures for **Check1** and **Check2,** and then run and test the code.

Adding Event Procedures for the Check Boxes

When a user clicks either one of the check boxes on the form, that event can be used to call **FlashSet. FlashSet** clears the text boxes, resets the index variable to a value of one (to start at the beginning of the data), and sets up the **Next** command buttons.

The complete event procedures for **Check1** and **Check2** are as follows:

```
SUB Check1_Click ()
  'Reset program and data set
  FlashSet
END SUB

SUB Check2_Click ()
  'Reset program and data set
  FlashSet
END SUB
```

Try your hand at adding these two event procedures. To do so, you will need to choose the **Event Procedures** command on the Edit menu. When the **Event Procedures** dialog box appears, scroll down the **Objects** list until **Check1** and **Check2** appear. Highlight `Check1`, select **Click** in the **Events** list, and click the **Edit in Active** button.

When the event procedure template displays, enter the **REM** statement and **FlashSet** on the empty line between the `SUB` and `END SUB` lines. Repeat this same process for **Check2,** and the corrected FlashCard application will be ready for testing.

The addition of **FlashSet** as a form-level subprocedure (and the insertion of the two check box procedures that call **FlashSet**) will fix the text box synch problem. If you wish, you might experiment with other changes to **Flash2.** You might try a completely different set of data or a different number of data items. How would could go about installing two data sets of different sizes? What changes would you have to make to the code to accommodate different sized data sets? (**Note:** There are many solutions, such as using two NmbrCards variables, inserting and detecting blanks or "no data" codes in the smaller set of data pairs, and so forth.) What is required to generalize the FlashCard application to handle any number of data sets?

If you continue to experiment with changes to FlashCard, repeat the steps outlined at the start of this chapter where you copy and rename the form. Then work with the renamed copy as you make changes, run experiments, and alter the way the application works.

Summary

In this chapter, you altered a Visual Basic application called FlashCard. You added two check box controls to an existing form, modified the main module and event procedure code, and developed a form-level subprocedure called **FlashSet.** You used the check boxes to control which data set to display and the order of the displayed data.

In making these changes, you used the same QBasic/QuickBasic keywords you used in the previous chapter (Chapter 3, "Creating Custom Applications"). In addition, you used the keywords REDIM and DECLARE. You used no new Visual Basic keywords.

You also explored the use of the Visual Basic debugging tools. You learned how to set a **Watchpoint** and view the **Watchpoint** results in the Debug window. To create the subprocedure **FlashSet,** you used the Edit menu **Cut, Copy,** and **Paste** commands. For a complete list of the key items you covered in this chapter, refer to this chapter's opening page.

In the next chapter, you build a group of small Visual Basic applications. These applications will be used to introduce new Visual Basic concepts and keywords. When you are ready, proceed to Chapter 5, "Exploring Visual Basic with Small Applications."

5 Exploring Visual Basic with Small Applications

In this chapter, you will continue your Visual Basic explorations by building two small applications. These applications extend your knowledge of the Visual Basic system and demonstrate several interesting features. You will build a simple calculation application that can be easily extended to handle a variety of computations. You will also examine an application that will test your mouse clicking skills.

Building a Calculator Application

In this section, you will build a small application that performs calculations and displays results. The application, called Calc, looks like Figure 5-1 when it is being used.

With this application, you learn how to use a text box control to capture a user's input data. You also use a multiline text box to display output results.

Calc Specifications

The Calc application uses a form, a frame, two labels, two text box controls, and four command buttons. These objects will be assembled to produce the application interface shown in Figure 5-1.

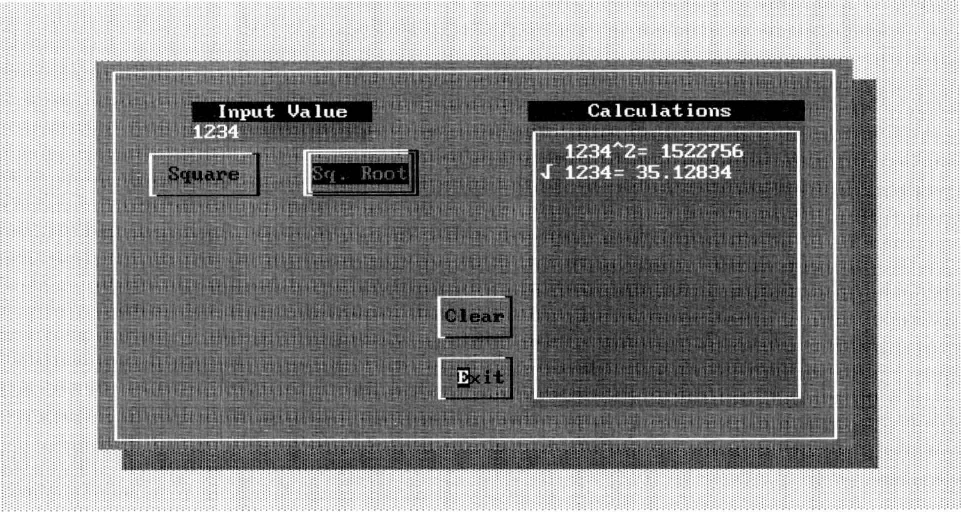

Figure 5-1 The Calc Application in use

The Calc Form Specification

The Calc form will house the frame, labels, text boxes, and command buttons for this application. The form's response to the **Load** event will be to execute code that clears the screen and sets a few desktop and form attributes.

The specifications for the Calc form are as follows.

Specification #5-1 (Form)

Calc Application

Form	Event(s) to be detected		Response(s)
Calc	Load		Clear screen
			Set Desktop/Form attributes
Properties:	Location	8,3	
	Size	63 × 19	
	BorderStyle	None	
	Colors	White (background)/black (foreground)	

Notes/Comments: This is the form for the application.

The Calc Frame Specification

The **BorderStyle** of the Calc form will be set to **None.** A frame object will then be used to add a border around the form's edge. When you use a frame control on a form, you need to place the frame on the form before installing other controls. The specifications for the frame follows (see page 114).

The Calc Label Specifications

Calc uses two labels as static design elements. One label identifies the user input region on the form. The second label sits over the output display region (see page 114).

Calc Text Box Specifications

You will install two text box controls on the Calc form. The first text box, used to capture user input values for the calculations, will be enabled to

Specification #5-1 (Frame)

Calc Application

Frame	Event(s) to be detected		Response(s)
Frame1	None		None
Properties:	Location	1,0	
	Size	61×19	
	Caption	Blank	
	Enabled	False	
	Colors	White (background)/black (foreground)	

Notes/Comments: Inner frame on the form; used as a design element.

Specification #5-1 (Labels)

Calc Application

Controls	Event(s) to be detected		Response(s)
Label1	None		None
Properties:	Location	8,2	
	Size	15×1	
	Colors	Gray (background)/bright white (foreground)	
	Caption	`Input Value`	
	Alignment	Center	
Label2	None		None
Properties:	Location	36,2	
	Size	23×1	
	Colors	Gray (background)/bright white (foreground)	
	Caption	`Calculations`	
	Alignment	Center	

Notes/Comments: None

accept keyboard input. The second text box, used to display multiple lines of calculation results, will not allow users to change the information that appears in the control.

Specification #5-1 (Text Boxes)

Calc Application

Controls	Event(s) to be detected		Response(s)
Text1	None		None
Properties:	Location	8,3	
	Size	15 × 1	
	Colors	Cyan (background)/black (foreground)	
	Text	Blank	
	BorderStyle	None	
	Enabled	True (1)	
Text2	None		None
Properties:	Location	36,3	
	Size	23 × 14	
	Colors	Cyan (background)/black (foreground)	
	Text	Blank	
	BorderStyle	None	
	MultiLine	True (1)	
	Enabled	False (0)	

Notes/Comments: Enabled set to True (0) means that the user can enter text into control from the keyboard.

Calc Command Button Specifications

The form Flash has four command buttons. Two buttons (**Command1** and **Command2**) control the application's defined calculations. The button with the caption `Square` computes the square of the current input value,

Specification #5-1 (Command Buttons)

Calc Application

Controls	Event(s) to be detected		Response(s)
Command1	Click		Gets input value
			Converts input to numeric data
			Computes square of input
			Displays results in display list
Properties:	Location	4,4	
	Size	10 × 3	
	Caption	`Square`	
Command2	Click		Gets input value
			Converts input to numeric data
			Computes square root of input
			Displays results in display list
Properties:	Location	17,4	
	Size	10 × 3	
	Caption	`Sq.Root`	
Command3	Click		Clears the text boxes
			Sets focus to Text1
Properties:	Location	28,11	
	Size	7 × 3	
	Caption	`Clear`	
Command4	Click		Hides form
			Exits application
Properties:	Location	28,14	
	Size	7 × 3	
	Caption	`Exit`	

Notes/Comments: None

and displays the results in the **Calculations** text box. The button captioned `Sq. Root` calculates the square root of the current input value. This button also displays results in the **Calculations** text box.

The third button (**Command3**) clears the input and calculations text boxes. This button is captioned `Clear`. The `Exit` button (**Command4**) hides the form and exits the application.

Figure 5-2 shows the Calc form and all of its control objects. Use this figure as a guide when you build your version of Calc.

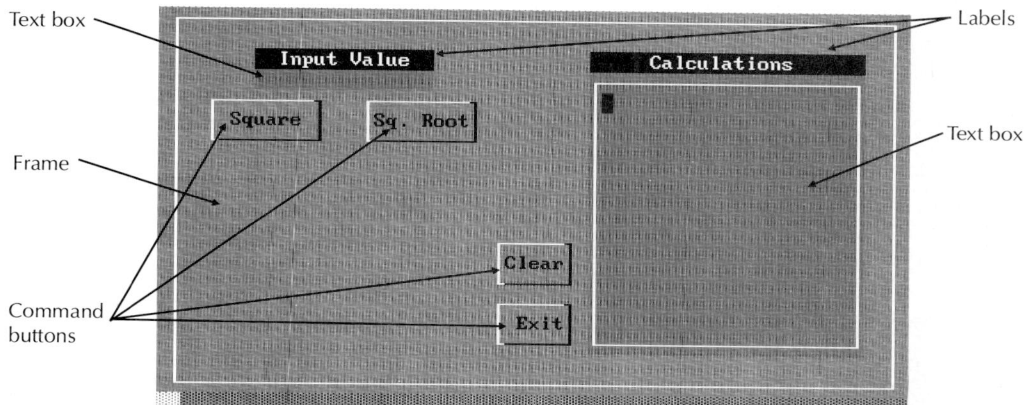

Figure 5-2 Calc application controls.

Building the Calc Form

To build the Calc form, do the following:

1. Start Visual Basic. The system displays a new project with an Untitled Code window.

2. Open the File menu and choose the **New Form** command. When the **New Form** dialog box appears, type `A:CALC.FRM` into the **File Name** text box, and click **OK.** Visual Basic switches from the programming environment to the Form Designer.

Customize the Calc Form

The new form, Calc, appears on the Form Designer screen along with the Toolbox and the Color Palette. Refer to the application's specifications and customize the form as follows:

1. Move the form to position 8,3 on the screen.
2. Adjust the form's size to 63 × 19 character positions.
3. Change the **BorderStyle** property to **None.**
4. Verify that the form's colors are set to those mentioned in the specifications (white background, black foreground) or to colors of your choice.

Figure 5-3 shows the Calc form after you finish the customization steps.

> ☑ If you use different property and control settings for your version of Calc, your screen images may not correspond to those shown in this book. We encourage you to experiment with alternate settings after you have successfully built the Calc application as outlined in this tutorial.

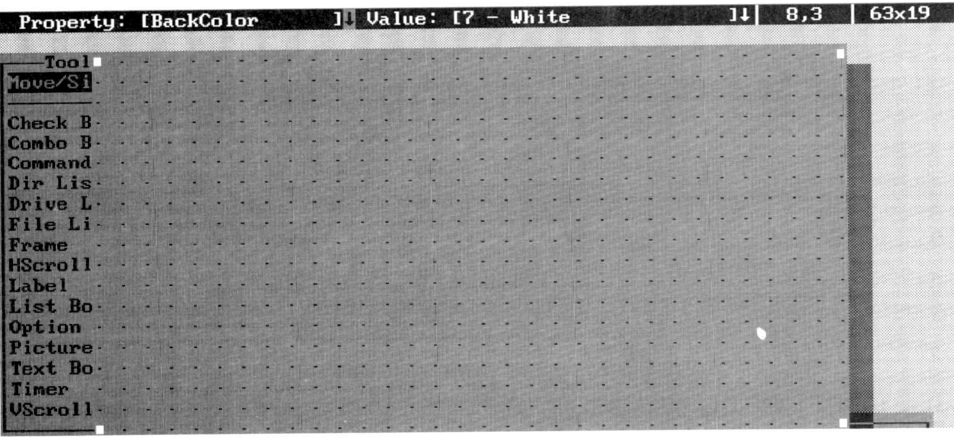

Figure 5-3 Calc form after customization.

Save the Project

Save your work before you proceed. To save the Calc project, do the following:

1. Open the File menu and choose the **Save Project** command.

2. Enter the following path and project file name into the text box on the dialog box:

   Type `A:CALC.MAK`

3. When you have entered the path and project file name, do the following:

   Click the `OK` button.

Visual Basic saves two files during this save operation: `CALC.MAK` and `CALC.FRM`. `CALC.MAK` is the project file for the Calc application. `CALC.FRM` is the form file you just created and customized.

When the save operation completes, Visual Basic displays the Form Designer and the customized Calc form. Your next step will be to add controls to the form and customize the controls for the Calc application.

Adding Controls to the Form

There are four sets of controls that go on the Calc form: a frame, two labels, two text boxes, and four command buttons. The next step will be to put a frame on the form.

Adding a Frame to the Form

Calc uses one frame control object. This frame will outline the rest of the controls and will serve as a border around the form itself. Proceed as follows to add and customize a frame for Calc:

1. Open the Tools menu and choose the **Frame** command. A frame control, Frame1, appears at the center of the form.
2. Click and drag this object to location 1,0.
3. Resize this object to size 61 × 19.
4. Open the **Property** list box menu (Property bar), choose **Caption,** and set the value of this property to a blank. The caption on the frame will disappear. Figure 5-4 shows the Calc form with the frame in place.
5. Verify that the form's colors are set to those mentioned in the specifications (white background, black foreground) or to colors of your choice.

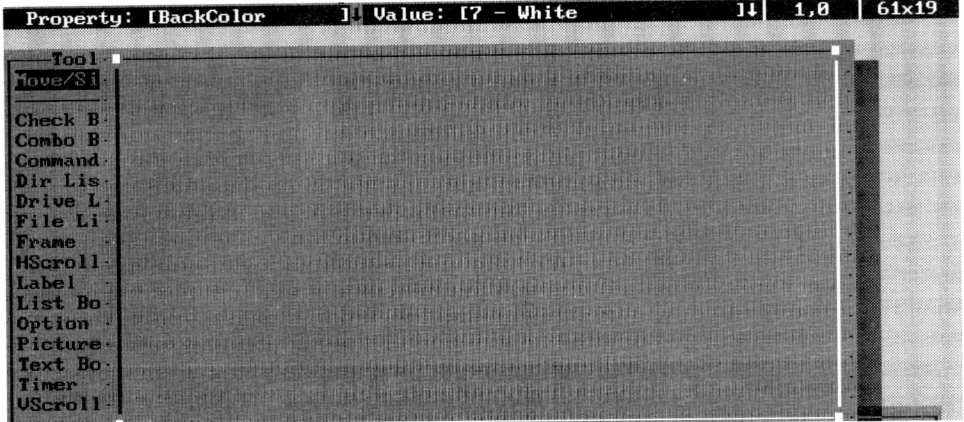

Figure 5-4 The Calc form with a frame.

6. Save the project by using the **Save Project** command on the File menu.

> ☑ As you add controls to a form, some may seem to "disappear" when you click a frame object. Press the **Tab** key repeatedly to "reveal" any objects that have "disappeared." Each time you press **Tab,** Visual Basic moves the focus to the next "hidden" object. Objects "hidden" behind other objects are "revealed" when Visual Basic gives them the focus.

Adding Labels to the Form

Calc has two labels. **Label1** (**Input Value**) identifies the user input region on the form. **Label2** (**Calculations**) marks the output display area.

To install **Label1,** follow these steps:

1. Open the Tools menu and choose the **Label** command. A label control object appears at the center of the form. This object's control name and caption is `Label1`.
2. Click and drag this object to location 8,2.
3. Resize this object to size 15 × 1.
4. Open the **Property** list box menu (Property bar), choose **Alignment** and change the value setting for the **Alignment** property to **Center.**

5. Open the **Property** list box menu, choose **Caption,** delete the current contents of the **Value** list box (`Label1`), and type this new caption for the label:

   Type `Input Value` and press **Enter.**

6. Set the **Background** property value to gray.
7. Set the **Foreground** property value to bright white.
8. Save the project.

To put **Label2** on the form, follow the same procedure you used to create, position, and modify **Label1.**

Adding Label2: Calculations

Follow these steps to put the Label2 on the form:

1. Open the Tools menu and choose the **Label** command. A label control object, `Label2`, appears at the center of the form.
2. Click and drag this object to location 36,2.
3. Resize this object to size 23 × 1.
4. Open the **Property** list box menu (Property bar), choose **Alignment,** and change the value setting for the **Alignment** property to **Center.**
5. Open the **Property** list box menu, choose **Caption,** delete the current contents of the **Value** list box (`Label2`), and type this new caption for the label:

   Type `Calculations` and press **Enter.**

6. Set the **Background** property value to gray.
7. Set the **Foreground** property value to bright white.
   Figure 5-5 shows Flash with the two labels, **Input Value** and **Calculations,** in place.
8. Save the project.

Installing the Text Boxes

Calc uses two text boxes. The first text box, **Text1,** sits directly below the **Label1** control (**Input Value**). The application uses this text box to capture user input values for calculations.

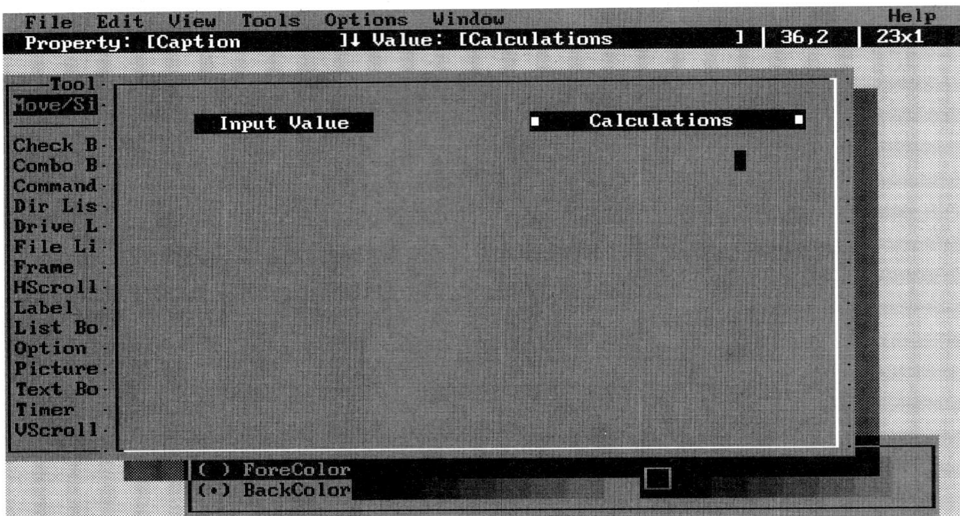

Figure 5-5 The Calc form with labels in place.

To install this text box object on the form, you proceed as with any other control object—open the Tools menu, choose the object, position the object, and customize its features. To place the first text box on the form Calc, do the following:

1. Open the Tools menu and choose the **Text Box** command. A text box control object, **Text1,** appears at the center of the form.
2. Click and drag this object to location 8,3.
3. Resize this object to size 15 × 1.
4. Open the **Property** list box menu (Property bar) and choose **Enabled.** Verify that the **Enabled** property is set to **True.** If it is not, change the value setting to **True.**
5. Open the **Property** list box menu (Property bar) and choose **MultiLine.** Verify that the **MultiLine** property is set to **False.** If it is not, change the value setting to **False.**
6. Open the **Property** list box menu (Property bar), choose **BorderStyle,** and set this property's value to **None.**
7. Open the **Property** list box menu, choose **Text,** delete the current contents of the **Value** list box (`Text1`), and press **Enter.**

8. Set the text box's **BackColor** and **ForeColor** properties to **Cyan** and **Black,** respectively.

   Figure 5-6 shows the form with Calc's first text box in place.

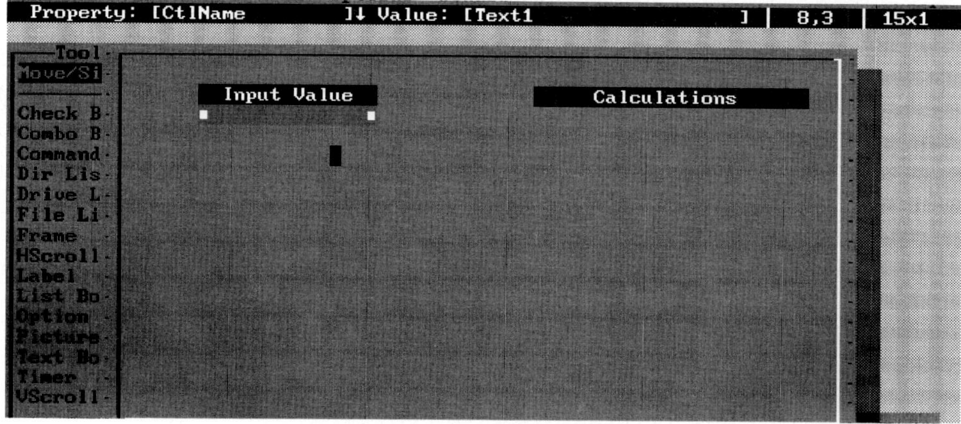

Figure 5-6 Text1 Text Box in place.

9. Save the project.

Installing the Second Text Box

To put the second text box on the form, follow the same steps you used to create the first text box, **Text1.** Do this task on your own, referring back to the steps in the previous section, as required.

The **Text2** text box is the same as **Text1,** with these exceptions:

- **Text2** is located at position 36,3.
- The size of **Text2** is 23 × 14.
- The **Enabled** property is set to **False.**
- The **MultiLine** property is set to **True.**
- The **BorderStyle** property is left at the default value, **Single Line.**

Figure 5-7 shows the Calc form with both text boxes in place.

Adding the Command Buttons

This application uses four command buttons to control the screen activities. Two buttons, **Command1** and **Command2,** sit below the input text

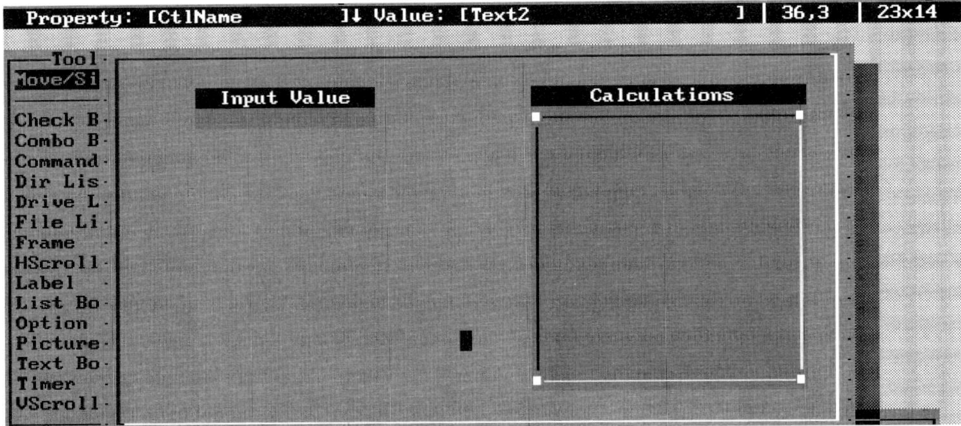

Figure 5-7 Calc with both text boxes in place.

box, **Text1.** The button on the left carries the caption `Square`. The button on the right has the caption `Sq. Root`. These two buttons will perform calculations on the current input value in **Text1** and will display results in the second text box, **Text2.**

Command3, captioned `Clear`, will clear the contents of the two text boxes and will put the focus on `Text1`. Command4, `Exit`, hides the form and exits the application.

To install the first command button, **Command1,** proceed as follows:

1. Open the Tools menu and choose the **Command Button** command. A command button, **Command1,** appears at the center of the form.
2. Click and drag this object to location 4,4.
3. Resize this object to size 10 × 3.
4. Open the **Property** list box menu (Property bar), choose **Caption,** delete the current contents of the **Value** list box (`Command1`), and enter the following caption:

   Type `Square` and press **Enter.**
5. Save the project.

Adding the Other Command Buttons

To put the remaining command buttons on the form, follow the same steps you used to create **Command1.** Do this task on your own, referring back to the steps in the previous section, as required.

Command2 is the same as **Command1,** with these exceptions:

- **Command2** is located at position 17,4.
- **Command2**'s caption is `Sq. Root`.

Command3 is the same as **Command1** with these exceptions:

- **Command3** is located at position 28,11.
- **Command3**'s size is 7 × 3.
- **Command3**'s caption is `Clear`.

Command4 is the same as **Command1,** with these exceptions:

- **Command4** is located at position 28,14.
- **Command4**'s size is 7 × 3.
- **Command4**'s caption is `Exit`.

When you have created and customized these last three command buttons, save the project. Figure 5-8 shows Calc with all of its controls installed.

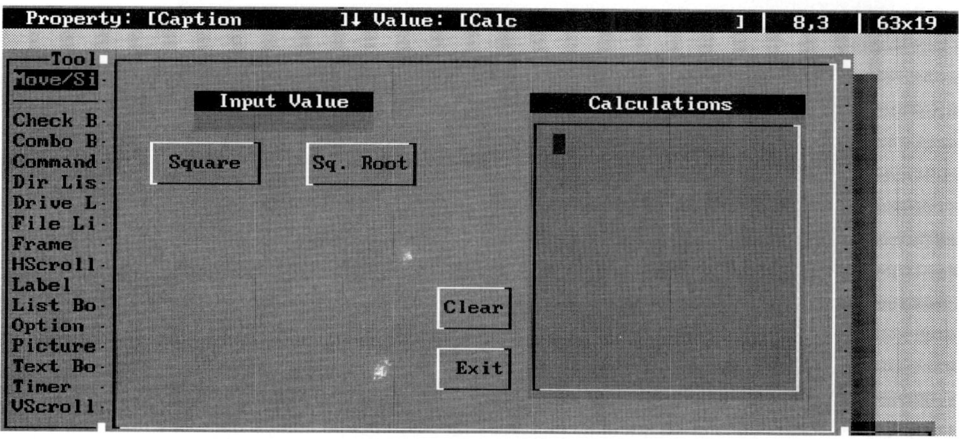

Figure 5-8 Calc with all controls installed.

These last few steps complete the design stage of the project. You are now ready to verify the form design and develop the code that will make the Calc perform its tasks.

Verify the Form Design

You can verify the form design before you write any code. To do so, follow these steps:

1. If you have not already done so, save the project.
2. Open the File menu and choose the **Exit** option. Visual Basic closes the Form Designer windows and opens the programming environment windows. The empty Code window, `CALC.FRM`, appears on the left side of the screen.
3. Open the Run menu and choose the **Start** command. The screen changes to a display of the Calc application (Figure 5-9). Compare your screen with the one shown in the figure. Do you need to make adjustments or changes?

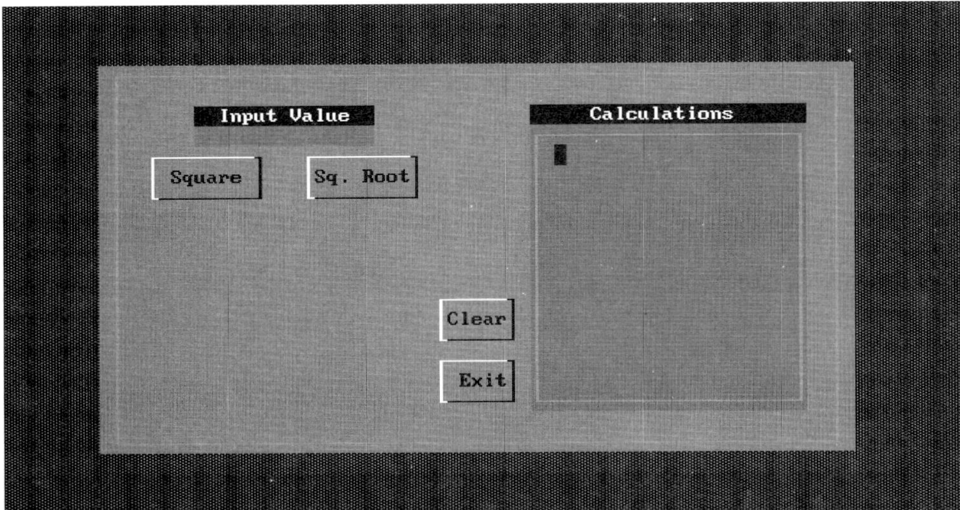

Figure 5-9 Calc application screen.

4. To exit from this screen, hold down **Ctrl** and press the **Break** key. Visual Basic restores the programming environment windows.

If you need to adjust your design, click the **Form** button on the Project window. The **Form** button switches you to the Form Designer screen, and displays the Calc form for editing. If you do make changes to your design, save the project to record the changes.

Developing the Calc Code

If you have not already done so, save the project. If you are not already in the Visual Basic programming environment, go there to begin to develop the project's event procedures. In the programming environment, the empty Code window, `CALC.FRM`, appears on the left side of the screen.

The `CALC.FRM` Code window will remain empty. Calc has no declarations or data that go in the application's main module.

The Form_Load Procedure

1. Open the Edit menu and choose **Event Procedures.**
2. Visual Basic displays an **Event Procedures** dialog box (Figure 5-10).

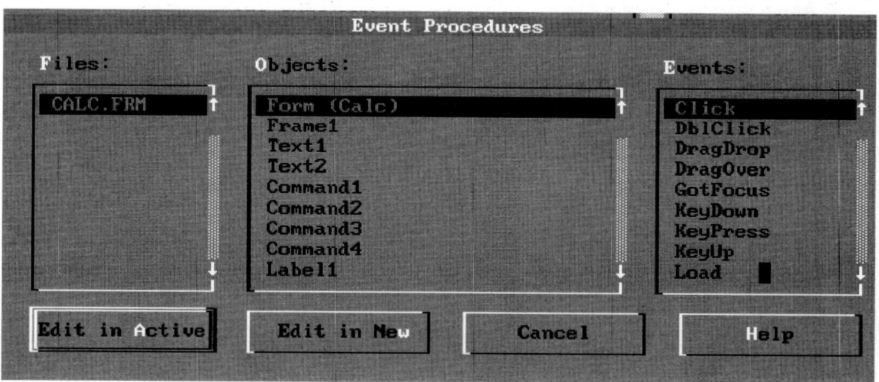

Figure 5-10 Event Procedures dialog box.

This dialog box has three lists: **Files, Objects,** and **Events.** The **Files** list has one file entry: `CALC.FRM`. This is the form file for the Calc application.

The **Objects** list displays a list of items: a form with the caption `Calc`, a frame control **(Frame1)**, two text boxes **(Text1, Text2)**, two labels **(Label1, Label2)**, and four command buttons (**Command1, Command2, Command3, Command4**).

The **Events** list displays the set of events that can be detected by the highlighted object in the **Objects** list. In Figure 5-10, the listed events are for the form Calc. The highlight in the **Events** list is on `Click`.

3. Move the highlight in the **Events** list to `Load`.

4. Click the **Edit in Active** button. When you click this button, Visual Basic dismisses the **Event Procedures** dialog box and displays the Code window shown in Figure 5-11.

Figure 5-11 Event procedure Form_Load window.

At the top of the Code window, you see the window title:

```
[1] CALC.FRM:Form_Load
```

In the text area of the Code window, you see a template for the procedure to be written into:

```
SUB Form_Load ()

END SUB
```

5. Enter the following code (shown in bold) into this event procedure template:

```
SUB Form_Load ()
  'Clear screen and set screen attributes
   CLS
  SCREEN.ControlPanel(7) = 178 'DESKTOP_PATTERN
  SCREEN.ControlPanel(5) = 14  'DESKTOP_BACKCOLOR
  SCREEN.ControlPanel(6) = 15  'DESKTOP_FORECOLOR
  SCREEN.ControlPanel(8) = 0   'DISABLED_ITEM_COLOR
END SUB
```

CLS clears any text entries from the text boxes on the form. The set of **SCREEN.ControlPanel** statements alters parts of the desktop display (pattern, and background, foreground, and disabled item colors). Compare the image in Figure 5-9 with the image shown in Figure 5-12. Figure 5-12 shows what the Calc application screen looks like with these **SCREEN.ControlPanel** settings applied.

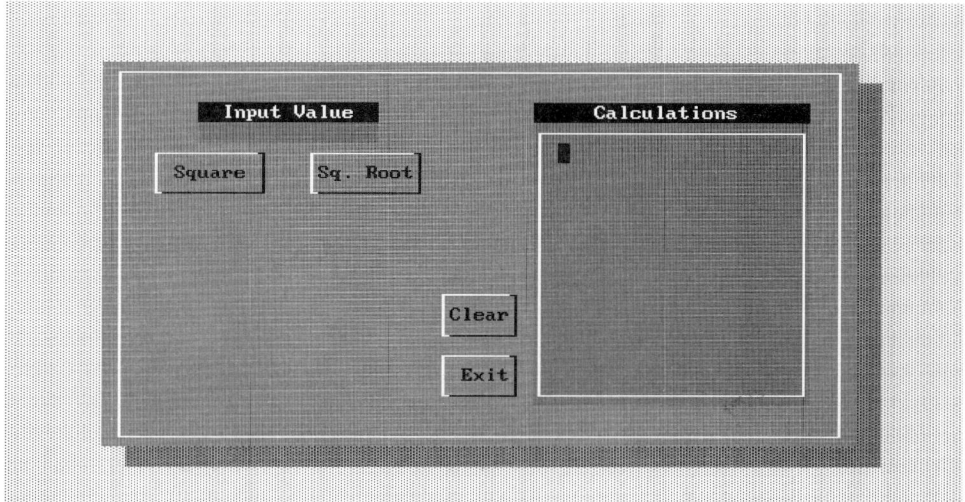

Figure 5-12 Calc with ControlPanel settings applied.

The desktop pattern is set to a pattern character (ASCII code 178). The color of the desktop is set to yellow (14). The foreground color is set to bright white (15). The foreground color of disabled items (such as **Text2**) is set to black (0).

6. After you enter this block of code, save the project.

Coding the Command Button Procedures

To code the command button procedures, complete the following steps:

1. Open the Edit menu and choose the **Event Procedures** command.
2. Visual Basic displays an **Event Procedures** dialog box.
3. Move the highlight in the **Objects** list to `Command1`.

4. Move the highlight in the **Events** list to `Click`.

5. Click the **Edit in Active** button. When you click this button, Visual Basic dismisses the **Event Procedures** dialog box and displays a new Code window.

   At the top of the Code window, you see the window title:

   ```
   [1] CALC.FRM:Command1_Click
   ```

   In the text area of the Code window, you see a template for the procedure to be written into:

   ```
   SUB Command1_Click ()

   END SUB
   ```

6. Enter the following code (shown in bold) into this event procedure template:

```
SUB Command1_Click ()
  'Convert input text to numeric value
  Number = VAL(Text1.Text)
  'Square the number
  Answer = Number ^ 2
  'Build the result string
  CalcText$ = " " + STR$(Number) + "^2="
  CalcText$ = CalcText$ + STR$(Answer) + CHR$(13)
  'Append result to the display list
  Text2.Text = Text2.Text + CalcText$
END SUB
```

This block of code begins by converting the contents of text box, **Text1,** to a numeric quantity. The result is stored in the variable **Number.** The procedure then squares **Number** and stores that result in **Answer.**

The procedure then builds an output string by converting the two results (**Number** and **Answer**) to text strings, and appending string components to form an equation that represents the calculation. The procedure places that output string in the **Text2** text box. The user sees an equation in **Text2** that includes the input value from **Text1** and the square of that value. The equation has the following form:

```
number^2= answer
```

7. After you enter this block of code, save the project.

Writing Code for the Remaining Buttons

Following the steps you used to create the code for the **Command1** event procedure, create code for **Command2, Command3,** and **Command4.**

The code (bold text) for each event procedure is as follows:

```
SUB Command2_Click ()
  'Convert input text to numeric value
  Number = VAL(Text1.Text)
  'Calculate square root of number
  Answer = SQR(Number)
  'Build the result string
  CalcText$ = CHR$(251) + STR$(Number) + "="
  CalcText$ = CalcText$ + STR$(Answer) + CHR$(13)
  'Append result to the display list
  Text2.Text = Text2.Text + CalcText$
END SUB

SUB Command3_Click ()
  'Clear the text boxes
  Text1.Text = ""
  Text2.Text = ""
  'Make the input text box the focus
  Text1.SETFOCUS
END SUB

SUB Command4_Click ()
  'Hide the form and exit the program
  SCREEN.HIDE
  END
END SUB
```

The **Command2** event procedure computes and displays the square root of the input value. The procedure builds an output string that looks like an equation with a root symbol, `CHR$(251)`, as the first character.

The **Command3** procedure clears the text boxes and sets the focus to **Text1.** When the user clicks **Command4,** the procedure hides the form and exits the application.

After you enter these blocks of code, save the project.

Run Calc

To run the program, open the Run menu and choose the **Start** command. If there are no syntax or run-time errors in the code, the form Calc will appear on the screen, with no entries in the text box areas.

Enter the value, 1234, into the input text box. Click **Square** and then click **Sq. Root.** Figure 5-13 shows what the Calc application produces after you take these actions.

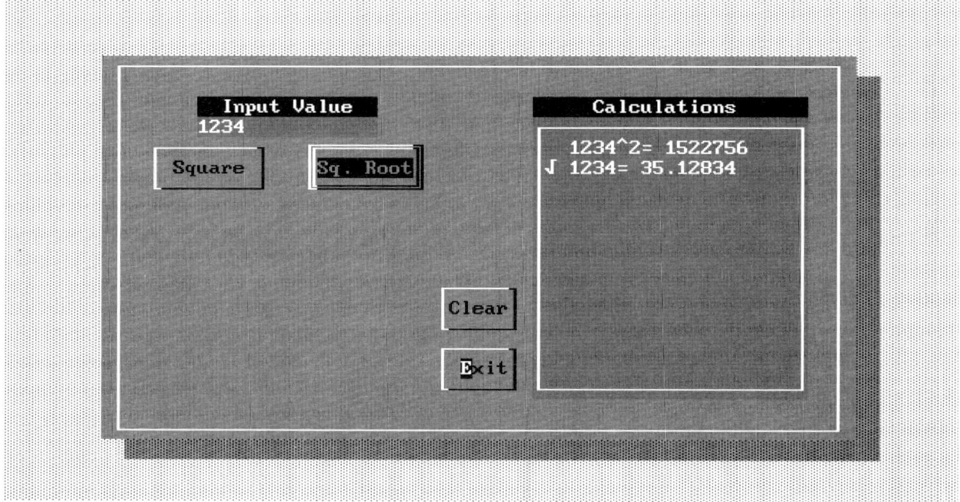

Figure 5-13 Calc Displays results.

Experiment with Calc and input other values. What happens if you enter a larger input value? What happens if you try to take the square root of a negative number?

In the first case, try entering the value 12345. When you click **Square,** Calc displays:

```
  12345^2=
1.52399E+08
```

Calc switched to *exponential* display notation, since the result exceeded seven digits. The actual result is 152399025. Visual Basic displays the first seven digits of the answer and moves the decimal point between the first and second digits. The notation at the end of the result (E+08) indicates how many places (8) to move the decimal point to show the result as a number. If the exponent is positive, you move the decimal point to the right; if negative, you move the decimal point to the left.

If you enter a negative number as an input value and click **Sq. Root,** the application stops and you see an illegal function call dialog box. The function **SQR** does not accept negative numbers. How would you alter the **Command2** event procedure to keep the program from stopping when users attempt to take the square root of negative numbers? Hint: You would test the sign of the number before passing it on to the **SQR** function.

Click the **Clear** button to verify that its event procedure clears the text boxes. When you are ready to leave the application, click **Exit** to verify that it performs as expected (hides the form and exits the application).

The CatchMe Application

In this section, you will build a small application that produces surprising results. The complete application, called CatchMe, looks like the one shown in Figure 5-14.

This application utilizes only two controls: a form and a picture box.

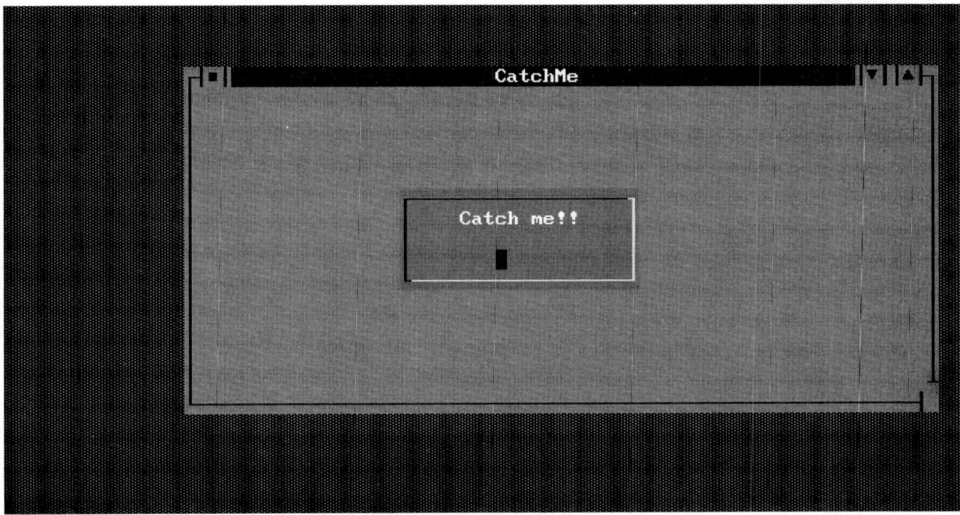

Figure 5-14 The CatchMe application.

CatchMe Specifications

The CatchMe application uses a form and a picture box control to create an interesting result: a screen object that moves unpredictably when you move the mouse. This simple application demonstrates one way for you to introduce movement and dynamic activity onto a form. It also demonstrates how Visual Basic gives you full control of screen objects for an active application.

The CatchMe Form Specification

The CatchMe form uses only one control object: a picture box. The form event procedures will respond to two events: **Load** and **MouseMove.**

The specifications for the CatchMe form are as follows.

Specification #5-2 (Form)

CatchMe Application

Form	Event(s) to be detected		Response(s)
CatchMe	Load		Seed random number generator
			Set picture box in place
			Turn on **AutoReDraw** feature
			Put text in picture box
	MouseMove		Move picture box to random location
Properties:	Location	15,3 (default)	
	Size	63 × 17 (default)	

Notes/Comments: This is the form for the application. The location and size settings are the default values when you enter the Form Designer.

CatchMe Picture Box Specification

A Visual Basic *picture box* can be used like a frame to enclose other controls. You can also direct text into a picture box using the **Print** method to create custom borders based on the characters that you print to the box.

In this example, you will learn how to direct text to a picture box. The control will respond to two events, **Click** and **MouseDown.** When clicked, the control will "beep" and display a message box. When the control detects a **MouseDown** event, it will move itself to a random form location.

The specification for CatchMe's picture box control is as follows:

Specification #5-2 (Picture Box)

CatchMe Application

Controls	Event(s) to be detected		Response(s)
Picture1	Click		Beep
			Display message box
	MouseDown		Move picture box to random location
Properties:	Location	20,5	
	Size	20 × 5	
	Colors	Yellow (background)/black (foreground)	

Notes/Comments: New control is a picture box. Choose **Picture Box** on the Tools menu to create the control.

Building CatchMe

Following the steps you have used to build previous applications, build CatchMe. The following is a summary of the steps you will take to develop the CatchMe form with a picture box control.

1. Start Visual Basic and create a new project.
2. Create a new form called CatchMe.
3. Add a picture box control, **Picture1,** to the form. Use the CatchMe picture form specifications to create this control.
4. Save the project as `CATCHME.MAK`.

5. Go to the programming environment and create the following event procedures. Text in bold will be the text you enter.

6. After you enter the code for each of these event procedures, save the project.

```
SUB Form_Load ()
  'Seed random number generator
  RANDOMIZE
  'Set initial picture box position
  picture1.MOVE 20, 5, 20, 5
  'Activate AutoReDraw feature
  picture1.AutoReDraw = -1
  'Put text into picture box
  picture1.PRINT " Catch me!"
END SUB

SUB Form_MouseMove (Button AS INTEGER, Shift
 AS INTEGER, X AS SINGLE, Y AS SINGLE)
  'Move picture box to random location
  picture1.MOVE INT(60 * RND), INT(15 * RND), 20, 5
END SUB

SUB Picture1_Click ()
  'Beep and display message box
  BEEP
  MSGBOX "You did it!"
END SUB

SUB Picture1_MouseDown (Button AS INTEGER,
Shift AS INTEGER, X AS SINGLE, Y AS SINGLE)
  'Move picture box to random location
  picture1.MOVE INT(60 * RND), INT(15 * RND), 20, 5
END SUB
```

Remember to save the project after you enter the code for each of these event procedures.

The Form Event Procedures

The **Form_Load** procedure seeds the random number generator, using the **RANDOMIZE** command. Then the procedure positions the picture box, using the **MOVE** method.

Next the **Load** procedure activates the picture box's **AutoReDraw** property. This property makes sure that a picture box (and its contents) is properly displayed when the control is moved or updated.

The final statement uses the **PRINT** method to insert text into the picture box.

The **Form_MouseMove** procedure moves the picture box control to a random location. This procedure activates when it detects the user moving the mouse.

Form_MouseMove has four *arguments* in its *parameter list:* Button, Shift, X, and Y. These arguments are passed to this procedure by the system. The *data type* for each argument is shown in the parameter list.

The Picture Box Procedures

Picture1_Click "beeps" and displays a message box each time it detects the user clicking the control. The problem, for the user, is that the control moves when the user moves the mouse on the form. Trying to click a moving target is not a simple task.

To compound the user's problem, the picture box control also reacts to a **MouseDown event.** Like the **MouseMove** event procedure at the form-level, **Picture1_MouseDown** also sends the picture box to random form locations with the **MOVE** method.

Run CatchMe

After you have entered this application's event procedures, save the project and start the application. Your initial CatchMe screen will show the picture box near the center of the form (Figure 5-15).

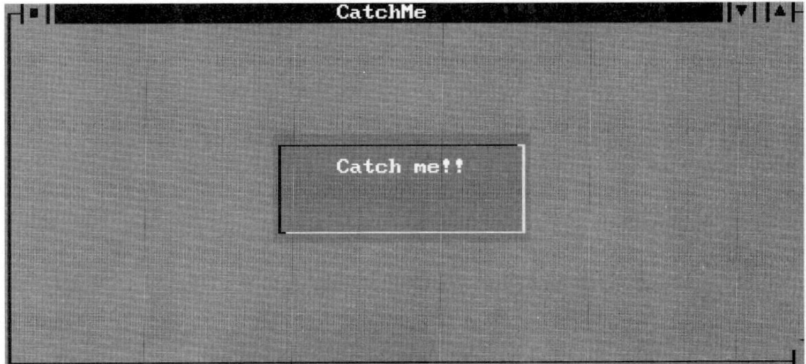

Figure 5-15 CatchMe application at start.

As soon as you move the mouse pointer onto the form, the picture box begins to dance around the form. If you try to "sneak up" on the picture box, it moves and dodges away. If you click the box and it detects a **MouseDown** event, it also moves.

Can you click the picture box and get a message box display like the one shown in Figure 5-16?

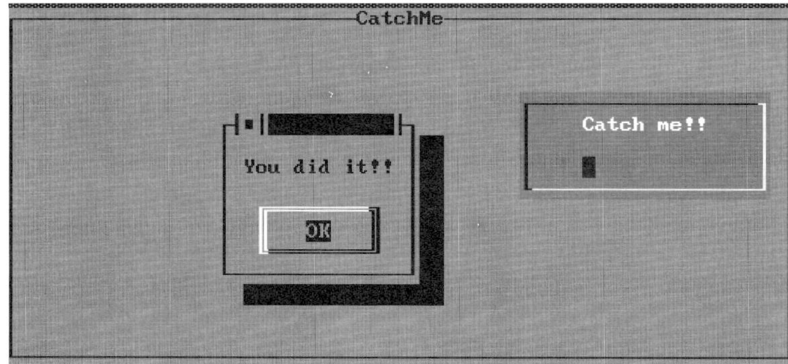

Figure 5-16 Picture box detects click.

If you want a bit more challenge, click the form's maximize control button in the upper right corner of the form. This action expands the form to full-screen size. Figure 5-17 shows CatchMe expanded to the full screen with a successful click detected.

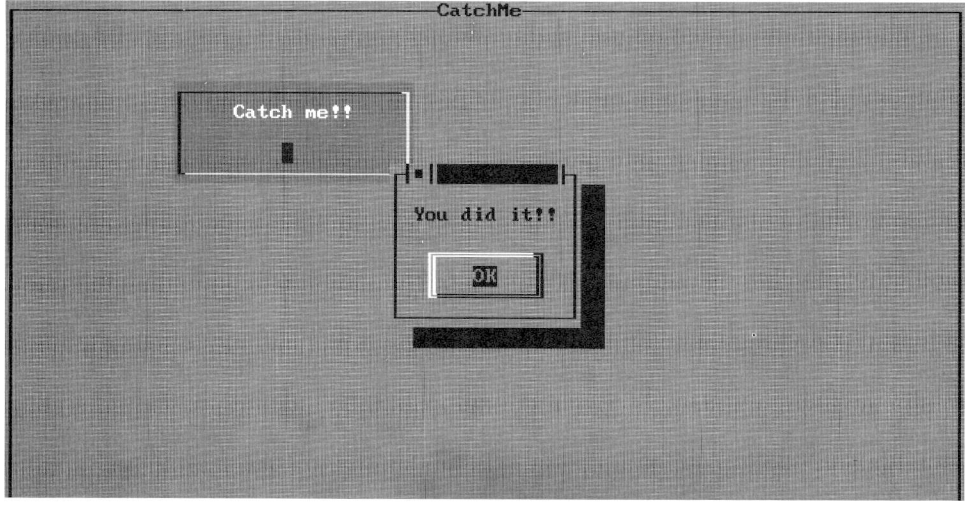

Figure 5-17 Full-screen CatchMe.

After you test your mouse clicking skills, double-click the form's system box (upper left corner of the form) to close the form and exit the application.

Summary

In this chapter, you built an application called Calc and another application called CatchMe. In the process of building these applications, you learned to use Visual Basic's text boxes for both input and output. You also used a picture box for the first time, along with two new event triggers, **MouseMove** and **MouseDown.** You developed event procedures for the **MouseDown** event and utilized several Visual Basic methods (**MOVE, AutoReDraw, PRINT**) to accomplish a variety of tasks.

You are encouraged to go ahead and build extra features into your Calc application. Add buttons that perform other types of computations and display the results in the Calculations output area.

Experiment with CatchMe. For example, what happens if you set the picture box's **BorderStyle** to **None**? Try it. For even more challenge:

- Remove the line of code in CatchMe's **Form_Load** procedure that prints text into the picture box.
- Set the color of the picture box to the color of the form.

These changes create an "invisible" object on the form. The object moves when you move the mouse and when the object detects a **MouseDown** event. The object will display a message box if you manage to click it.

In the next few chapters, you will build a larger, more complex Visual Basic application. When you are ready, proceed to Chapter 6 and begin your design and development of that application.

6 Building a Multiform Application

To this point, you have only built and run applications based on a single form. In this chapter, you build an application that uses two forms.

Concepts and Terminology

QBasic/QuickBasic Keywords

New Visual Basic Keywords

Visual Basic Event Procedures

The application will display an electronic version of the Periodic Table of Elements. You will build an initial version of the table in this chapter, and add features to the application that require the use of a second form. You do not have to be a chemistry major to perform this task. In fact, you do not need to know anything about chemistry to successfully build this application.

In the next chapter, you will expand the functionality of the Periodic Table application to let users view related data in several different ways.

The Periodic Table

The main form for the application, captioned `Periodic Table`, looks like the one shown in Figure 6-1. This table displays the atomic numbers and symbols for 109 elements.

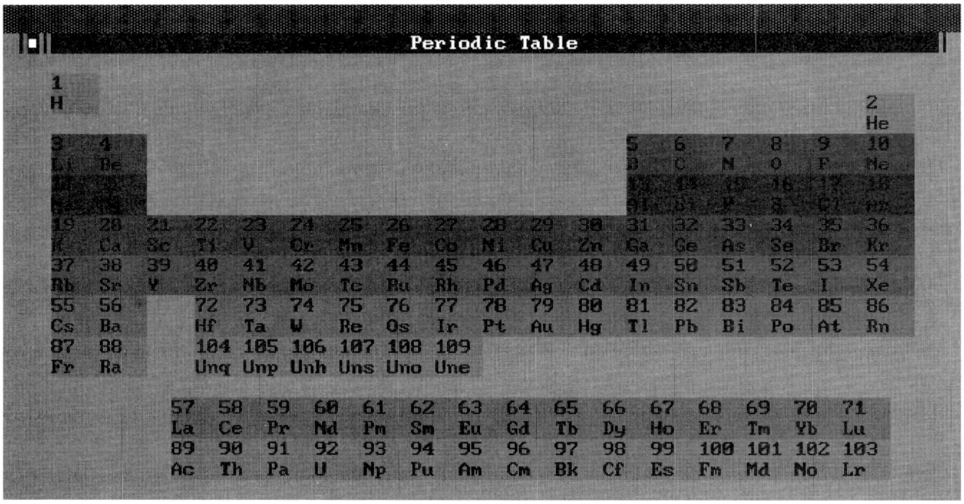

Figure 6-1 The Periodic Table form.

The table layout looks similar to periodic tables found in chemistry books. This version of the table uses different colors for each table row. The two rows of entries across the bottom of the form represent the lanthanide and actinide series of elements that logically fit into the table where there are two empty spots. The colors of the two lanthanide and actinide rows match the colors of the two rows where the series would be inserted into the main part of the table.

To design this table (form and controls), you follow the same procedures that you have done previously to build earlier applications. First, examine the specifications for the form and its controls. Next, add whatever code is required to make the application work.

Periodic Table Specifications

To create the display shown in Figure 6-1, you use a form and a single picture box control. Look over the specifications for the Periodic application, and then develop the needed form and control.

The Periodic Form Specification

The Periodic form uses a single picture box control, in the mode of a *control array*, to create the display shown in Figure 6-1. A control array is a set of controls of the same type that are referenced by the same name and that share the same event procedures. The form responds to the **Load** event with code that actually creates most of the screen display from the single picture box control.

The specifications for the Periodic form are as follows.

Specification #6-1 (Form)

Periodic Application

Form	Event(s) to be detected		Response(s)
Periodic	Load		Read table data
			Create picture box controls
			Put data into controls
Properties:	Location	0,2	
	Size	80 × 23	
	BorderStyle	Fixed Solid	
	Caption	`Periodic Table`	
	MaxButton	False	
	MinButton	False	

Notes/Comments: Form fills all but the two top rows of the screen.

The Periodic Picture Box Specification

The Periodic form uses a single picture box control. You place this control on the form during the design stage. Event procedure code, attached to the form, generates the remaining control objects when the application first loads. The objects that are created when the form loads will become a control array of picture boxes that are displayed on the form.

Specification #6-1 (Picture Box)

Periodic Application

Picture Box	Event(s) to be detected		Response(s)
Picture1	None		None
Properties:	Location	3,1	
	Size	4×2	
	Index	0	
	AutoReDraw	True	
	BorderStyle	None	
	Colors	Gray (background)/black (foreground)	

Notes/Comments: The Index property establishes this object as the first one in a control array of picture boxes named Picture1.

Figure 6-2 shows the Periodic form and its single control object. Use this figure as a guide when you build your version of Periodic.

Building the Periodic Form

To build the Periodic form, do the following:

1. Start Visual Basic. The system displays a new project with an Untitled Code window.

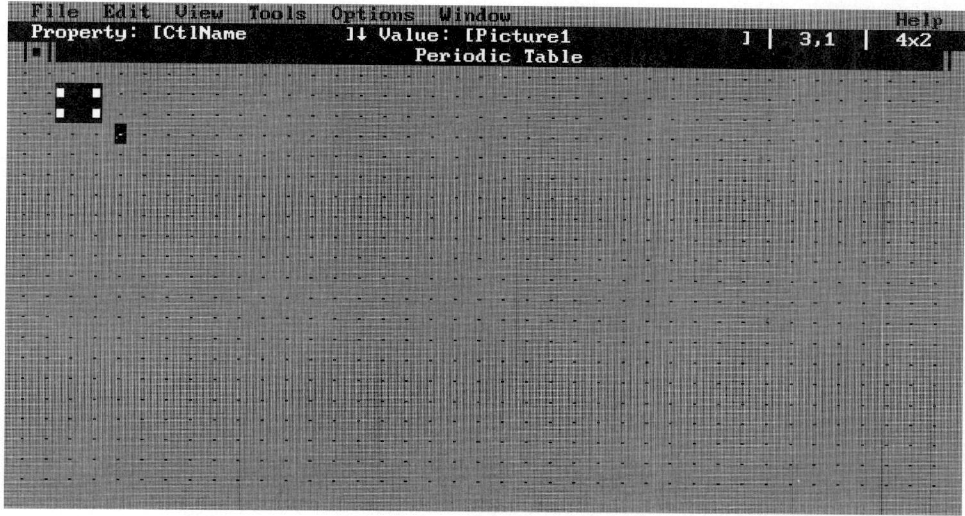

Figure 6-2 Periodic form with picture box control.

2. Open the File menu and choose the **New Form** command. When the **New Form** dialog box appears, type `A:PERIODIC.FRM` into the **File Name** text box and click **OK.** Visual Basic switches from the programming environment to the Form Designer.

Customize the Periodic Form

The new form, Periodic, appears on the Form Designer screen along with the Toolbox and the Color Palette. Refer to the application's specifications and customize the form as follows:

1. Move the form to position 0,2 on the screen.
2. Adjust the form's size to 80 × 23 character positions.
3. Change the **BorderStyle** property to **Fixed Solid.**
4. Set the **Caption** property to **Periodic Table.**
5. Set the **MaxButton** property to **False.**
6. Set the **MinButton** property to **False.**

Figure 6-3 shows the Periodic form after you finish the customization steps. When you set the **MaxButton** and **MinButton** properties to **False,** those two items disappear from the title bar.

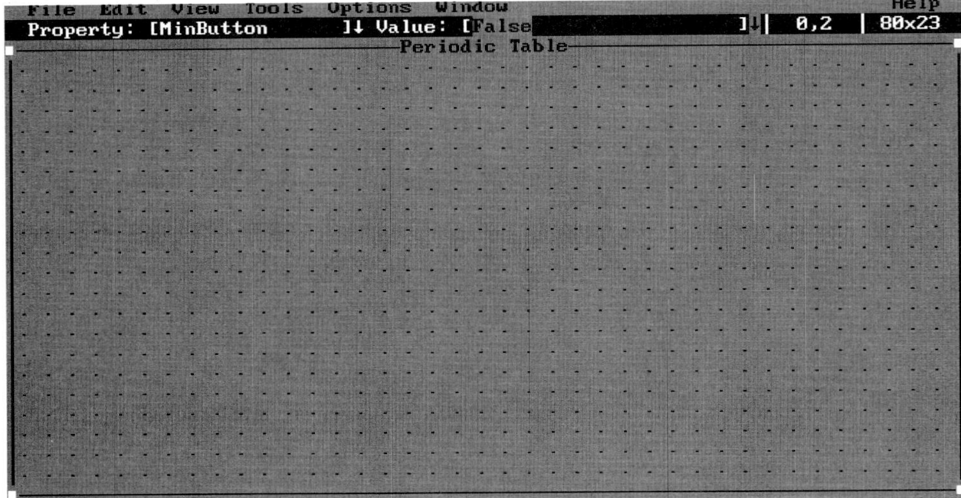

Figure 6-3 Periodic form after customization.

> ☑ If you use different property and control settings for your version of Periodic, your screen images may not correspond to those shown in this book. We encourage you to experiment with alternate settings after you have successfully built the Periodic application as outlined in this tutorial.

Save the Project

Save your work before you proceed. To save the Periodic project, do the following:

1. Open the File menu and choose the **Save Project** command.
2. Enter the following path and project file name into the text box on the dialog box:

   Type `A:PERIODIC.MAK`

3. When you have entered the path and project file name, do the following:

   Click the **OK** button.

Visual Basic saves two files during this save operation: `PERIODIC.MAK` and `PERIODIC.FRM`. When the save operation completes, Visual Basic displays the Form Designer and the customized Periodic form. Your next step will be to add a picture box control to the form.

Adding a Picture Box to the Form

The Periodic form requires a single picture box control. Proceed as follows to add this control to the form:

1. Open the Tools menu and choose the **Picture Box** command. A picture box control, **Picture1,** appears at the center of the form.
2. Click and drag this object to location 3,1.
3. Resize this object to size 4 × 2.
4. Set the object's Index property to 0. This establishes the object as a control array with the **CtlName** Picture1.
5. Open the **Property** list box menu (Property bar), choose **AutoReDraw,** and set the value of this property to **True.**
6. Set the **BorderStyle** property to **None.**
7. Set the **BackColor** property to **Gray.** (Figure 6-4 shows the Periodic form with the picture box control in place.)
8. Save the project by using the **Save Project** command on the File menu.

Developing the Code for the Periodic Application

If you have not already done so, save the project. If you are not already in the programming environment, go there to begin to develop the project's event procedures. In the programming environment, the empty Code window, PERIODIC.FRM, appears on the left side of the screen.

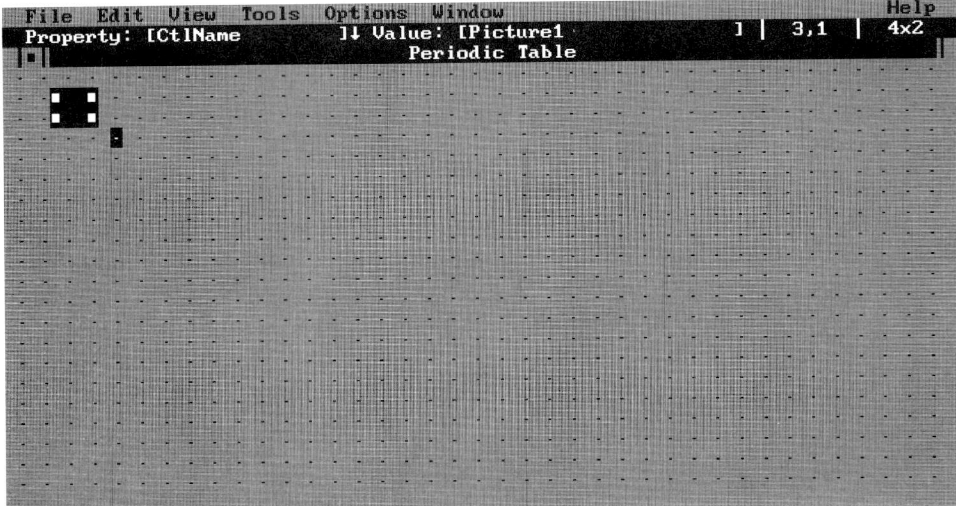

Figure 6-4 The Periodic form with a picture box.

The Form-Level Code

As you may have guessed from the simplicity of this application's design steps, the application is not going to require a lot of complex code. Right now, there are only two controls, a form and a picture box. For this first exploration, only the form will have code.

The bulk of the code for the application will be a set of **DATA** statements. These statements will contain information that the program will use to generate the entire periodic table of 109 elements.

The PERIODIC.FRM Code window will be the place you put the table data. The first data value (109) is used by the **Form_Load** event procedure to read the table data and generate the rest of the application's display.

To test the application, you may choose to enter only some of the data values. If you take this approach, you will have to change the first data item (109) to the number of table elements you plan to use.

The bulk of data entries for the application involve a set of values that specify the location of the data on the table, the color of the object that contains the data, the chemical symbol for the element, and the element's name. For example, the data entry for the first element in the **DATA** list looks like this:

```
DATA 3,1,8, "H  ",Hydrogen
```

The first two numbers, 3 and 1, specify the **Left** and **Top** properties for the control. The third number, 8, sets the control's background color (gray in this case). "H " is a string value for the element's chemical symbol. The last piece of data is the element's name. In the **DATA** list, the data are ordered by atomic number from 1 (Hydrogen) to 109 (Unnilennium).

The character strings for the chemical symbols are padded at the end with blank spaces to make all the entries three characters wide. This convention is being established now to accommodate some planned features that you will implement later in this chapter.

Here are the data for this application. Enter this data into the PERIODIC.FRM window:

```
'Declarations
DEFINT A-Z
CONST TRUE = -1
CONST FALSE = 0
'Data for the periodic table
'Number of elements
DATA 109
'Left, Top, Color, Symbol, Element
DATA 3,1,8, "H  ",Hydrogen
DATA 71,2,8, "He ",Helium
DATA 3,4,9, "Li ",Lithium
DATA 7,4,9, "Be ",Beryllium
DATA 51,4,9, "B  ",Boron
DATA 55,4,9, "C  ",Carbon
DATA 59,4,9, "N  ",Nitrogen
DATA 63,4,9, "O  ",Oxygen
DATA 67,4,9, "F  ",Fluorine
DATA 71,4,9, "Ne ",Neon
DATA 3,6,10, "Na ",Sodium
DATA 7,6,10, "Mg ",Magnesium
DATA 51,6,10, "Al ",Aluminum
DATA 55,6,10, "Si ",Silicon
DATA 59,6,10, "P  ",Phosphorus
DATA 67,6,10, "Cl ",Chlorine
DATA 71,6,10, "Ar ",Argon
DATA 3,8,11, "K  ",Potassium
DATA 7,8,11, "Ca ",Calcium
DATA 11,8,11, "Sc ",Scandium
DATA 15,8,11, "Ti ",Titanium
DATA 19,8,11, "V  ",Vanadium
DATA 23,8,11, "Cr ",Chromium
DATA 27,8,11, "Mn ",Manganese
DATA 31,8,11, "Fe ",Iron
DATA 35,8,11, "Co ",Cobalt
```

```
DATA 39,8,11, "Ni ",Nickel
DATA 43,8,11, "Cu ",Copper
DATA 47,8,11, "Zn ",Zinc
DATA 51,8,11, "Ga ",Gallium
DATA 55,8,11, "Ge ",Germanium
DATA 59,8,11, "As ",Arsenic
DATA 63,8,11, "Se ",Selenium
DATA 67,8,11, "Br ",Bromine
DATA 71,8,11, "Kr ",Krypton
DATA 3,10,12, "Rb ",Rubidium
DATA 7,10,12, "Sr ",Strontium
DATA 11,10,12, "Y  ",Yttrium
DATA 15,10,12, "Zr ",Zirconium
DATA 19,10,12, "Nb ",Niobium
DATA 23,10,12, "Mo ",Molybdenum
DATA 27,10,12, "Tc ",Technetium
DATA 31,10,12, "Ru ",Ruthenium
DATA 35,10,12, "Rh ",Rhodium
DATA 39,10,12, "Pd ",Palladium
DATA 43,10,12, "Ag ",Silver
DATA 47,10,12, "Cd ",Cadmium
DATA 51,10,12, "In ",Indium
DATA 55,10,12, "Sn ",Tin
DATA 59,10,12, "Sb ",Antimony
DATA 63,10,12, "Te ",Tellurium
DATA 67,10,12, "I  ",Iodine
DATA 71,10,12, "Xe ",Xenon
DATA 3,12,13, "Cs ",Cesium
DATA 7,12,13, "Ba ",Barium
DATA 13,17,13, "La ",Lanthanum
DATA 17,17,13, "Ce ",Cerium
DATA 21,17,13, "Pr ",Praseodymium
DATA 25,17,13, "Nd ",Neodymium
DATA 29,17,13, "Pm ",Promethium
DATA 33,17,13, "Sm ",Samarium
DATA 37,17,13, "Eu ",Europium
DATA 41,17,13, "Gd ",Gadolinium
DATA 45,17,13, "Tb ",Terbium
DATA 49,17,13, "Dy ",Dysprosium
DATA 53,17,13, "Ho ",Holmium
DATA 57,17,13, "Er ",Erbium
DATA 61,17,13, "Tm ",Thulium
DATA 65,17,13, "Yb ",Ytterbium
DATA 69,17,13, "Lu ",Lutetium
DATA 15,12,13, "Hf ",Hafnium
DATA 19,12,13, "Ta ",Tantalum
DATA 23,12,13, "W  ",Tungsten
DATA 27,12,13, "Re ",Rhenium
```

```
DATA 31,12,13, "Os ",Osmium
DATA 35,12,13, "Ir ",Iridium
DATA 39,12,13, "Pt ",Platinum
DATA 43,12,13, "Au ",Gold
DATA 47,12,13, "Hg ",Mercury
DATA 51,12,13, "Tl ",Thallium
DATA 55,12,13, "Pb ",Lead
DATA 59,12,13, "Bi ",Bismuth
DATA 63,12,13, "Po ",Polonium
DATA 67,12,13, "At ",Astatine
DATA 71,12,13, "Rn ",Radon
DATA 3,14,14, "Fr ",Francium
DATA 7,14,14, "Ra ",Radium
DATA 13,19,14, "Ac ",Actinium
DATA 17,19,14, "Th ",Thorium
DATA 21,19,14, "Pa ",Protactinium
DATA 25,19,14, "U  ",Uranium
DATA 29,19,14, "Np ",Neptunium
DATA 33,19,14, "Pu ",Plutonium
DATA 37,19,14, "Am ",Americium
DATA 41,19,14, "Cm ",Curium
DATA 45,19,14, "Bk ",Berkelium
DATA 49,19,14, "Cf ",Californium
DATA 53,19,14, "Es ",Einsteinium
DATA 57,19,14, "Fm ",Fermium
DATA 61,19,14, "Md ",Mendelevium
DATA 65,19,14, "No ",Nobelium
DATA 69,19,14, "Lr ",Lawrencium
DATA 15,14,14, "Unq" ,Unnilquadium
DATA 19,14,14, "Unp" ,Unnilpentium
DATA 23,14,14, "Unh" ,Unnilhexium
DATA 27,14,14, "Uns" ,Unnilseptium
DATA 31,14,14, "Uno" ,Unniloctium
DATA 35,14,14, "Une" ,Unnilennium
```

The Form_Load Procedure

To create the **Form_Load** procedure for this application, do the following:

1. Open the Edit menu and choose the **Event Procedures** command.
2. Visual Basic displays an **Event Procedures** dialog box (Figure 6-5).

   This dialog box has three lists: **Files, Objects,** and **Events.** The Files list shows a file entry labeled `PERIODIC.FRM`. This is the form file for the Periodic application.

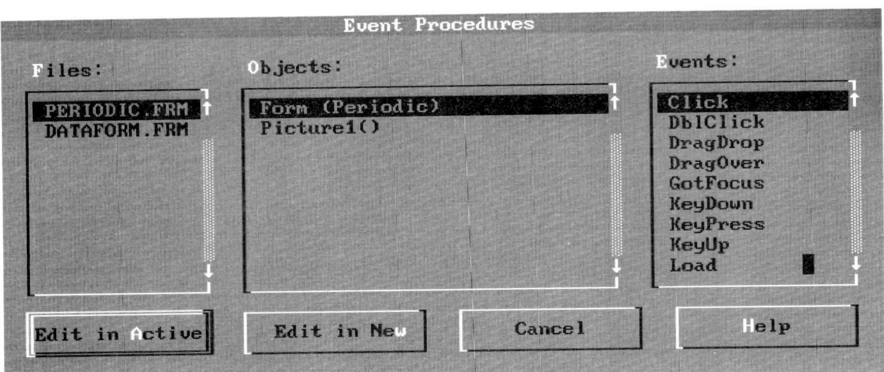

Figure 6-5 Event Procedures dialog box.

The **Objects** list displays a list with two items: a form with the caption `Periodic`, and a picture box control, **Picture1.**

The **Events** list displays the set of events that can be detected by the highlighted object in the **Objects** list. In Figure 6-5, the listed events are for the form Periodic. The highlight in the **Events** list is on `Click`.

3. Move the highlight in the **Events** list to `Load`.
4. Click the **Edit in Active** button. When you click this button, Visual Basic dismisses the **Event Procedures** dialog box and displays the Code window shown in Figure 6-6.

Figure 6-6 Event procedure Form_Load Window.

At the top of the Code window, you see the window title:

```
[1] PERIODIC.FRM:Form_Load
```

In the text area of the Code window, you see a template for the procedure you are about to create:

```
DEFINT A-Z
SUB Form_Load ()

END SUB
```

5. Enter the following code (shown in bold) into this event procedure template:

```
DEFINT A-Z
SUB Form_Load ()
 Num$ = SPACE$(3)           'element number variable
 CR$ = CHR$(13)             'Carriage return
 READ NumElem               'Get number of elements

 'Begin loop that reads element data
 'and generates the periodic table
 FOR index = 1 TO NumElem
   'Get data for an element
   READ L, T, Bcolor, Sym$, Ename$

   'Create picture box in control array
   LOAD Picture1(index)

   'Set picture box properties
   Picture1(index).BackColor = Bcolor
   Picture1(index).Visible = TRUE
   Picture1(index).AutoReDraw = TRUE

   'Create display text
   'Trim initial space and left justify in Num$
   LSET Num$ = LTRIM$(STR$(index))
   'Display element number and symbol
   Picture1(index).PRINT Num$ + CR$ + Sym$

   'Store data as Tag property value
   Picture1(index).Tag = Sym$ + Num$ + Ename$

   'Position the picture box
   Picture1(index).MOVE L, T, 4, 2
 NEXT index

 ' Hide original picture box
 Picture1(0).Visible = FALSE
END SUB
```

This block of code reads and uses the information in the **DATA** statements in the form code window. This code performs the following actions:

a. Sets up the `Num$` and `CR$` variables, reads the value for the number of elements in the table, and stores that value in the variable `NumElem`.
b. Starts a FOR-NEXT loop based on `NumElem`; the loop counter is `index`.
c. Reads a line of data from the DATA section. The data values are for the **Left** and **Top** control properties, the background color, the chemical symbol, and the element name. These values are read into the variables `L`, `T`, `Bcolor`, `Sym$`, and `Ename$`, respectively.
d. Creates a new picture box control with the **LOAD** command. This new control becomes part of a control array, `Picture1(index)`. A control array is a set of controls of the same type that share the same name and event procedures. These controls have the same **CtlName** property value (Picture1 in this case), but have a unique index number (`index` in this case). The index number can be used to identify and manipulate a specific control.
e. The rest of the code in the loop structure modifies properties of the control that was just created with the **LOAD** command. The control's color is set to the value in `Bcolor`. Its **Visible** and **AutoReDraw** properties are set to **True. AutoReDraw** enables automatic "repainting" of an object that is being moved, resized, or updated with the **PRINT** method. The index value is transformed into a three character string variable, `Num$`, with spaces filling out the width for smaller values of the index.

   The **PRINT** method is used to display the index value and the chemical symbol inside the control. The chemical symbol, index value, and element name are stored in the control's **Tag** property. You can attach a small amount of data to a control by storing that data in the object's Tag area.

   Finally, the **MOVE** method is used to position the control on the form based on the left (`L`) and top (`T`) values. In the **DATA** statements, the values for each control's **Left** and **Top** properties has been planned out so that the picture boxes fit tightly against each other on the screen. During a move operation, you can also resize a control. In this case, each control's width and height is set to the same values (4 × 2) as the initial control in the array.

f. The last line of code hides the original picture box object that was placed on the form in the design stage.

6. After you enter this block of code, save the project.

This completes the initial set of code modules for this application. If you have entered the code, you are ready to run and test the application.

Run Periodic

To run the program, open the Run menu and choose the **Start** command. If there are no syntax or run-time errors in the code, the form Periodic will appear on the screen along with 109 picture box controls. The most likely problem will be typographical errors in the **DATA** statements that will cause the **READ** statements to work incorrectly. Use the **Instant Watch** features on the Debug menu to look at the `Ename$` and `index` variables to help locate problems in the **DATA** statements.

When you designed the form, you put a single picture box control on the form. The code in the **Form_Load** procedure uses the **DATA** statements and generates the 109 additional picture box controls and information displays.

The result is a colorful display of the Periodic Table of Elements, as shown in Figure 6-7.

Adding a Second Form

The Periodic application display you just created is colorful but not very interactive. If you click on the form or on any of the 109 picture boxes, nothing happens.

With Visual Basic, you can easily add a second form to the application that displays element data each time you click one of the picture box controls. The second form, configured as a dialog box, can be designed to fit neatly into the space between Hydrogen and Helium. Figure 6-8 shows what the Periodic application will look like after you make this addition.

The second form for this application uses two control objects: a multiline text box and a command button. Here are the specifications for this new form.

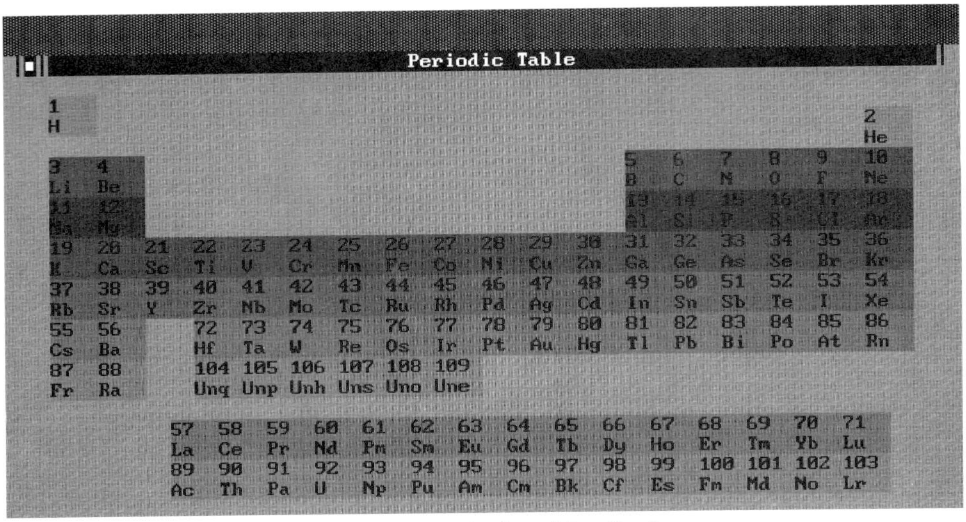

Figure 6-7 Periods table display.

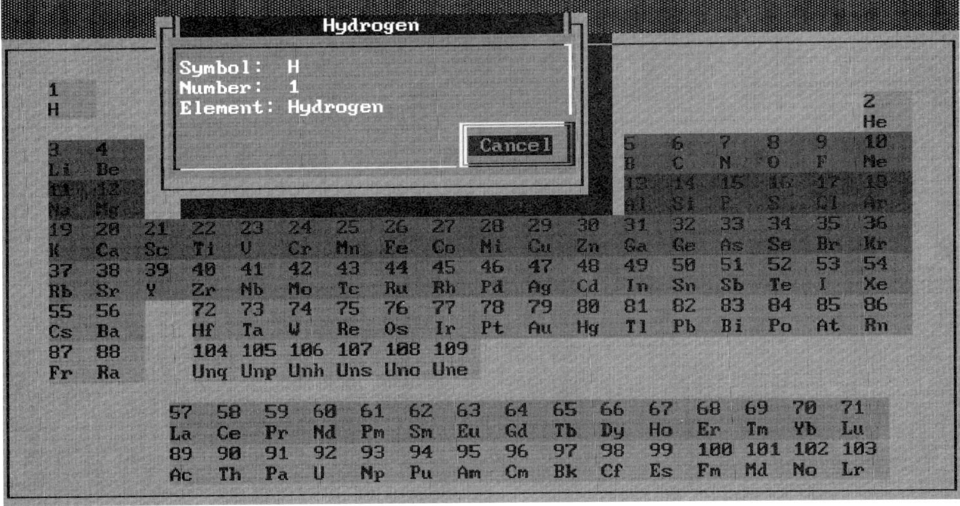

Figure 6-8 Periodic application with a second form.

The DataForm Specifications

The Periodic application will use a second form, **DataForm,** as a dialog box that appears each time the user clicks one of the picture boxes on the main form. **DataForm** will contain two controls: a text box and a command button.

DataForm Specifications

The specifications for the **DataForm** form are as follows.

Specification #6-2 (Form)

Periodic Application

Form	Event(s) to be detected		Response(s)
DataForm	None		None
Properties:	Location	13,1	
	Size	36,9	
	BorderStyle	Fixed Single	
	Caption	`DataForm`	
	MaxButton	False	
	MinButton	False	

Notes/Comments: This form will be used as a dialog box by the Periodic application.

DataForm Text Box Specification

DataForm will use a text box control as the primary display area for the Periodic Table data. The specification for the text box control is as follows (see page 158).

DataForm Command Button Specification

DataForm will show a single command button that can be used to dismiss the dialog box. The specification for the command button control follows (see page 158).

Building DataForm

Following the steps you have used to build the Periodic form, build **DataForm.** The following is a summary of the steps you will take to develop the **DataForm** form with its controls:

Specification #6-2 (Text Box)

Periodic Application DataForm Form

Controls	Event(s) to be detected		Response(s)
Text1	None		None
Properties:	Location	0,0	
	Size	34×7	
	BorderStyle	Single line	
	MultiLine	True	
	Colors	Cyan (background)/black (foreground)	

Notes/Comments: Application will display element data here.

Specification #6-2 (Command Button)

Periodic Application

DataForm Form

Controls	Event(s) to be detected		Response(s)
Command1	Click		Hide DataForm
Properties:	Location	24,4	
	Size	10×3	
	Caption	`Cancel`	
	Default	True	
	Colors	Cyan (background)/black (foreground)	

Notes/Comments: Default property sets button as default on form.

1. Start Visual Basic and open the Periodic project.
2. Add a new form called **DataForm** to the project. Use the DataForm specifications to set the form's properties and then to establish the size and location of the form. Note that once you move the form to 13,1 and resize it, the top of the form overlaps the Properties bar. Once the bar is covered, you will have to click the visible part of the bar each time you wish to adjust a property value. When you click the visible part of the bar, the complete Properties bar appears on the screen.
3. Add a text box control, **Text1,** to the form. Use the **DataForm** text box specifications to create and locate this control.
4. Add a command button, **Command1,** according to the specifications.
5. Save the project after you add this form and its controls.

Figure 6-9 shows what **DataForm** looks like after you customize it and add the controls.

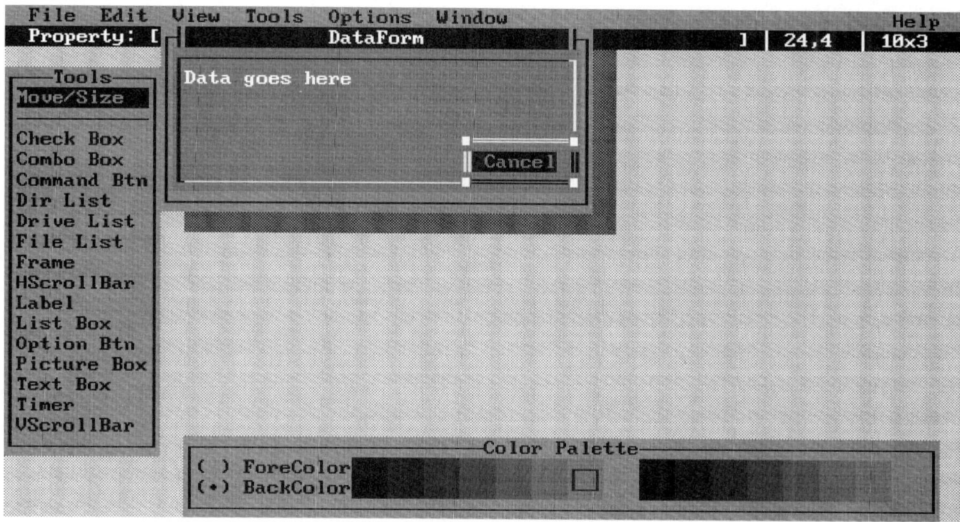

Figure 6-9 DataForm and its controls.

Update the Application's Code

Return to the programming environment, and create the following event procedures. Text in bold will be the text you enter.

Put the following code into the **Picture1_Click** event procedure on the Periodic form. This event procedure will respond to a **Click** event on any of the objects in the control array Picture1. The code calls up a dialog box (**DataForm**) and puts a string of element data into the text box and caption areas on **DataForm.**

```
DEFINT A-Z
SUB Picture1_Click (index AS INTEGER)
  CR$ = CHR$(13)                    'Carriage return
  DataForm.SHOW                     'Display the dialog box

  'Get element data from tag and extract name
  Dat$ = Picture1(index).Tag
  Cap$ = RIGHT$(Dat$, LEN(Dat$) - 6)

  'Build output strings and display data
  Out$ = "Symbol: " + LEFT$(Dat$, 3) + CR$
  Out$ = Out$ + "Number: " + MID$(Dat$, 4, 3) + CR$
  Out$ = Out$ + "Element: " + Cap$
  DataForm.Text1.Text = Out$

  'Change dialog box caption
  DataForm.Caption = Cap$

  'Give command button the focus
  DataForm.Command1.SETFOCUS
END SUB
```

This event procedure is activated when the user clicks one of the picture boxes on the Periodic form. The argument `index` indicates which picture box in the control array has been clicked.

The procedure displays the dialog box (**DataForm**) with the **SHOW** method. It then takes the data stored in the **Tag** property of the clicked picture box control and isolates the three data items: the element name, the chemical symbol, and the atomic number. To perform these data operations, the procedure uses the `RIGHT$`, `LEFT$`, and `MID$` string functions.

After building an output string of the element data (`Out$`), the procedure transfers the data to the **DataForm** text box (**Text1**) by modifying that control's **Text** property. It then updates the caption on the dialog box to match the displayed data.

As a final step, the code uses the **SETFOCUS** method to give the focus to the dialog box's **Cancel** button.

The code that goes into **DataForm's Cancel** button procedure follows (the code you enter is shown in bold). Put this code in the **Command1_Click** event procedure for **DataForm.**

```
SUB Command1_Click
    'Remove dialog box
    UNLOAD DataForm
END SUB
```

This completes the new code required to activate the dialog box and its features. When you have entered the code, save the project and try running the application.

If you look in the code module for **PERIODIC.FRM** (the **DATA** statement area), you will see the following code entry at the top of the window:

```
'$FORM DataForm
```

This statement is a $FORM metacommand which lets the code in the current form access an external form's properties and controls. Visual Basic inserted this code when you created DataForm. The metacommand insures that the references to DataForm in the **Picture1_Click** event procedures will work.

Run Periodic

After you have updated this application's event procedures, save the project and start the application. Your initial Periodic screen will look like the image in Figure 6-10. This screen looks exactly like the original Periodic application display.

Click any one of the 109 element areas on the display. When you do so, the dialog box (**DataForm**) appears on top of the Periodic form, in the area at the top of the table. Figure 6-11 shows the display after the user has clicked one of the picture box controls.

The dialog box displays the data for the element that was selected on the table. The caption on the dialog box changes to match the selection. The dialog box will remain on the screen until the user clicks the **Cancel** button. If the user continues to click elements on the table, the dialog box remains on the screen and shows new data each time a selection is made.

Figure 6-12 shows the Periodic application display after the user clicks a second table element.

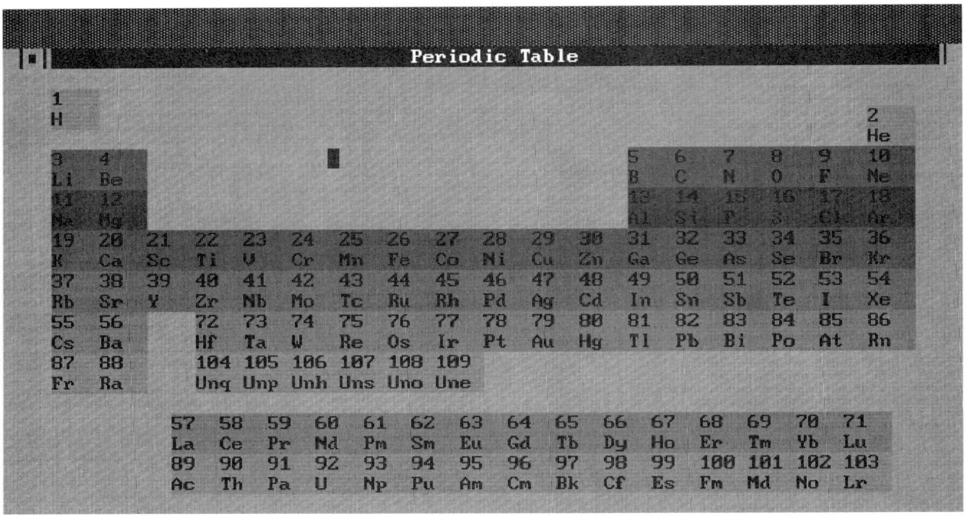

Figure 6-10 Periodic application at start up.

Experiment with your version of this application. Try clicking each element. Do you notice any problems or odd results? If so, check the **DATA** statements for errors, and correct any data entry mistakes.

To exit the running application, click **Cancel** to remove the dialog box and double-click the control box in the upper left corner of the Periodic form. Then press a key (**Enter**) to return to the programming environment.

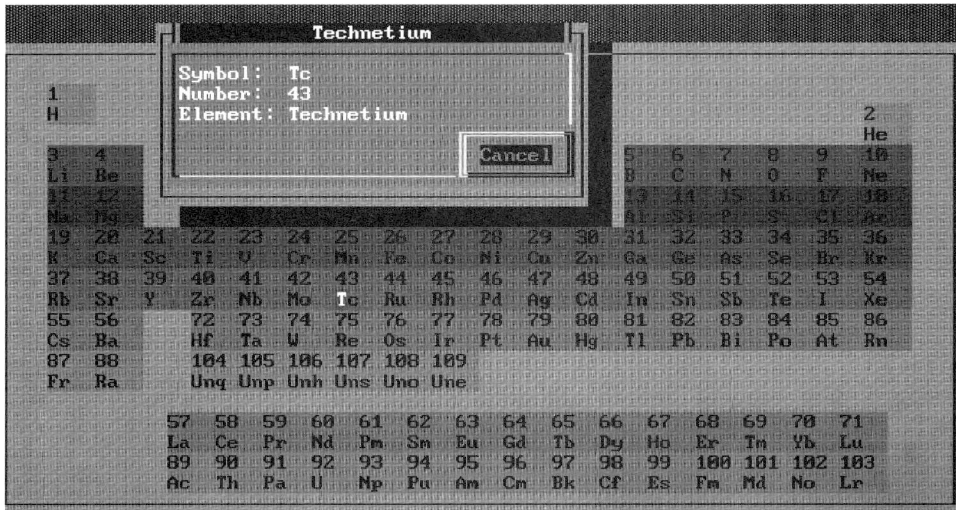

Figure 6-11 Display after user clicks a picture box control.

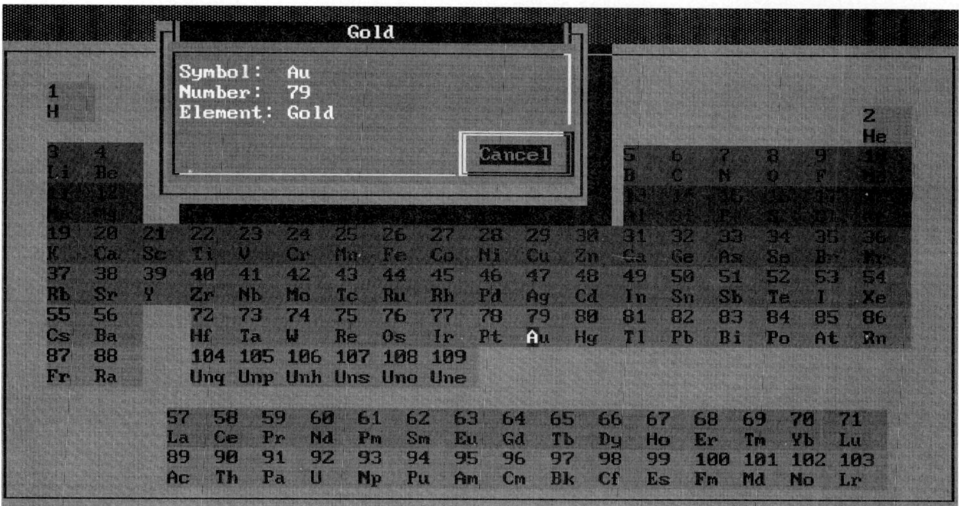

Figure 6-12 Display after user clicks another element.

If you only entered a portion of the table data, this would be a good place to enter the rest, now that you have a working application. If you make changes, save the project to record edits and corrections.

Summary

In this chapter, you built an application called Periodic that utilizes two forms: Periodic and **DataForm.** You developed code for the main form that called upon Visual Basic's powerful control array features to generate most of the user display. You designed and installed one picture box control on the form, and the code generated another 109 controls using a small amount of event procedure code (and quite a bit of data).

You then added a second form to the application: **DataForm.** You designed this form as a dialog box to pop up over the main form and display information based on where the user clicked the mouse. In implementing these features, you used several new Visual Basic commands and learned how to manipulate the properties of objects on an external form.

In the next chapter, you will expand the features of the Periodic application to provide users with additional data display options. Before leaving this application, here is a challenge that you might like to explore:

How might you alter the **DATA** statements and associated code in the **Form_Load** event procedure to simplify the data? *Hint:* Look carefully at the data for the third, fourth, and fifth rows of the table, as well as the rows at the bottom (the lanthanides and actinides). Note how most of the controls for these areas are right next to each other (have the same **Top** property values), are the same color, and are the same size. The position (**Left** property value) changes, but does so by a constant value, based on the position of the controls. By altering and adding code to the **Form_Load** procedure, you can greatly simplify the data used to generate the table.

7 Adding Features to the Multiform Application

In the previous chapter, you built a multiform application called Periodic. That application displayed a version of the Periodic Table of Elements. Periodic used one form for its main display, and used a second form, as a dialog box, to show more detailed information.

In this chapter, you will extend the functionality of the Periodic application in two ways. First, you will add controls to the main form that allow the user to alter that form's display. Next, you will add controls and

Concepts and Terminology

QBasic/QuickBasic Keywords

New Visual Basic Keywords

Visual Basic Event Procedures

features to the application's dialog box to let users view related data in several different ways.

Adding Controls to the Periodic Application

The main form for the application, captioned `Periodic Table`, and its dialog box are shown in Figure 7-1. The table displays the atomic numbers and symbols for 109 elements.

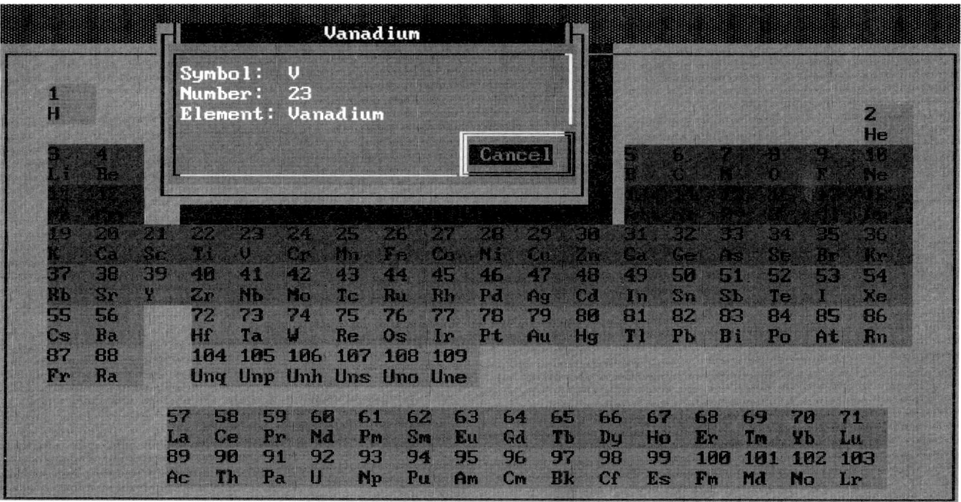

Figure 7-1 The Periodic Table form.

The two rows of entries across the bottom of the form represent the lanthanide and actinide series of elements. These elements logically fit into the two empty spots on the sixth and seventh rows of the table.

Let's add two label controls in the two empty table locations. When clicked, each of these controls will hide and show its corresponding row of picture boxes. For example, Figure 7-2 shows the two labels in place, the `Lan` label clicked, and the lanthanide series removed from the screen.

Update to Periodic Specifications

To create the display shown in Figure 7-2, you will add two label controls to the Periodic form and two event procedures to the application. You will also add two lines of simple code to the **Form_Load** procedure.

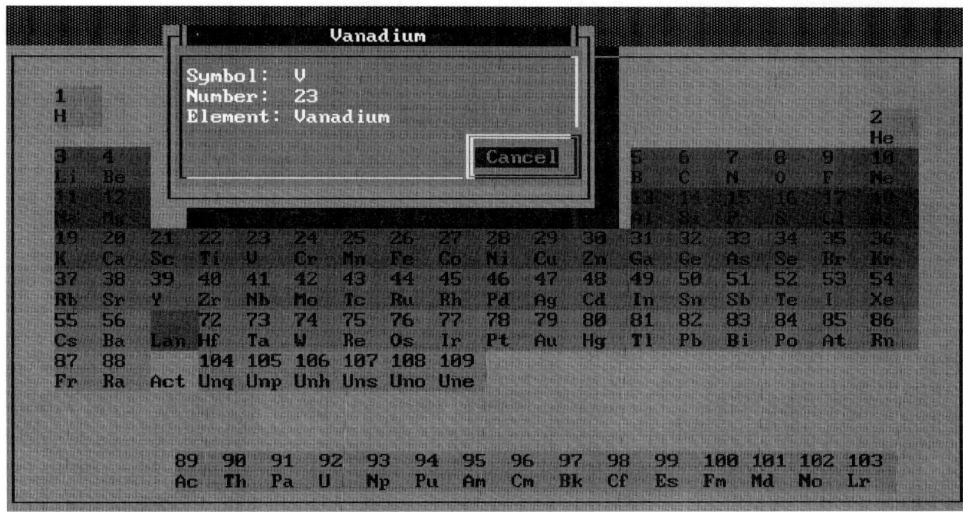

Figure 7-2 Periodic form with label controls activated.

The Label Specifications

The Periodic form will use two label controls that, when clicked, will hide and show the picture boxes associated with the lanthanide and actinide elements. The labels will respond to a **Click** event to perform their hide/show operations.

The specifications for the two labels are as follows (see page 168).

Adding the Labels to the Periodic Form

Before starting your modifications to the Periodic application, you may want to make copies of the application's project files, `PERIODIC.FRM`, `DATAFORM.FRM`, and `PERIODIC.MAK`. In this chapter, you will be making quite a few changes to the original application. If you want to keep the original application files intact, make copies of them now.

To add the first label to the Periodic form, do the following:

1. Start Visual Basic. The system displays a new project with an Untitled Code window.

2. Open the File menu and choose the **Open Project** command. When the **Open Project** dialog box appears, type `A:PERIODIC.MAK` into

Specification #7-1 (Labels)

Periodic Application

Controls	Event(s) to be detected		Response(s)
Label1	Click		Hide/show lanthanide series
			Change label color each click
Properties:	Location	11,12	
	Size	4×2	
	BorderStyle	None	
	BackColor	Bright white	
	Caption	`Lan`	
Label2	Click		Hide/show actinide series
			Change label color each click
Properties:	Location	11,14	
	Size	4×2	
	BorderStyle	None	
	BackColor	Bright white	
	Caption	`Act`	

Notes/Comments: Labels are separate objects, not a control array.

the File Name text box, and click **OK.** Visual Basic loads the Periodic application, which includes the forms `PERIODIC.FRM` and `DATA-FORM.FRM`.

3. Select the PERIODIC.FRM entry in the Project window, and click the **Form** button to go to the Form Designer area. The Periodic form appears on the screen, as shown in Figure 7-3.
4. Open the Tools menu and choose the **Label** command. A label control, `Label1`, appears at the center of the form.
5. Click and drag this object to location 11,12.
6. Resize this object to size 4×2.

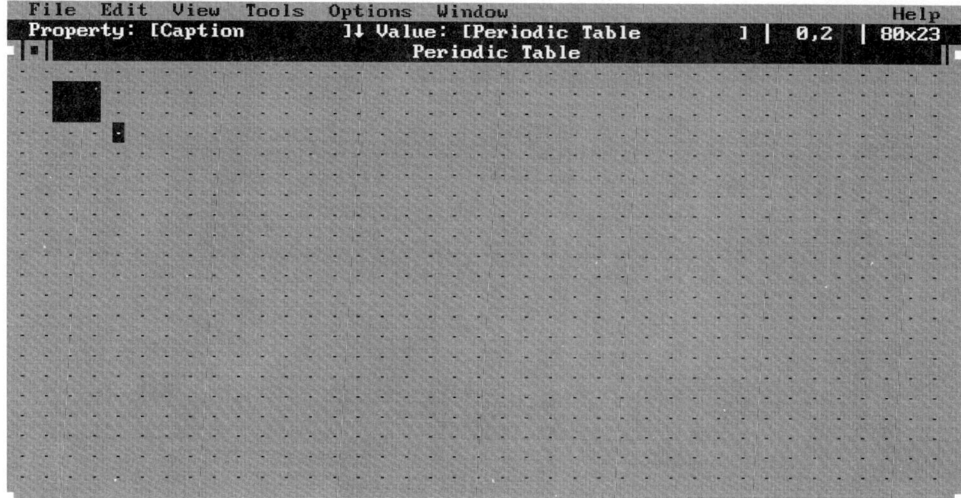

Figure 7-3 Periodic form.

7. Use the Property bar to set the labels properties: **Caption** (`Lan`), **BorderStyle** (**None**), **BackColor** (**Bright White**).

Add the Second Label

Follow steps 4 through 7 that you used to put `Label1` on the form, and create a second label control, `Label2`. Refer back to the label specifications as you create this control. After you add this second label, the form looks like the one shown in Figure 7-4.

Save the Project

Save your work before you proceed. To save the Periodic project, do the following:

1. Open the File menu and choose the **Save Project** command.

Visual Basic updates the form file, `PERIODIC.FRM`, during this save operation. You are now ready to add two event procedures for the label controls.

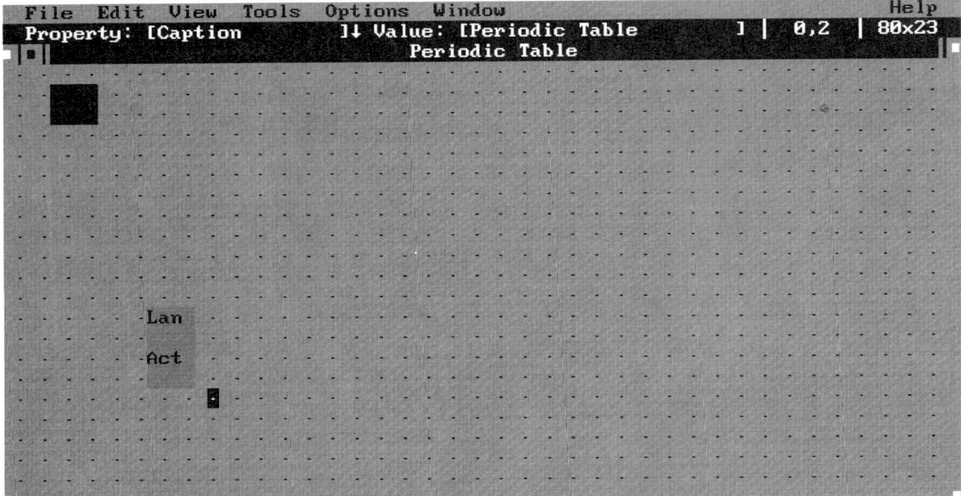

Figure 7-4 The Periodic form with label controls.

Adding Code to the Periodic Application

If you have not already done so, save the project. If you are not already in the programming environment, go there to add event procedures for the two label controls.

You will create two event procedures for `Label1` and `Label2`, and add two lines of code to the Periodic form's **Form_Load** procedure. Otherwise, all of the Periodic application's existing code can be used as is.

The Label1 Procedure

To create the Label1 event procedure, do the following:

1. Open the Edit menu and choose the **Event Procedures** command.

2. Visual Basic displays an **Event Procedures** dialog box (Figure 7-5).

   This dialog box has three lists: **Files, Objects,** and **Events.** The **Files** list has three entries: `PERIODIC.FRM`, `DATAFORM.FRM`, and `DATAWIND.FRM`. These are the form files for the Periodic application. You will create the `DATAWIND.FRM` later in this chapter.

   With `PERIODIC.FRM` selected, the **Objects** list displays a list with four items: a form with the caption `Periodic`, a picture box control, `Picture1`, and the two label controls.

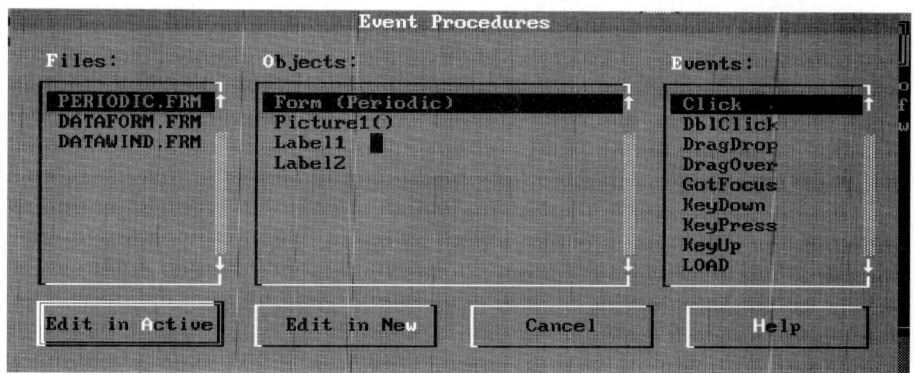

Figure 7-5 Event Procedures dialog box.

3. Move the highlight in the **Objects** list to `Label1`, then move the highlight in the **Events** list to `Click`.

4. Click the **Edit in Active** button. When you click this button, Visual Basic dismisses the **Event Procedures** dialog box and displays the Code window for the **Label1_Click** event procedure.

   At the top of the Code window, you see the window title:

   ```
   [1] PERIODIC.FRM:Label1_Click
   ```

   In the text area of the Code window, you see a template for the procedure you are about to create:

   ```
   SUB Label1_Click ()

   END SUB
   ```

5. Enter the following code (shown in bold) into this event procedure template:

   ```
   SUB Label1_Click ()
      'Hide or show the lanthanides
      'Check if lanthanides are visible
      IF Picture1(57).Visible = TRUE THEN
           'Controls visible; change label color
           'Hide controls
           Label1.BackColor = 3
           FOR index = 57 TO 71
                Picture1(index).Visible = FALSE
           NEXT Index
   ```

```
    ELSE
        'Controls invisible; change label color
        'Show controls
        Label1.BackColor = 15
        FOR index = 57 TO 71
            Picture1(index).Visible = TRUE
        NEXT Index
    END IF

    IF DataForm.Visible = TRUE THEN
        DataForm.SETFOCUS 'Give dialog box the focus
    END IF
END SUB
```

6. Save the project.

This code looks at the **Visible** property of the picture box control array element, **Picture1(57)**. If that array element is visible, the procedure hides all the elements 57 through 71, and changes the color of **Label1** to cyan (**3**).

If the array element is invisible, the procedure shows elements 57 through 71, and changes the color of **Label1** back to bright white (**15**).

The last three lines of code give the focus to the dialog box, **DataForm,** if that object is visible.

Add the code for Label2

Choose the **Events Procedure** command on the Edit menu, and create the **Label2_Click** event procedure. The code for that procedure follows (enter the text in bold):

```
SUB Label2_Click ()
    'Hide or show the actinides
    'Check if actinides are visible
    IF Picture1(89).Visible = TRUE THEN
        'Controls visible; change label color
        'Hide controls
        Label2.BackColor = 3
        FOR index = 89 TO 103
            Picture1(index).Visible = FALSE
        NEXT Index
    ELSE
        'Controls invisible; change label color
        'Show controls
        Label2.BackColor = 15
        FOR index = 89 TO 103
```

```
            Picture1(index).Visible = TRUE
        NEXT Index
    END IF

    IF DataForm.Visible = TRUE THEN
        DataForm.SETFOCUS 'Give dialog box the focus
    END IF
END SUB
```

This procedure operates just like the **Label1_Click** procedure. The only difference involves the controls that are shown and hidden. **Label2_Click** uses the **Visible** property of **Picture1(89)** as the trigger for hiding and showing the elements 89 through 103.

After you enter this block of code, save the project.

Update the Code in Form_Load

You need to add two lines of code to the **Form_Load** event procedure. These lines of code adjust the captions of `Label1` and `Label2` to match the rest of the table entries.

The code for the **Form_Load** subroutine is reproduced below. The new lines that you are to enter appear in bold:

```
SUB Form_Load ()
    Num$ = SPACE$(3)        'element number variable
    CR$ = CHR$(13)          'Carriage return
    READ NumElem            'Get number of elements

    'Begin loop that reads element data
    'and generates the periodic table
    FOR index = 1 TO NumElem

        'Get data for an element
        READ L, T, Bcolor, Sym$, Ename$

        'Create picture box in control array
        LOAD Picture1(index)

        'Set picture box properties
        Picture1(index).BackColor = Bcolor
        Picture1(index).Visible = TRUE
        Picture1(index).AutoReDraw = TRUE

        'Create display text
        'Trim initial space and left justify in Num$
        LSET Num$ = LTRIM$(STR$(index))
        'Display element number and symbol
        Picture1(index).PRINT Num$ + CR$ + Sym$

        'Store data as Tag property value
```

```
        Picture1(index).Tag = Sym$ + Num$ + Ename$

        'Position the picture box
        Picture1(index).MOVE L, T, 4, 2
    NEXT index

    'Hide original picture box
    Picture1(0).Visible = FALSE

    'Set label captions
    Label1.Caption = CR$ + "Lan"
    Label2.Caption = CR$ + "Act"
END SUB
```

As you can see, most of the code in **Form_Load** remains the same, as does the code for **Picture1_Click,** the event procedure that displays the dialog box and its information.

Save the project, and run the application to test out the new code entries.

Run Periodic

To run the program, open the Run menu and choose the **Start** command. If there are no syntax or run-time errors in the code, the form Periodic will appear on the screen. The two new label controls will appear, as shown in Figure 7-6.

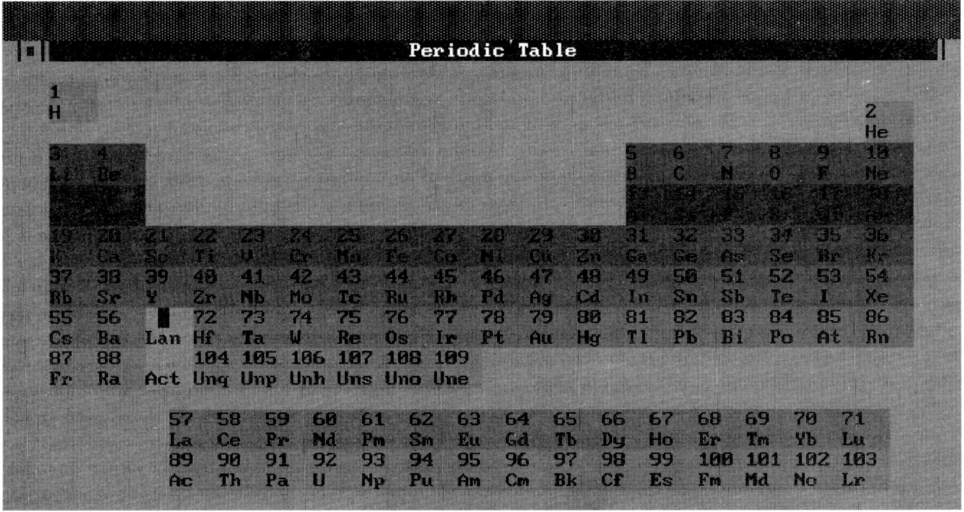

Figure 7-6 Periodic application with new label controls.

Click the label control captioned `Lan`. Figure 7-7 shows the screen after you click this control.

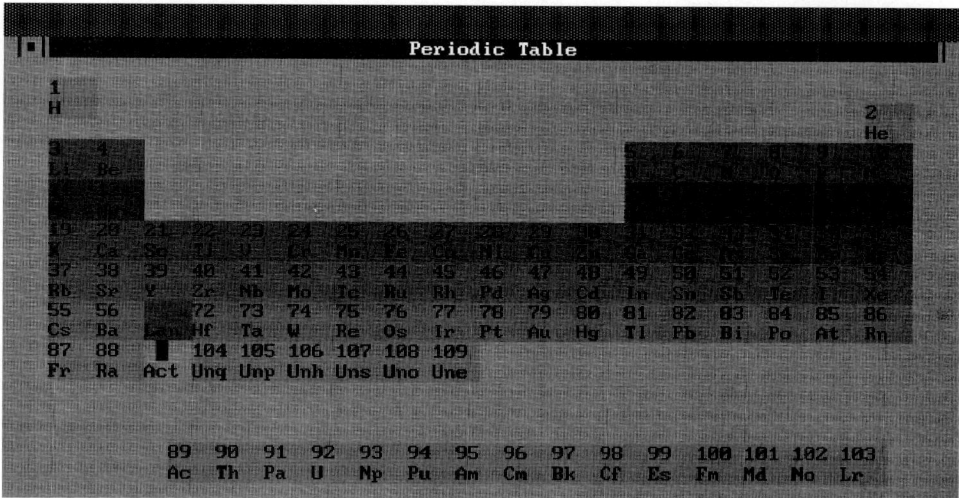

Figure 7-7 Display after Lan is clicked.

Since the lanthanides were visible, the **Label1_Click** event procedure hid that row of elements and changed the color of the **Label1** (`Lan`) control to cyan.

Try clicking the second label control, **Label2** (`Act`). Since the actinides are visible, **Label2_Click** hides that row of elements and changes the color of **Label2** to cyan. Figure 7-8 shows the Periodic form after **Label2** has been clicked.

If you now click either one of the label controls, the corresponding row of elements will become visible, and the control you click will change color to bright white. Try it. Verify that both label controls work properly in hiding and showing the picture box controls across the bottom of the table.

Adding a Third Form to the Application

In the previous chapter, you added a second form, DataForm, to the Periodic application. You designed and implemented **DataForm** as a dialog box that appeared when the user clicked an element on the table.

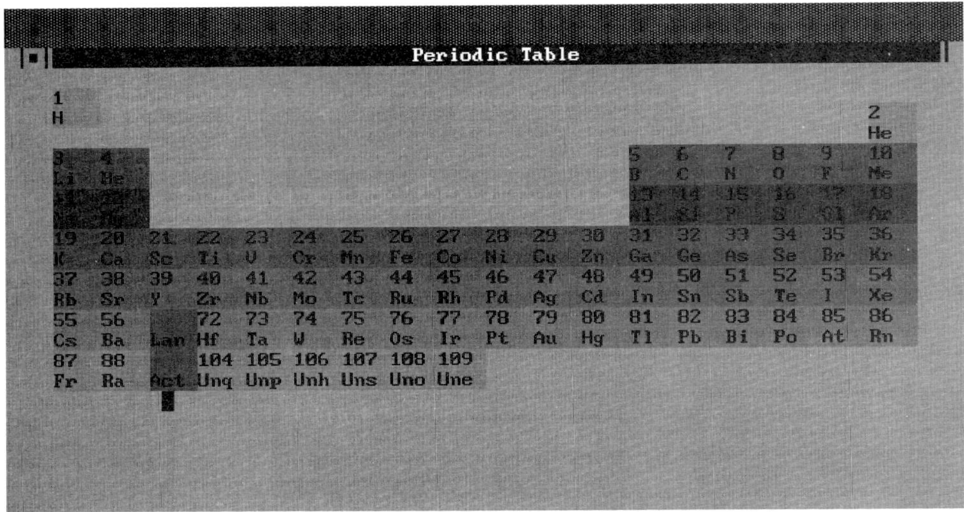

Figure 7-8 Display after Act is clicked.

Figure 7-9 shows the current version of the application with DataForm displayed.

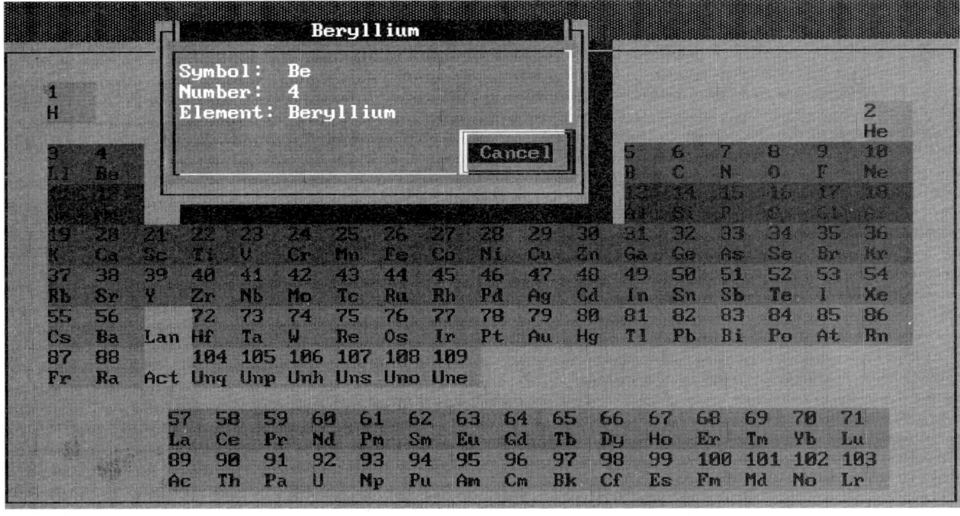

Figure 7-9 Application with dialog box displayed.

The next set of activities involves adding additional controls to the dialog box and a third form to this application. Figure 7-10 shows the application display with the new controls on the dialog box.

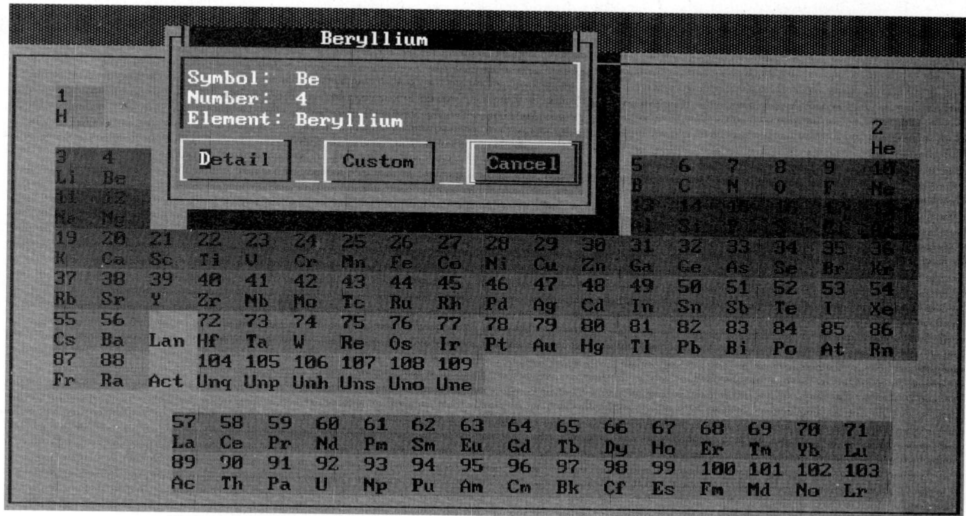

Figure 7-10 Dialog box with new controls.

The new **Detail** button will be used to bring up a third form, DataWind, which will display additional information about the element selected on the table. DataWind will be designed and implemented as a window that appears and displaces the table and dialog box displays. Figure 7-11 shows the screen after you click the **Detail** button.

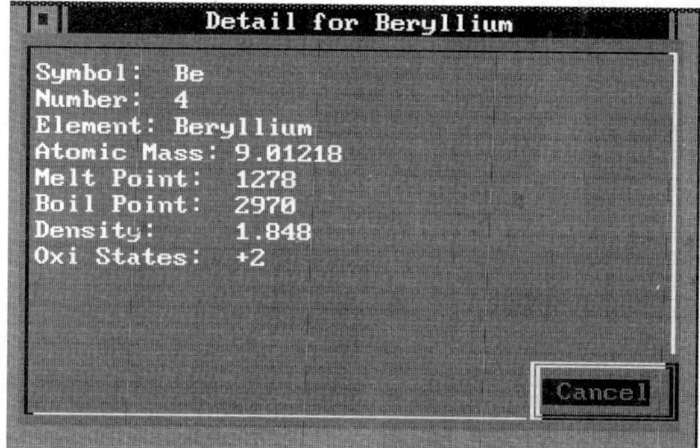

Figure 7-11 DataWind window.

The new **Custom** button will be installed as you update DataForm. Custom will be a button you can use to add more features to this application.

Update to the DataForm Specifications

You will add two new command buttons to the **DataForm** dialog box. The addition of these two controls does not change the form's specifications or alter its current event procedures. These additions will add one event procedure to DataForm, **Command2_Click.** At the form level, DataForm will also be used as a storage area for some new **DATA** statements that contain data to be displayed on the new form, DataWind.

New DataForm Command Buttons

Here are the specifications for the two new command buttons to go on DataForm. DataForm already uses a single command button, **Cancel** (**Command1**) (see page 179).

The New DataWind Specification

DataWind will appear each time the user clicks the **Detail** button on the **DataForm** dialog box. The form will have a multiline text box for information display, and one command button, **Cancel.** The command button will unload the window and bring back the application's table display and dialog box. The specifications for the third application form, DataWind, are as follows (see page 180).

DataWind Text Box Specification

DataWind will use a multiline text box control as a display area for detailed periodic table information. The specification for this text box control is as follows (see page 180).

DataWind Command Button Specification

DataForm uses a single command button to dismiss the dialog box and restore the main screen display. The specification for this command button control follows (see page 181).

Updating DataForm and Building DataWind

Follow the steps you have used to build the other forms for this application to modify DataForm and build DataWind. The following is a summary of the steps you will take to update the DataForm form with its controls:

<u>Specification #7-2 (Command Buttons)</u>

Periodic Application

DataForm Form

Controls	Event(s) to be detected		Response(s)
Command2	Click		Show DataWind window
			Build display on DataWind
			Hide main screen objects
Properties:	Location	0,4	
	Size	10 × 3	
	Caption	`Detail`	
	Colors	Cyan (background)/black (foreground)	
Command3	None		None
Properties:	Location	12,4	
	Size	10 × 3	
	Caption	`Custom`	
	Colors	Cyan (background)/black (foreground)	

Notes/Comments: **Command3** is not going to be activated now.

1. If you are in the programming environment, select DataForm in the Project window and click the **Form** button to go to the Form Designer area.
2. Using the set of #7-2 specifications, add the two command buttons to DataForm.
3. Save the project.

Figure 7-12 shows what DataForm looks like after you add the two new command buttons.

To add the third form, DataWind, and its controls, here is an outline of the steps you will perform:

Specification #7-3 (Form)

Periodic Application

DataWind Form

Form(s)	Event(s) to be detected		Response(s)
DataWind	None		None
Properties:	Location	16,3	
	Size	45 × 17	
	BorderStyle	Fixed solid	
	Caption	`DataWind`	
	MaxButton	False	
	MinButton	False	

Notes/Comments: This form will be used as a information window. The **Detail** button on the **DataForm** dialog box activates the display of this window.

Specification #7-4 (Text Box)

Periodic Application

DataWind Form

Controls	Event(s) to be detected		Response(s)
Text1	None		None
Properties:	Location	0,0	
	Size	43 × 15	
	BorderStyle	Single line	
	MultiLine	True	
	Colors	Bright green (background)/black (foreground)	

Notes/Comments: Application will display detail element data here.

<u>Specification #7-5 (Command Button)</u>

Periodic Application

DataForm Form

Controls	Event(s) to be detected		Response(s)
Command1	Click		Hide DataWind
			Restore main screen objects
Properties:	Location	33,12	
	Size	10 × 3	
	Caption	`Cancel`	
	Default	True	
	Colors	Bright green (background)/black (foreground)	

Notes/Comments: Default property sets button as default on form.

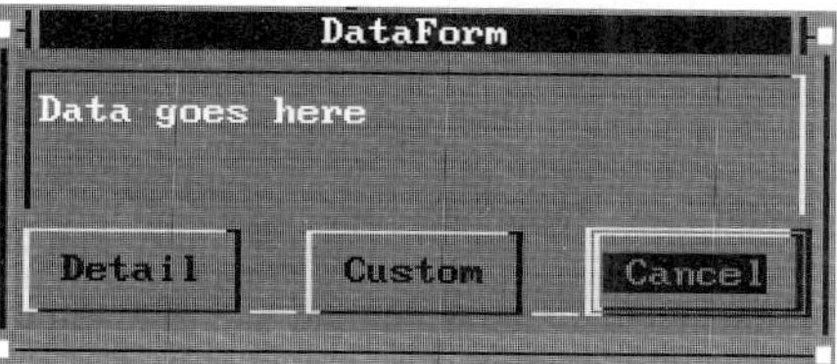

Figure 7-12 DataForm with two new controls.

1. Add a new form called DataWind to the project. Use the DataWind specifications (#7-3) to establish the size and location of the form.
2. Add a text box control, **Text1,** to the form. Use the DataWind text box specifications (#7-4) to create and locate this control.
3. Add a command button, **Command1,** according to the specifications (#7-5).
4. Save the project after you add this form and its controls.

Figure 7-13 shows what DataWind looks like after you build it and add its single command button.

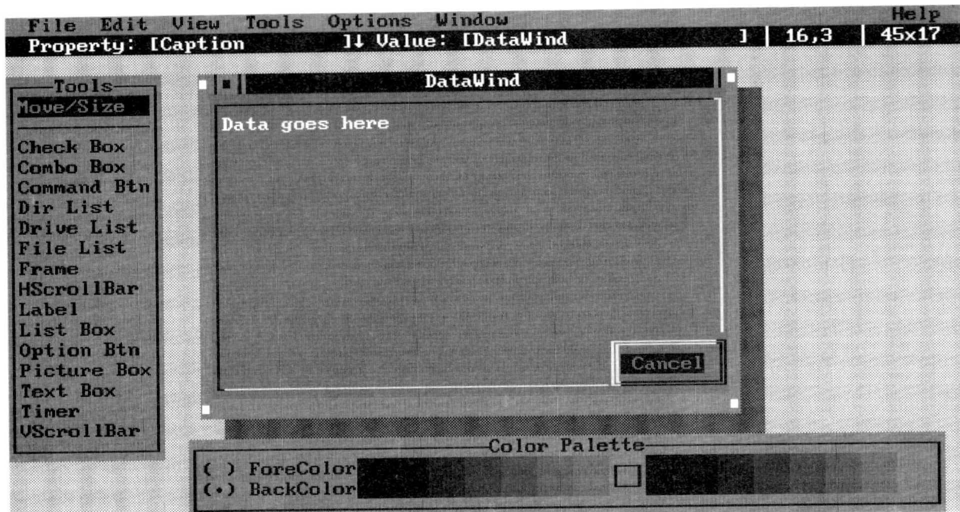

Figure 7-13 Completed DataWind form.

Update the Application's Code

Return to the programming environment and add the following code and event procedures to the application.

Periodic Form Code Changes

A couple of lines of code need to be added to the **Picture1_Click** procedure attached to the Periodic form. The code for this procedure follows. The lines in bold are the lines you need to add.

```
SUB  Picture1_Click (index AS INTEGER)
     CR$ = CHR$(13)               'Carriage return
     DataForm.SHOW                'Display the dialog box

     'Get element data from tag and extract name
     Dat$ = Picture1(index).Tag
     Cap$ = RIGHT$(Dat$, LEN(Dat$) - 6)

     'Build output strings and display data
     Out$ = "Symbol: " + LEFT$(Dat$, 3) + CR$
     Out$ = Out$ + "Number: " + MID$(Dat$, 4, 3) + CR$
     Out$ = Out$ + "Element: " + Cap$
     DataForm.Text1.Text = Out$
```

```
      'Change dialog box caption
      DataForm.Caption = Cap$

      'Give buttons the focus; highlight Command1
      DataForm.Command2.SETFOCUS
      DataForm.Command3.SETFOCUS
      DataForm.Command1.SETFOCUS
END SUB
```

These code additions make sure that the three **DataForm** command buttons appear on top of the text box on the display, and leave **Command1** highlighted when the dialog box appears.

Update the DataForm Code

DataForm has two new blocks of code. One block is a set of **DATA** statements that provide detailed information for the DataWind display. The second block of code is the event procedure for the **Detail** button (**Command2**).

Here is the block of **DATA** statements that goes onto DataForm's Code window (form-level code). Enter this code into the DATAFORM.FRM Code window.

```
'Detail data stored here
DetailData:
    'Number of entries
DATA 6
'Atomic Mass, Melting Point, Boiling Point,
'Density, and Oxidation States
DATA 1.00794,-259.14,-252.87,0.00008988, "+1"
DATA 4.00260,-272.2,-268.934,0.001785, ""
DATA 6.941,180.54,1342,0.534, "+1"
DATA 9.01218,1278,2970,1.848, "+2"
DATA 10.81,2079,3675,2.34, "+3"
DATA 12.011,3550,4827,2.267, "-4, +2, +4"
```

To simplify your data entry tasks, detailed data for only the first six elements (hydrogen to carbon) have been created and put into this DATA block labeled `DetailData`. If you want to enter data for the rest of the elements, locate a chemistry book and fill out the rest of the entries. Change the number of entries (`DATA 6`) to match the number of data items you create.

The element data in this section are atomic mass units, melting point (°C), boiling point (°C), density (g/cm^3; gases at Standard Temperature and

Pressure), and major oxidation states. These data can be found in most Chemistry books.

Add Code for the Detail Button

The second block of code to add to DataForm is the event procedure code for the **Detail** button (**Command2**). That code appears next, with the lines you type shown in bold:

```
SUB Command2_Click ()
    'Dimension string variables
    DIM Amass$, MeltPt$, BoilPt$, Density$, OxStates$
    CR$ = CHR$(13)                 'Carriage return

    SCREEN.HIDE                    'Hide the current objects
    DataWind.SHOW                  'Display the Detail window

    'Get element data from dialog box
    Dat$ = DataForm.Text1.Text
    'Put data into text box on window
    DataWind.Text1.Text = Dat$

    'Get element name from dialog box caption
    Cap$ = DataForm.Caption
    'Display new caption for window
    DataWind.Caption = "Detail for " + Cap$

    'Get detail data
    RESTORE DetailData             'Restore data block
    READ NumElem                   'Read number of entries
    'Redimension the string arrays
    REDIM Amass$(NumElem), MeltPt$(NumElem)
    REDIM BoilPt$(NumElem), Density$(NumElem)
    REDIM OxStates$(NumElem)

    'Read the data into the arrays
    FOR index = 1 TO NumElem
        READ Amass$(index), MeltPt$(index)
        READ BoilPt$(index), Density$(index)
        READ OxStates$(index)
    NEXT Index

    'Retrieve current window text
    Out$ = DataWind.Text1.Text

    'Retrieve element number
    index = VAL(MID$(Dat$, 23, 3))
    IF index >= NumElem THEN
       'If detailed data available, then add it to
       'the output string for the window
       Out$ = Out$ + CR$ + "Atomic Mass: " + Amass$(index)
```

```
        Out$ = Out$ + CR$ + "Melt Point: " + MeltPt$(index)
        Out$ = Out$ + CR$ + "Boil Point: " + BoilPt$(index)
        Out$ = Out$ + CR$ + "Density:    " + Density$(index)
        Out$ = Out$ + CR$ + "Oxi States: " + OxStates$(index)
    END IF

    'Display the detail information
    DataWind.Text1.Text = Out$

    'Give command button the focus
    DataWind.Command1.SETFOCUS
END SUB
```

This event procedure responds to a **Click** event with the following actions:

- Hides all of the current screen objects.
- Shows the DataWind window.
- Retrieves text stored in the dialog box.
- Updates the caption on the window (`DataWind`).
- Restores the data block stored on DataForm.
- Redimensions the string arrays to match the number of data entries.
- Reads in the detailed data.
- Builds the detailed information display.
- Displays the detailed data.

The simple result of all of these actions is that when the user clicks the **Detail** button, the screen clears and detailed information appears in a separate window, DataWind.

The DataWind Code

The only code you need to create for the DataWind form is the event procedure code for the **Cancel** button (**Command1** on DataWind). The code for that button follows (what you type appears in bold):

```
SUB Command1_Click ()
    'Display the form, dialog box, and window
    SCREEN.SHOW
    DataForm.SETFOCUS     'Give dialog box the focus
    UNLOAD DataWind       'Unload the window
END SUB
```

When the user clicks **Cancel** on the window (DataWind), this procedure restores all of the screen objects, gives the focus to the dialog box (**DataForm**), and unloads the window (DataWind).

This entry completes all of the new code required to implement the **Detail** button feature on the dialog box (**DataForm**). When you have entered the code, save the project and try running the application. If the code works properly, you should be able to duplicate the screen displays shown in Figures 7-9, 7-10, and 7-11.

More $FORM Metacommands

If you look in the code module for `DATAFORM.FRM` (the **DATA** statement area) and `DATAWIND.FRM`, you see these code entries at the top of the window:

```
'$FORM DataWind          — on DataForm
'$FORM DataForm          — on DataWind
```

These statements are **$FORM** metacommands. Visual Basic inserts these code lines because there are linkages between objects on the two forms. The **Detail** button on DataForm references DataWind objects and properties. The **Cancel** button on DataWind references DataForm. The metacommands make sure that these cross linkages between the forms work properly.

Summary

In this chapter, you extended the features of the Periodic application in two ways. You added two label controls and code that lets the user hide and show the two rows of picture boxes across the bottom of the table.

You then added command buttons to the dialog box (**DataForm**), as well as a third form (DataWind) with a text box control and a command button. You updated the code for DataForm that lets the user call up the detail information window (DataWind). You added code to DataWind that sends the user back to the main screen display (the table of elements and the dialog box).

The dialog box (**DataForm**) has an unused command button (**Command 3,** captioned `Custom`). You are encouraged to go ahead and add other display or computational features to the Periodic application. Give the user access to these new features when they click the **Custom** button.

In the next chapter, you will explore Visual Basic's graphics and sound capabilities. When you are ready to "listen to the music" and see a few colorful displays, turn to Chapter 8, "Sound and Graphics."

8 Sound and Graphics

Visual Basic supports access to the computer's sound and graphics features. Using Visual Basic, you can play music and display colorful graphic images from within your applications.

This chapter introduces you to combining Visual Basic forms with music and graphics. You build a simple music application that simulates an electronic keyboard, on the screen. Then you design, build, and code a graphics generator that shows you how to display graphics from within

Concepts and Terminology

QBasic/QuickBasic Keywords

(continued)

Visual Basic. This application introduces several new Visual Basic controls and features.

Listen to the Music

In this section, you will build the Music application. Figure 8-1 shows what this application looks like when all of its controls are in place and also when a "key" on the keyboard is being clicked. Each time you click one of Music's "keys," the program activates your computer's sound feature and plays the indicated note. You can play simple, one-note tunes with Music.

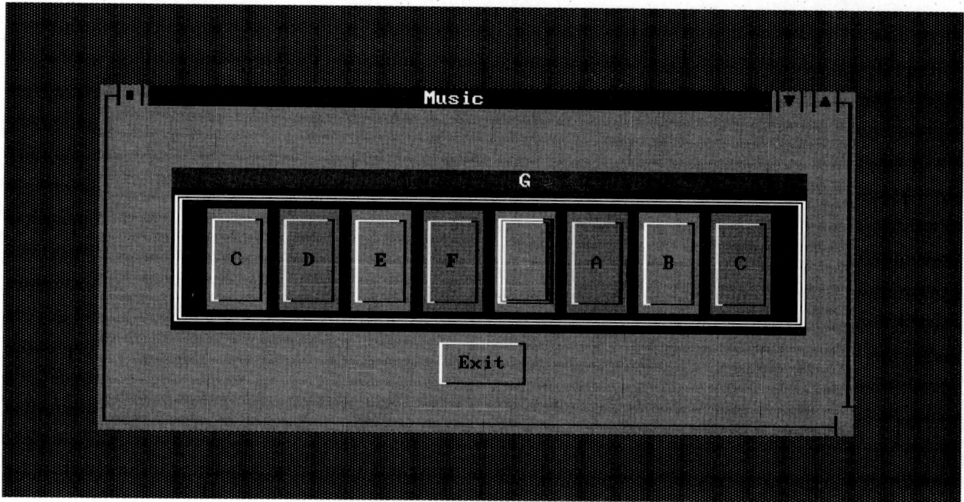

Figure 8-1 Music application screen.

Music uses the following set of controls:

- A text box across the top of the keyboard area.
- A picture box to enclose the keyboard "keys."
- A command button control array for the eight "keys."
- A **Exit** command button.

To begin, review the Music specifications. Then proceed to build the Music form and install the indicated controls. Finally, add the code that controls the user's interactions and plays the music.

Music Application Specifications

Music houses the controls that lets the user click objects (a control array of eight command buttons) that play notes on the musical scale. The Music form that contains these controls has the following specifications. The form itself does not respond to any events (see page 192).

Music Application Control Specifications

Music has a text box control, a picture box, a control array of eight command buttons, and a command button that lets the user exit the application. Figure 8-2 identifies Music's controls and how they appear on the form.

Specification #8-1 (Form)

Music Application

Controls	Event(s) to be detected		Response(s)
Music	None		None
Properties:	Location	8,4	
	Size	63 × 17 (default)	
	Caption	`Music`	

Notes/Comments: Form only used to house controls.

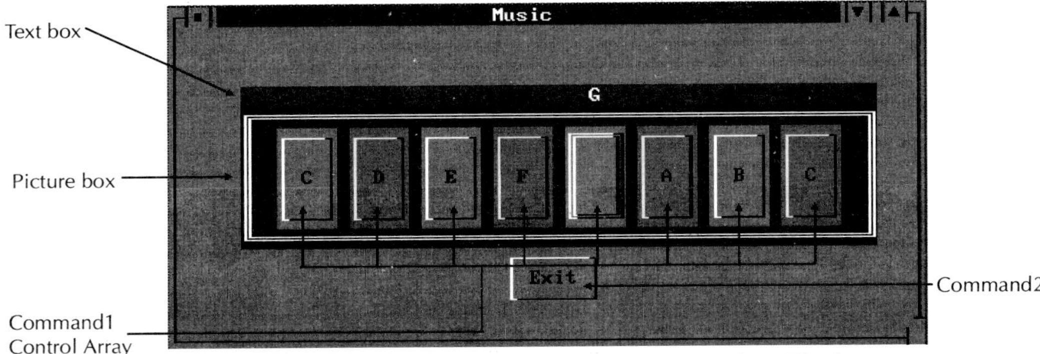

Figure 8-2 Music form with controls identified.

The following specifications indicate where you place these controls and the required event procedures.

Music Text Box Specification

Music uses a single text box control. The control appears as a color band across the top of the keyboard. The application displays the character of the note being played (C, D, E,...) in this text box region (see page 193).

Music Picture Box Specification

Music's picture box control encloses the control array of eight command buttons that play the notes. As you build the application, put the picture box down first, before you add the control array elements (see page 193).

Specification #8-2 (Text Box)

Music Application

Controls	Event(s) to be detected		Response(s)
Text1	None		None
Properties:	Location	5,3	
	Size	53 × 1	
	BorderStyle	None	
	Enabled	False	
	Text	None (remove default text)	
	BackColor	Cyan	

Notes/Comments: Used for display only.

Specification #8-3 (Picture Box)

Music Application

Controls	Event(s) to be detected		Response(s)
Picture1	None		None
Properties:	Location	5,4	
	Size	53 × 7	
	BorderStyle	Double line	
	Enabled	False	
	BackColor	Bright blue	

Notes/Comments: Used to enclose the "keys" on the keyboard.

Music Command Buttons Specification

Music has two command button controls on the form. One control, **Command1()**, is a control array that produces the eight "keys" on Music's keyboard. The second control, **Command2,** serves as the **Exit** button.

The specifications for these controls follow.

Specification #8-4 (Command Buttons)

Music Application

Controls	Event(s) to be detected		Response(s)
Command1()	Click		Play assigned note
Properties:	Location	8,5; 14,5; 20,5; 26,5; 32,5; 38,5; 44,5; 50,5	
	Size	5 × 5	
	Caption	`C, D, E, F, G, A, B, C`	
	BackColor	Alternating white and gray	
Command2	Click		Exit application
Properties:	Location	27,11	
	Size	8 × 3	
	Caption	`Exit`	

Notes/Comments: Control array, **Command1(),** has eight different locations and captions.

Build the Music Form

You build the Music application just as you have built earlier applications. The only new items to be covered in this section will be:

- Use of the Edit menu commands (**Copy** and **Paste**) to create copy and paste controls onto the form.
- The creation of a control array.

To begin, review this application's specifications and then do the following:

1. Start Visual Basic. The system displays a new project with an Untitled Code window.
2. Open the File menu and choose the **New Form** command. When you see the **New Form** dialog box:

   Type `A:MUSIC.FRM` and press **Enter.**

You will be placed in the Form Designer area with a form captioned `Music`.

3. Based on the Music form specification (#8-1), customize the form for the application.
4. Add the form's text box control, **Text1,** using specification #8-2 as a guide.
5. Add the picture box control, **Picture1,** using specification #8-3 to guide your efforts.
6. Save the project.

At this stage of development, your form should look like the one shown in Figure 8-3.

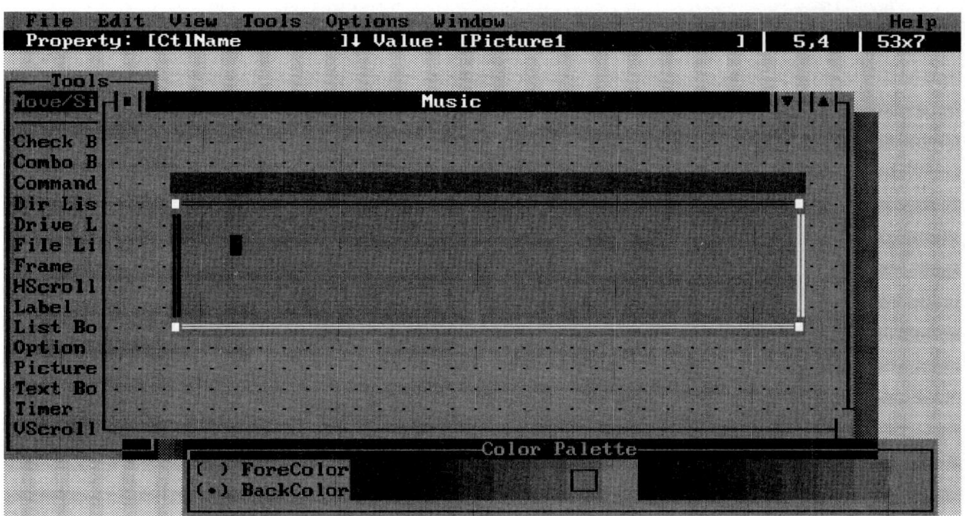

Figure 8-3 Music form with text and picture box controls.

Add the Control Array

In this section, you add the eight controls that act as the "keys" on the Music keyboard. The controls are a single command button control array, **Command1().**

To add this control array to the Music form, review the specifications (#8-4) and then proceed as follows:

1. Open the Tools menu and choose the **Command Button** command. A command button, **Command1,** appears at the center of the form.

2. Click and drag this object to location 8,5.
3. Resize this object to size 5 × 5.

   Figure 8-4 shows the Music form with **Command1** in place.

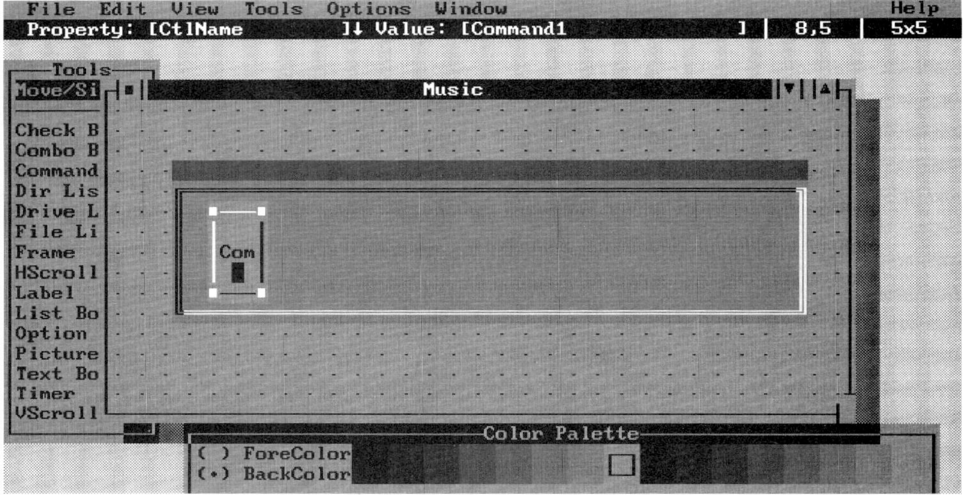

Figure 8-4 Music form with Command1 in place.

4. While the command button is selected, choose the **Copy** command on the Edit menu. This choice copies **Command1** to the Clipboard.
5. Choose the **Paste** command on the Edit menu. A dialog box appears, asking if you want to create a control array. Figure 8-5 shows this dialog box and its message.

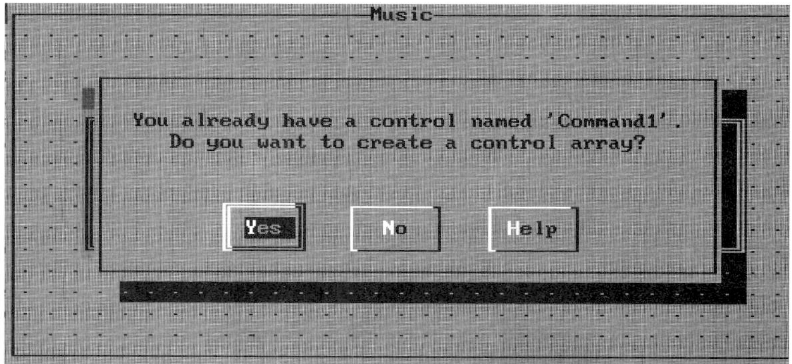

Figure 8-5 Control array message dialog box.

6. Click the **Yes** button to tell Visual Basic you want to create a control array.

   A copy of the **Command1** button appears in the upper left corner of the form.

7. Click and drag this button onto the picture box control to location 14,5. Figure 8-6 shows the Music form with the first two control array objects in place.

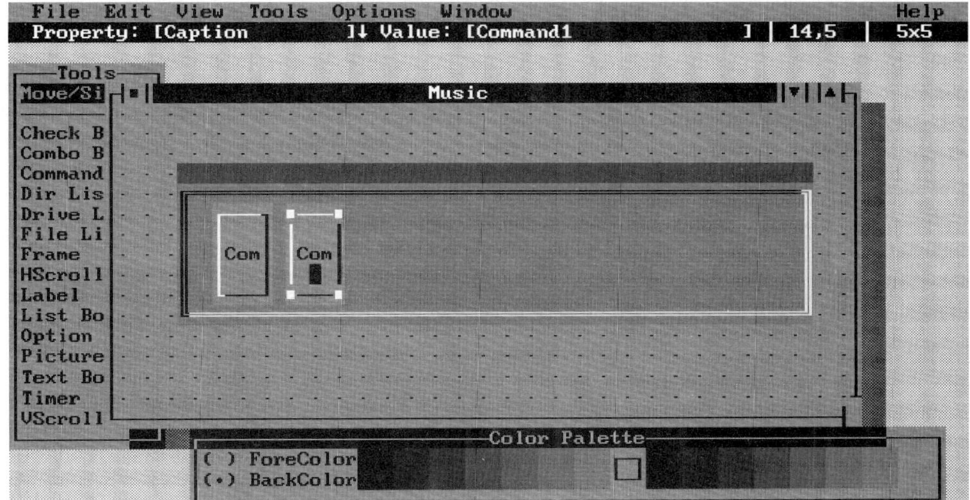

Figure 8-6 Music form with two control array objects.

Use Edit Commands to Create Remaining Control Array Objects

You used the **Copy** and **Paste** commands to create the second **Command1** control. You can use these same commands to create the rest of the **Command1()** control array.

1. Click the first **Command1** object to select that control.

2. Then **Ctrl-click** (hold down the **Ctrl** key and click) the second **Command1** object.

   At this point, you have both of the **Command1** objects selected. Figure 8-7 shows the two objects after you complete the previous two steps.

3. Choose the **Copy** command on the Edit menu. This action will copy both of the selected objects to the Clipboard.

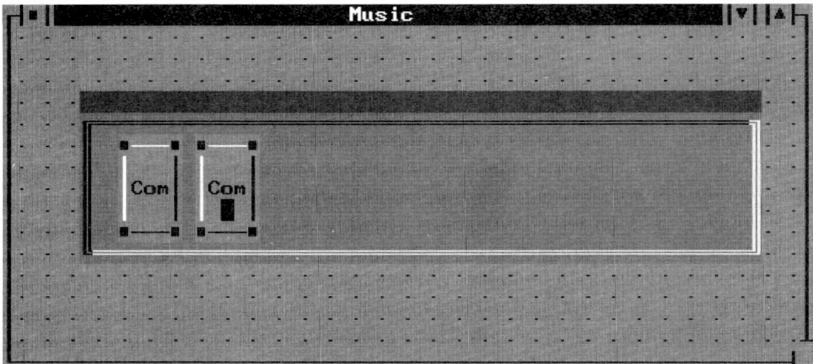

Figure 8-7 Both Command1 objects selected.

4. Choose the **Paste** command on the Edit menu. A copy of the two controls appears in the upper left corner of the form. Figure 8-8 shows the screen after you complete the paste operation.

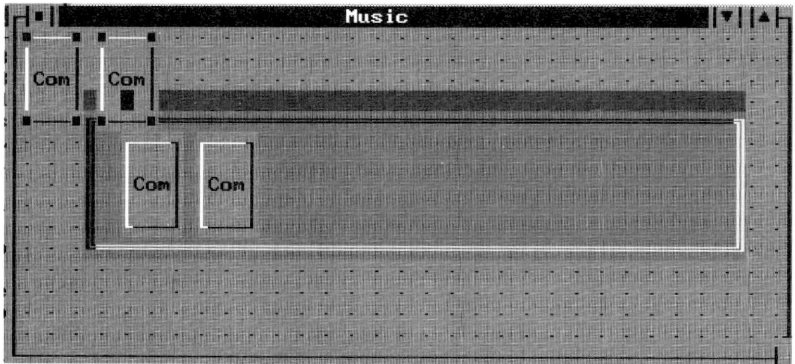

Figure 8-8 Copied objects pasted onto form.

5. The two objects in the upper left corner are both selected. You can click and drag the pair of objects, as a group, onto the keyboard region of the form. Do that: Click and drag the two objects and place them next to the first two control array objects. Figure 8-9 shows the form after you perform this action.

6. Save the project.

Copy and Paste the Last Four Control Array Objects

Using the same copy and paste technique, make a copy of the first four control array objects, paste them onto the form, and move them into position.

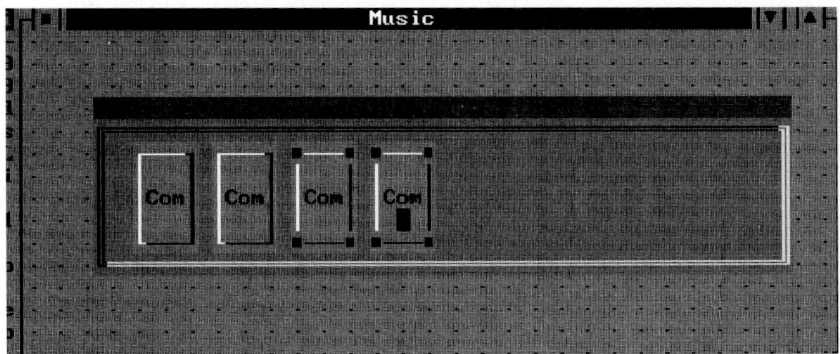

Figure 8-9 Copied objects moved into position.

1. Click the first **Command1** object (the left-most control) to select it.
2. Using **Ctrl-clicks,** add each of the other **Command1** controls to the selection, moving from left to right across the screen.
3. When all four controls are selected, as a group, copy those objects to the Clipboard.
4. Paste the contents of the Clipboard onto the form.
5. Click and drag the pasted controls, as a group, down onto the keyboard region.
6. Save the project.

   Figure 8-10 shows the Music form with the entire control array in place.

Figure 8-10 Music form with control array in place.

7. Adjust the captions and colors of the control array objects according to the specification. The captions from left to right should be `C`, `D`, `E`, `F`, `G`, `A`, `B`, `C`. The colors alternate between white and gray.
8. Save the project after you make these final changes.

Add the Exit Command Button

After you generate the **Command1()** control array, add the **Exit** command button (specification #8-4) to the form. Then save the project and go to the programming environment.

The Code for the Music Application

The Music application has only three short blocks of code:

- A DATA table declaration at the form code level.
- An event procedure that handles a **Click** event for any of the eight control array objects in the **Command1()** control array.
- An event procedure for the **Exit** button (**Command2**).

Form Level Declarations

The code for the DATA table declaration follows. The data are frequency values to be used with the Visual Basic **SOUND** statement. The values correspond to indicated musical notes. Place this code on the MUSIC.FRM code window and then save the project.

```
'Frequency values for notes: C, D, E, F, G, A, B, C
FreqTable:
DATA 262, 294, 330, 349, 392, 440, 494, 523
```

Code for the Control Array Objects

The code for the **Command1** control array event procedure follows. The code you enter appears in bold. Visual Basic creates the `SUB` and `END SUB` lines when you use the **Event Procedures** command on the Edit menu to start the creation of this code module.

```
SUB Command1_Click (Index AS INTEGER)
    'Dimension frequency array
    DIM freq(7)             'frequency array

    'Get frequency values for DATA table
    RESTORE FreqTable       'restore DATA table
    FOR I = 0 TO 7          'begin loop
        READ freq(I)        'read frequency values
    NEXT I                  'end loop

    'Build text string for text box
```

```
        'Position character with spaces
        Text1.Text = SPACE$(5 + Index * 6)
        'Add the character from the caption property
        Text1.Text = Text1.Text 1 Command1(Index).Caption

        'Play the note
        SOUND freq(Index), 9
END SUB
```

This block of code handles a **Click** event on any of the eight elements of the **Command1()** control array. The code dimensions an array, freq(), to hold the frequency values. The procedure then restores the DATA table and reads the frequency values into the freq() array.

The procedure uses the **Text1** text box as a display area. Each time the user clicks a "key" on the keyboard, that array control's caption is moved into the text box. **SPACE$** adds spaces to the text string so that the character in the text box appears above the clicked "key."

The Visual Basic **SOUND** statement causes a sound to play. The sound produced is a function of two values: *frequency* and *duration*. Frequency values are measured in *hertz* (cycles per second) and can be in the range 37 to 32,767. Duration values are measured in clock ticks, with 18.2 clock ticks per second. Duration values can be in the range 0 to 65,535. The frequency values used in this application correspond to one octave of musical notes. The duration is set to 9, or about one-half of a second.

Exit Command Button Code

The **Exit** command button, **Command2**, terminates the application by hiding the form. The code for that event procedure follows (you enter text in bold):

```
SUB Command2_Click ()
      SCREEN.HIDE
      END
END SUB
```

Save the project and run the application. Based on your musical skills, you can play simple melodies with your complete Music application.

Shapes Ahoy!

In this section, you build the colorful graphics Shapes application. Figure 8-11 shows what the Shapes form looks like with its controls and options. The user uses this form to select the type of shape (**Box, Circle, Oval**) and

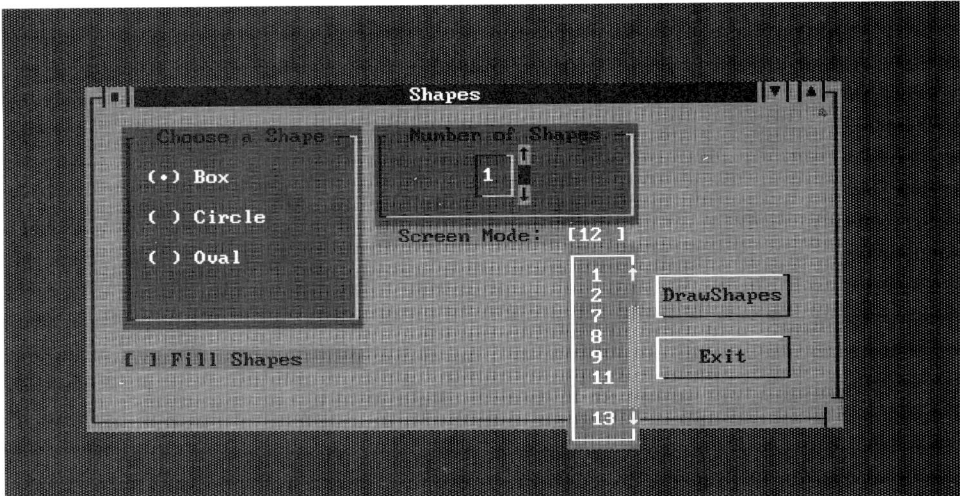

Figure 8-11 The Shapes application.

the number of shapes to be generated. The user can choose to fill the shapes with colors and can select a mode of screen display available on his or her computer.

In Visual Basic for MS-DOS, all of the screens are basically text screens. To display graphics within a Visual Basic application, you have to unload any Visual Basic forms and switch to one of the graphic screen modes. After viewing the graphics, you have to switch the system back to the text screen mode and restore the forms to the screen.

To perform this set of tasks, you would normally use a combination of Visual Basic form-level code plus routines and code in an external code module (.BAS code module).

In this section, you will develop and explore an application that requires you to build both form-level code and an external code module. In the process, you will discover how to handle graphics with Visual Basic for MS-DOS and a few new Visual Basic controls and features.

Shapes Application Specifications

The Shapes application form contains a collection of controls you have used and a few new controls. The form utilizes two frame objects, three option buttons, a check box, a text box, a vertical scroll bar, a label, a combo box, and two command buttons. The option buttons, vertical scroll bar, and combo box are new control objects that you have not seen in previous chapters.

Specification #8-5 (Form)

Shapes Application

Controls	Event(s) to be detected		Response(s)
Shapes	Load		Call video configuration code; initialize scroll bar and text box.
Properties:	Location	7,4	
	Size	63 × 17 (default)	
	Caption	`Shapes`	

Notes/Comments: Form houses controls and reacts to **Load** event.

Shapes Application Control Specifications

The Shapes application has 12 controls on the form. The forms displays two frames. One frame surrounds the three option buttons that let the user choose the type of shape (**Box, Circle, Oval**). The second frame surrounds the text box and vertical scroll bar that selects the number of shapes to be drawn.

A check box sits just below the cluster of **Choose a Shape** option buttons. This check box controls whether or not the drawn shapes are filled with colors. Attached to the bottom of the **Number of Shapes** frame is a label (`Screen Mode:`) and a *combo box* control. A combo box is like a combination text box and list box. The user can click the arrow to reveal a list of items, and make a selection from that list.

The form uses two command buttons: **DrawShapes** and **Exit.** Figure 8-12 shows the Shapes form and identifies the various controls that you will be using.

The following specifications tell you where you place controls, how those controls are customized for this application, and what event procedures are required.

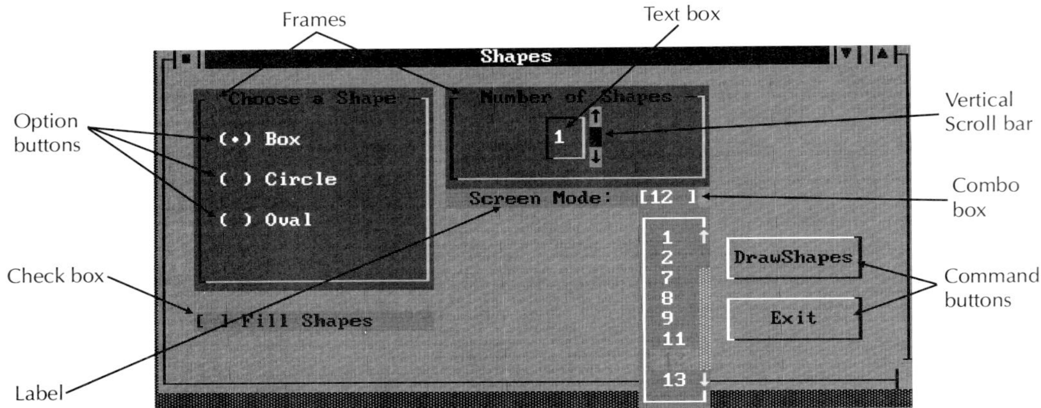

Figure 8-12 Shapes form with controls identified.

Shapes Frame Specifications

Shapes uses two frames to surround and organize two clusters of user controls. When you start to put controls on the form, make sure you position the frame controls first and then add the other control objects that go on top of the frames. This action insures that control objects, such as the option buttons, work as group when the user is making selections (see page 205).

Shapes Option Button Specifications

The three option buttons let the user select the one type of shape to be used on the graphics screen (**Box, Circle, Oval**). When you create and install the option buttons on Frame1, the frame control, the buttons work as group. Only one button out of the three can be selected and made active. Visual Basic automatically handles this task for you, since the buttons are in a group (see page 206).

Notice that the **CtlName** properties of these three buttons have been changed from the default values (**Option1, Option2, Option3**) to explicit names: **optBox, optCircle,** and **optOval.**

Up to this point, you have always used the default **CtlName** values for objects. With smaller, simpler applications, that tactic works fine. With more complex applications, you will want to start using a naming scheme that helps you identify controls easily.

One way to do this is to prefix the control name with a short, three-letter code that represents the control type. The rest of the control

Specification #8-6 (Frames)

Shapes Application

Controls	Event(s) to be detected		Response(s)
Frame1	None		None
Properties:	Location	2,1	
	Size	20 × 10	
	Enabled	False	
	Caption	`Choose a Shape`	
	BackColor	Cyan	
Frame2	None		None
Properties:	Location	23,1	
	Size	22 × 5	
	Enabled	False	
	Caption	`Number of Shapes`	
	BackColor	Cyan	

Notes/Comments: Frame1 used to enclose the three option buttons; Frame2 used to enclose the text box and vertical scroll bar.

name can then be made descriptive and can be related to the application tasks.

Table 8-1 shows a suggested scheme for naming Visual Basic objects (see page 207).

Shapes Check Box Specification

This application uses a single check box. The check box lets the user determine whether or not the drawn images are filled with colors. If the box is on (shows an "x"), the shapes are filled with colors. If the box is set to off (no "x" showing), the shapes are filled with the background color.

This control has the following specification (see page 207).

Specification #8-7 (Option Buttons)

Shapes Application

Controls	Event(s) to be detected		Response(s)
optBox	None		None
Properties:	Location	4,2	
	Size	16 × 3	
	Caption	`Box`	
	CtlName	optBox	
	BackColor	Cyan	
optCircle	None		None
Properties:	Location	4,4	
	Size	16 × 3	
	Caption	`Circle`	
	CtlName	optCircle	
	BackColor	Cyan	
optOval	None		None
Properties:	Location	4,6	
	Size	16 × 3	
	Caption	`Oval`	
	CtlName	optOval	
	BackColor	Cyan	

Notes/Comments: Buttons grouped together on Frame1.

Shapes Text Box and Scroll Bar Specification

This application has a text box and a vertical scroll bar positioned on top of Frame2. These two objects work together to let the user select the number of shapes to be drawn. Actions on the scroll bar updates the value in the text

Table 8-1

Control Object	Prefix	Example
Form	frm	frmShapes
Check box	chk	chkFillShape
Combo box	cbo	cboScrnMode
Command button	cmd	cmdExit
Directory list box	dir	dirListBox
Drive list box	drv	drvListBox
File list box	fil	filListBox
Frame	fra	fraShapes
Horizontal scroll bar	hsb	hsbNumShapes
Label	lbl	lblScreenMode
List box	lst	lstShapes
Menu	mnu	mnuEditShapes
Option button	opt	optCircle
Picture box	pic	picKeyboard
Text box	txt	txtNumShapes
Timer	tmr	tmrHelp
Vertical scroll bar	vsb	vsbNumShapes

Specification #8-8 (Check Box)

Shapes Application

Controls	Event(s) to be detected	Response(s)
chkFillShape	None	None

Properties:

Location	2,12
Size	20×1
Caption	`Fill Shapes`
CtlName	chkFillShape
BackColor	Yellow

Notes/Comments: Set to On means fill the shapes with colors.

box. The value in the text box (and other settings on this form) are used by the routine that draws the shapes.

These controls have the following specifications.

Specification #8-9 (Text Box and Scroll Bar)

Shapes Application

Controls	Event(s) to be detected		Response(s)
txtNumShapes	KeyDown		Updates scroll bar value
Properties:	Location	31,2	
	Size	4 × 3	
	BorderStyle	Single line	
	CtlName	txtNumShapes	
	BackColor	Cyan	
vsbNumShapes	Change		Updates text box value
Properties:	Location	35,2	
	Size	1 × 3	
	CtlName	vsbNumShapes	

Notes/Comments: These two objects work together; actions on scroll bar updates text box contents. Text box updates scroll bar values.

Shapes Label and Combo Box Specification

Shapes uses a combo box control to record the current screen mode and to let the user select other screen modes. The combo box is part text box (section at top that displays the current setting) and part list box (user can display list by clicking the arrow on the right end of the combo box).

A label object sits to the right of the combo box to tell the user what the combo box controls. The specifications for these two objects follows.

Specification #8-10 (Combo Box and Label)

Shapes Application

Controls	Event(s) to be detected		Response(s)
cboScrnMode	None		None
Properties:	Location	39,6	
	Size	6 × 1	
	Text	None	
	CtlName	cboScrnMode	
	BackColor	Yellow	
lblScrnMode	None		None
Properties:	Location	23,6	
	Size	16 × 1	
	CtlName	lblScrnMode	
	BorderStyle	None	
	BackColor	Yellow	
	Alignment	Center	
	Caption	`Screen Mode:`	

Notes/Comments: These two objects look like a single unit on the screen. The combo box automatically responds to user actions. The combo box setting is used by the configuration subroutine in the external module.

Shapes Command Button Specifications

Shapes has two command buttons: **DrawShapes** and **Exit.** Both buttons respond to **Click** events. When clicked, **DrawShapes** unloads the Shapes form and calls the external routine that draws the shapes. This button's event procedure also restores the form to the screen when the user exits the graphics screen.

Exit unloads the form when the user indicates that he or she wants to exit the application. Here are the specifications for these two controls.

Specification #8-11 (Command Buttons)

Shapes Application

Controls	Event(s) to be detected		Response(s)
cmdDrawShape	Click		Unloads form; calls graphics routine; restores display upon return.
Properties:	Location	46,8	
	Size	12 × 3	
	CtlName	cmdDrawShape	
	Caption	`DrawShapes`	
cmdExit	Click		Unloads form; exits to system.
Properties:	Location	46,11	
	Size	12 × 3	
	CtlName	cmdExit	
	Caption	`Exit`	

Notes/Comments: None

Build the Shapes Form and Controls

Using the specifications (#8-5 through #8-11), create the Shapes form and its associated controls. Follow these steps to design and develop the form and controls:

1. Start with a new project.
2. Create a new form called Shapes.

3. Customize Shapes based on the #8-5 specifications. Save the project and save again after each of the following steps.
4. Add the frame controls to the form (specifications #8-6).
5. Add the option button controls (specifications #8-7—**optBox, optCircle, optOval**).
6. Add the check box control (specifications #8-8—**chkFillShape**).
7. Add the text box control and vertical scroll bar (specifications #8-9—**txtNumShapes, vsbNumShapes**).
8. Add the combo box and label controls (specifications #8-10—**cboScrnMode, lblScrnMode**).
9. Add the command buttons (specifications #8-11—**cmdDrawShape, cmdExit**).
10. Save the project and switch to the programming environment.

Develop the Code for the Shapes Form and Controls

The Shapes application utilizes six short blocks of form-level code:

- Declarations that go on the form code window `SHAPES.FRM`.
- An event procedure for the **Load** event.
- Two event procedures that work together to let the user scroll through and set the number of shapes to be drawn.
- Two event procedures for the two command buttons on the form.

In addition, the application uses an external (.BAS) code module with two subroutines: **VidConfig** and **DrawShapes.**

Code Declarations for the Shapes Form

The declaration statements for the form-level application code follows. There are two **DECLARE SUB** statements that reference the two external subroutines called from this form's event procedures. The remaining statements set up six constants used in the event procedure code. Put this code on the `SHAPES.FRM` code window.

```
DECLARE SUB DrawShapes ()
DECLARE SUB VidConfig ()

'Logical constants
CONST TRUE = -1
CONST FALSE = 0

'Constants for key up/down
CONST KEY_UP = 12
CONST KEY_DOWN = 13

'Constants for NumShapes scroll bar
CONST SCROLL_MIN = 1
CONST SCROLL_MAX = 15
```

Code for the Control Array Objects

The code for the **Load** event procedure follows. The code you enter appears in bold. Visual Basic creates the SUB and END SUB lines when you use the **Event Procedures** command on the Edit menu to define this code module.

```
SUB Form_Load ()
     'Set screen mode options
     VidConfig

     'Set NumShapes scroll bar limits
     vsbNumShapes.Min = SCROLL_MIN
     vsbNumShapes.Max = SCROLL_MAX

     'Initialize NumShapes text box
     txtNumShapes.Text = FORMAT$(SCROLL_MIN)
END SUB
```

This procedure calls the external **VidConfig** subroutine, which determines the screen modes available on the computer system. **VidConfig** installs the number codes for the available screen modes into the Shapes form combo box (**cboScrnMode**). The assignment statements establish the limits of the scroll bar control (**vsbNumShapes**) and the initial value of the text box object (**txtNumShapes**).

Note: The bulk of the **VidConfig** code and part of the structure of the **Shapes** event procedures were modeled after a sample Visual Basic project: TORUS.MAK. To learn more about screen modes and using graphics with

Visual Basic for MS-DOS, look at the TORUS.MAK project that comes with Visual Basic.

Text Box and Scroll Bar Code

The code for the text box control (**txtNumShapes**) and the vertical scroll bar (**vsbNumShapes**) work together in the following way:

- **txtNumShapes** detects the user's actions on the scroll bar (clicking the **up** and **down arrow** keys), and updates the scroll bar's **Value** property.
- **txtNumShapes** update of the scroll bar's **Value** property triggers a **Change** event for that object (**vsbNumShapes**). The scroll bar's event procedure, triggered by the **Change** event, updates the text box's **Text** property. The **Text** property value represents the number of shapes to be drawn.

The code for these two event procedures follows (you enter text in bold). The first code block is the **KeyDown** event procedure for **txtNumShapes.**

```
'Keydown event procedure for textbox.
'Traps up arrow and down arrow keys to increase or
'decrease current value.
SUB txtNumShapes_KeyDown (KeyCode AS INTEGER, Shift
 AS INTEGER)

    'error means value is out of range of scrollbar,
    'so do nothing
    ON LOCAL ERROR GOTO NoChange

    SELECT CASE KeyCode
    'Key Up
    CASE KEY_UP:
        vsbNumShapes.value = vsbNumShapes.value + 1
    'Key Down
    CASE KEY_DOWN:
        vsbNumShapes.value = vsbNumShapes.value - 1
    END SELECT

NoChange:
    EXIT SUB
END SUB
```

The following code is the **Change** event procedure for **vsbNumShapes,** the vertical scroll bar object:

```
'Change event procedure for scrollbar
SUB vsbNumShapes_Change ()

      'Sets textbox value to current scrollbar value.
      txtNumShapes.Text = FORMAT$(vsbNumShapes.value)

END SUB
```

DrawShapes Command Button Code

The **DrawShapes** command button, **cmdDrawShape,** responds to a **Click** event by hiding the form, calling the external routine DrawShapes, and waiting for the user to press a key to resume. This event procedure uses the **SLEEP** command to pause the system until the user presses a key. When a key press is detected, the procedure restores the Visual Basic normal screen mode (**SCREEN 0 — text screen**), the 80-character screen width (**WIDTH 80**), and shows the hidden form (**SCREEN.SHOW**). The code for this event procedure follows (you enter text in bold):

```
SUB cmdDrawShape_Click ()

      SCREEN.HIDE             'Hide the current form
      DrawShapes              'Call shape draw routine
      SLEEP                   'Wait for key press
      SCREEN 0                'Reset screen mode and width
      WIDTH 80
      SCREEN.SHOW             'Restore form

END SUB
```

Exit Command Button Code

The **Exit** command button, **cmdExit,** terminates the application by hiding the form. The code for that event procedure follows (you enter text in bold):

```
SUB cmdExit_Click ()

      'Unload form and exit program
      UNLOAD shapes

END SUB
```

Save the project. Now you will build an external code module (`SHAPEDRW.BAS`) that contains the code for the external subroutines **VidConfig** and **DrawShapes.**

Develop Code for External Module

To build the code for the external module, follow these steps:

1. Make sure you have saved the Shapes project files (`SHAPES.FRM` and `SHAPES.MAK`) by using the **Save Project** command on the File menu.
2. Choose the **New Project** command to clear all of the code windows and form descriptions. You will see an `UNTITLED.FRM` Code window.
3. Enter the declaration statements for the external module onto the `UNTITLED.FRM` Code window.
4. Choose the **New Sub** command on the Edit menu, and enter the code for the **VidConfig** subroutine.
5. Save this module as `SHAPEDRW.BAS` by choosing the **Save File As** command on the File menu.
6. Choose the **New Sub** command on the Edit menu, and enter the code for the **DrawShapes** subroutine.
7. Save the code for `SHAPEDRW.BAS` with the **Save File** command on the File menu.

When you have performed these steps and entered the code for the external module, you will then merge the form-level code with this module to create the Shapes application. To start, follow the steps and enter the code for each part of the external module.

Declaration Statements for the External Module

Enter the following declaration statements onto the `UNTITLED.FRM` Code window. The **$FORM** declaration lets the code in this module reference objects on the Shapes form. If you do not enter this line of code, Visual Basic will insert it when you attempt to run the application.

The screen mode constants will be used by the **VidConfig** subroutine. This routine determines the available screen modes for the computer system being used. The shape type constants will be used by the **DrawShapes** subroutine as it determines which shapes to draw. This same routine also uses the draw region constants to control where the limits of where shapes are drawn (**xMax, yMax**), size limits (**rMax**), and the orientation of oval shapes (**oMax**).

```
'$FORM Shapes
'Logical constants
CONST TRUE = -1
CONST FALSE = 0

'Constants for best available screen mode
CONST VGA = 12
CONST MCGA = 13
CONST EGA256 = 9
CONST EGA64 = 8
CONST MONO = 10
CONST HERC = 3
CONST CGA = 1

'Constants for shape type
CONST BX = 0
CONST CIRC = 1
CONST OVL = 2

'Constants for draw region limits
CONST xMax = 640
CONST yMax = 480
CONST rMax = 100
CONST oMax = 5
```

VidConfig Subroutine Code

After you enter the declarations, choose the **New Sub** command on the Edit menu. You will see a dialog box that asks you to name the subroutine you are about to create. Enter the following name:

Type `VidConfig` and click the **Edit in Active** button.

As mentioned earlier, most of the following code and the structure of this code was modeled after the TORUS.MAK project code that comes with Visual Basic. You are encouraged to look at that project's code for more information about setting up screen modes and putting graphics on the screen.

For example, the Shapes application (**VidConfig**) code does not fully link the information about available screen modes and keeping the drawn objects on the visible screen area. For some screen modes, Shapes will draw objects off the edges of the screen. The complete code in TORUS.MAK addresses this issue and always keeps the torus image within the available screen limits.

Enter the lines of code shown in bold to create the **VidConfig** subroutine. **VidConfig** determines which screen modes are available on the current computer system and installs the codes for those modes in the **Shapes** combo box (**cboScrnMode**). In effect, this block of code customizes the application to match the hardware upon which the application is being used.

```
DEFINT A-Z
' ============================ VidConfig =============
'   Determine best video mode for this system.
' ====================================================
'
SUB VidConfig ()

   'Assume best possible screen mode
   BestMode = VGA
   Available$ = "12789BCD"

   ON LOCAL ERROR GOTO VideoErr
   'Fall through error trap until a mode works
   SCREEN BestMode
   'If EGA, then check pages to see whether more than 64K
   ON LOCAL ERROR GOTO EGAErr
   IF BestMode = EGA256 THEN SCREEN 8, , 1

   ON ERROR GOTO 0

   'Reset text mode
   SCREEN 0, , 0
   WIDTH 80, 25

   FOR tmp% = 1 TO LEN(Available$)
        scrnVal = VAL("&H" + MID$(Available$, tmp%, 1))
        Shapes.cboScrnMode.ADDITEM FORMAT$(scrnVal)
        IF scrnVal = BestMode THEN
           Shapes.cboScrnMode.ListIndex = tmp% - 1
        END IF
   NEXT

   EXIT SUB
```

```
'Error trap to make screen independent
VideoErr:
   SELECT CASE BestMode 'Fall thru until something works
      CASE VGA
         BestMode = MCGA
         Available$ = "12BD"
      CASE MCGA
         BestMode = EGA256
         Available$ = "12789"
      CASE EGA256
         BestMode = CGA
         Available$ = "12"
      CASE CGA
         BestMode = MONO
         Available$ = "A"
      CASE MONO
         BestMode = HERC
         Available$ = "3"
      CASE ELSE
         PRINT "Graphics support not available. Cannot
run Shapes program."
         END
   END SELECT
   RESUME

'Trap to detect 64K EGA
EGAErr:
   BestMode = EGA64
   Available$ = "12789"
   RESUME NEXT
END SUB
```

The string variable **Available$** starts off with a string of characters that represent the most common screen modes: 1, 2, 7, 8, 9, 11(B), 12(C), and 13(D) for a system with VGA graphics capabilities. The code attempts to set the system to the best screen mode for VGA capabilities (screen mode 12). If a failure occurs, the error code labeled **VideoErr** is used to seek out the correct system graphics options.

Once a system graphics option has been identified, the FOR-NEXT loop in the middle of the subroutine installs the screen mode options into the combo box (**cboScrnMode**) on the Shapes form. The **ADDITEM** method is used to perform this task.

Save the Module Code

At this point, choose the **Save File As** command on the File menu, and save your work onto the file `SHAPEDRW.BAS`. After you enter the next subroutine, **DrawShapes,** you will merge this code module with the form code to create the Shapes application.

DrawShapes Subroutine Code

DrawShapes is called by Shapes when the user is ready to draw images on the screen. This subroutine looks at the various settings on the Shapes form to determine what types of shapes to draw, whether the shapes are to be filled with colors, and how many shapes to create.

The first action by the routine is to set the screen mode based on the combo box setting. Then the code gets the number of shapes to be drawn and the setting of the check box (**chkFillShape**).

The code then looks at the option buttons and sets a variable, **typeShape,** based on the option button settings. After that, a FOR-NEXT loop controls the shape drawing activities. Within the loop, shapes are assigned random screen locations and random colors if they are to be filled, and then are drawn on the screen. In the SELECT CASE code block, each CASE module draws either an unfilled or a filled shape. After all the shapes are drawn, the code places a message on the screen telling the user to press a key to return to the main screen.

Choose the **New Sub** command on the Edit menu, enter the name of this subroutine (**DrawShapes**), and then enter the lines of code shown in bold.

```
SUB DrawShapes ()
'Set screen display mode
scrnVal = VAL(Shapes.cboScrnMode.Text)
SCREEN scrnVal

'Get number of shapes, fill setting
numShapes = VAL(Shapes.txtNumShapes.Text)
fillVar = Shapes.chkFillShape.value

'Determine type of shapes to draw
typeShape = BX
IF Shapes.optCircle.value = TRUE THEN typeShape = CIRC
IF Shapes.optOval.value = TRUE THEN typeShape = OVL

'Draw the shapes
FOR I = 1 TO numShapes       'begin draw loop
    shapeCol = RND * 15      'random color
    xPos = RND * xMax        'random x-value
    yPos = RND * yMax        'random y-value

    SELECT CASE typeShape    'create shapes
```

```
      CASE BX                   'boxes
        IF fillVar = FALSE THEN
         LINE (xPos, xPos)-(yPos, yPos), B
        ELSE
         LINE (xPos, xPos)-(yPos, yPos), shapeCol, BF
        END IF
      CASE CIRC                 'circles
        IF fillVar = FALSE THEN
         CIRCLE (xPos, yPos), RND * rMax
        ELSE
         CIRCLE (xPos, yPos), RND * rMax, shapeCol
         PAINT (xPos, yPos), shapeCol
        END IF
      CASE OVL
        IF fillVar = FALSE THEN
         CIRCLE (xPos, yPos), RND * rMax,, RND * oMax
        ELSE
         CIRCLE (xPos, yPos), RND * rMax, shapeCol,, RND * oMax
         PAINT (xPos, yPos), shapeCol
        END IF
    END SELECT
NEXT I

'Print message about key press
LOCATE 25, 3
PRINT "Press any key to restore main screen."
END SUB
```

After you enter the code for the **DrawShapes** subroutine, save the SHAPEDRW.BAS module. Save this code on the disk or in the directory you have been using for your Visual Basic project files.

Create the Complete Shapes Application

Now that you have developed the code for both the Shapes form (SHAPES.FRM) and the external module (SHAPEDRW.BAS), you are ready to merge these two blocks of code. To merge the code blocks and create the complete Shapes applications, do the following:

1. Make sure you have saved the SHAPEDRW.BAS module.

2. Choose **New Project** on the File menu to clear all of the code windows.

3. Choose **Open Project** on the File menu and open the Shapes project (`SHAPES.MAK`). This action should bring the `SHAPES.FRM` and its associated code into the programming environment.
4. Now choose the **Add File** command on the file menu and add `SHAPEDRW.BAS` to the project.
5. Save the project (`SHAPES.MAK`).

You are now ready to run and test the Shapes application.

Run Shapes

If all of your form objects and code modules are in place, you can run the application. If there are no immediate problems with the code, you will see the application's form as shown in Figure 8-13.

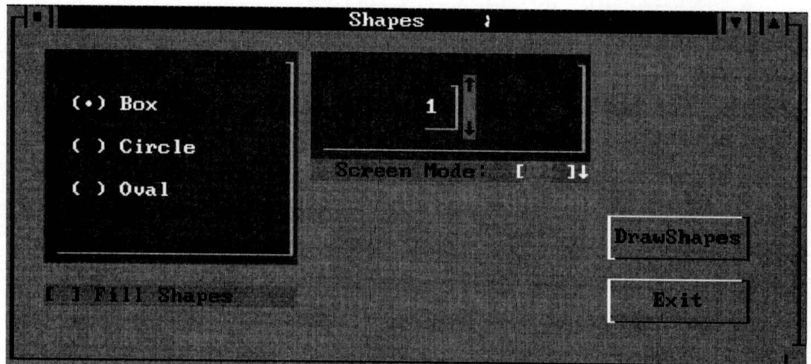

Figure 8-13 Shapes application form.

Try clicking the various controls and verify that they work. Click the **Circle** option button. The **Box** button should turn **Off,** and the **Circle** button should turn **On.** Click the **Oval** button. **Circle** should turn **Off,** and **Oval** should turn **On.** Since these option buttons are grouped on a frame control, Visual Basic treats then as a unit and does not allow more than one button to be activated. You wrote no code to handle this task. Visual Basic performs this task automatically.

Click the check box (**Fill Shapes**). Does it turn on and off? Here again, Visual Basic handles the detection of a user **Click** event, and updates the check box on/off indicator.

Try clicking the **up** and **down arrows** on the scroll bar. Does the text box for the number of shapes change as you click the scroll bar?

Click the arrow next to the combo box (**Screen Mode**). Does the list of screen mode codes appear? On the example screen, screen mode 12 has been set by the **VidConfig** subroutine during the **Load** event.

The final test involves clicking the **DrawShapes** button and looking at the drawn shapes on the graphics screen.

The following series of figures shows various screen displays of the Shapes form and the graphics screens with shape images. For the examples, the number of shapes was set to 7. Figure 8-14 shows the Shapes form with the number of shapes set to 7 and **DrawShapes** about to be clicked.

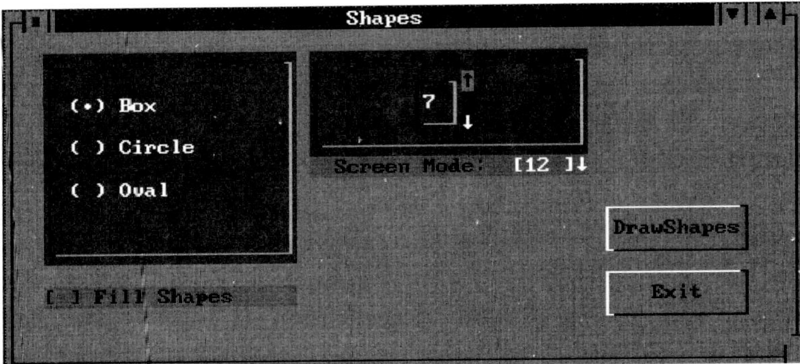

Figure 8-14 Shapes form to produce 7 box shapes.

Figure 8-15 shows the screen display with the unfilled box shapes. Your screen will look different based on the screen mode you are using and because of the random placement and size of the boxes.

When you finish viewing the graphics screen, press a key (**Enter**) to return to the main screen. When the Shapes form appears, click the **Circle** option button and the **Fill Shape** check box. Figure 8-16 shows the Shapes form with these settings.

When you click the **DrawShapes** button on the Shapes form, the program produces a screen display that looks something like the one in Figure 8-17.

If your computer has color, your screen will show a cluster of bright, colorful circle shapes.

Keep experimenting with the Shapes application. Try the **Oval** option. Try displaying more shapes. Look at both filled and unfilled shape dis-

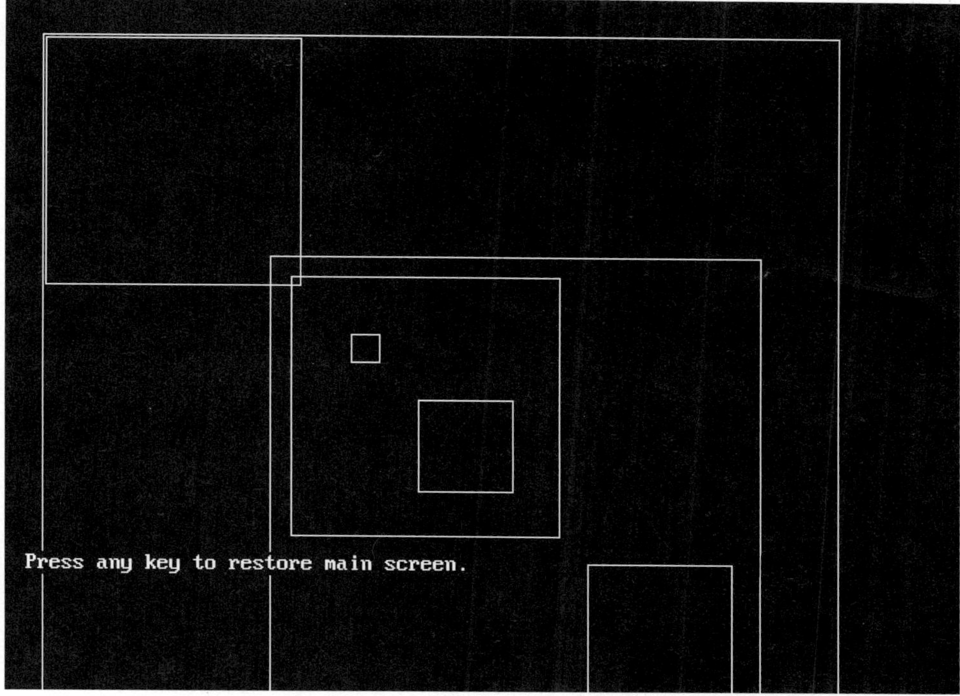

Figure 8-15 Unfilled box shapes displayed.

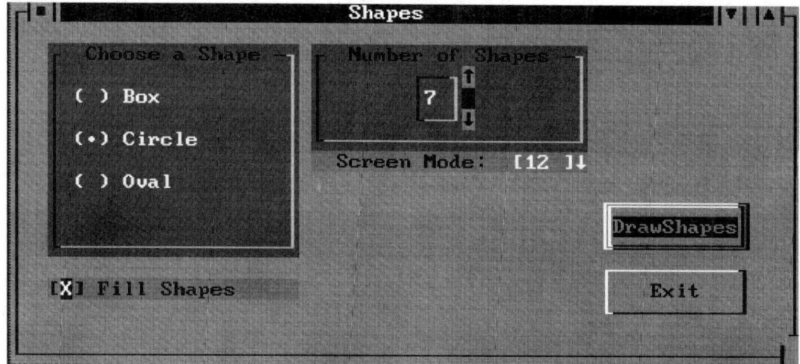

Figure 8-16 Shapes form to produce 7 filled circles.

Figure 8-17 Filled circle shapes displayed.

plays. Try different screen modes by picking another screen mode on the combo box control.

Summary

In this chapter, you built two Visual Basic applications: Music and Shapes. Music simulates a simple electronic keyboard and lets a user play an octave of musical notes. Shapes utilizes the Visual Basic graphics features to draw a variety of colorful shapes (boxes, circles, and ovals) on the screen.

In building Music, you used a command button control array and the Visual Basic **SOUND** statement. To create the Shapes application, you used several new controls and Visual Basic features (option buttons, scroll bars, and combo boxes), and you built an external code module that contained two external subroutines. In building Shapes, you learned several new techniques for controlling objects on the screen and transferring property values between different blocks of code.

When you complete the Music and Shapes applications, move on to Chapter 9, "Files." In this chapter, you will explore the Visual Basic file features and objects that let you build file handling controls on a form.

9 Using Data Files

Visual Basic has a set of statements and functions that help you:

- Write information from an application onto a disk
- Print information onto a printer
- Read information stored on a disk into an application.

In this chapter, you will learn how to call upon and use a data file from within a Visual Basic application. *Data files* are blocks of information stored at physical locations on your disks. You will examine two different ways of

Concepts and Terminology

QBasic/QuickBasic Keywords

External Modules

New Visual Basic Keywords

Visual Basic Event Procedures

retrieving the information stored in a data file, and then go on to look at Visual Basic file controls that you can put on a form.

You will examine the Visual Basic Common Dialog Toolkit. The toolkit contains a form, controls, and code for seven of the most common types of dialog boxes. Included in the toolkit are examples of dialog boxes that handle file operations.

Visual Basic File Types

The type of data that Visual Basic statements and functions can store and retrieve includes any information that an application uses or generates. For the data files that you create, you can name the files and tell Visual Basic which one of its three types of files you want to use.

Visual Basic supports three file types: sequential, random, and binary. *Sequential files* are generally used for storing and retrieving plain text information where the number of data items may vary or the size of the data items varies in length. In a sequential file, each byte of data corresponds to a character of text that can be displayed or printed.

Random files are used to store data where each data item or collection of data items (called a *record*) is of uniform length. In a file with records of uniform length, any record can be retrieved or written into directly, since the location of each record can be calculated and new information cannot be longer than the data it replaces.

Binary files store information as a sequence of individual bytes. The information stored in a binary file might be, for example, text data, the actual runtime code for a program, or the information used to create a graphic image.

Visual Basic's input/output statements and functions are just like those used in QBasic and QuickBasic. If you have used these type of statements and functions before, you will have no problems using them in Visual Basic. If this is your first experience with data files, the following examples show you how easy it is to use these Visual Basic features with a forms-based application. For more details regarding the use of files with Visual Basic, you are referred to Chapter 12 of the *Visual Basic Programmer's Guide*, "Interacting with Files and Devices."

Including a Data File in an Application

Back in Chapter 6, "Building a Multiform Application," you encountered a rather large DATA table. The data in the table were needed to supply the labels and display information for the 109 elements in the Periodic application.

In the Periodic application, the data were placed in **DATA** statements in the code declarations at the form-level. The first few lines of data table code in that application appeared as follows:

```
'Data for the periodic table
'Number of elements
DATA 109
'Left, Top, Color, Symbol, Element
DATA 3,1,8, "H  ",Hydrogen
DATA 71,2,8, "He ",Helium
DATA 3,4,9, "Li ",Lithium
DATA 7,4,9, "Be ",Beryllium
DATA 51,4,9, "B  ",Boron
DATA 55,4,9, "C  ",Carbon
DATA 59,4,9, "N  ",Nitrogen
DATA 63,4,9, "O  ",Oxygen
•
•
• (rest of DATA table for 109 elements)
```

Creating the Include Data File

Visual Basic has a command that will let you put the entire block of **DATA** statements for this application into a text file, and include that file when you run the program. To use this command, do the following:

1. Start Visual Basic and open the Periodic project.
2. Locate the lines of code for the DATA table on the PERIODIC.FRM Code window.
3. Copy the entire block of code to the Clipboard (**Copy** command on the Edit menu). Include comment lines as well as the **DATA** statements. *Do not* include the **$FORM** metacommand line (`'$FORM DataForm`) and the **DEFINT** and **CONST** declarations.
4. Choose **New Project** on the File menu.
5. Paste the contents of the Clipboard onto the `UNTITLED.FRM` Code window.
6. Choose the **Save Text** command on the File menu.
7. When the **Save Text** dialog box appears:

   Type `A:PERIODIC.TXT` and press **Enter.**

You now have a sequential type data file, called `PERIODIC.TXT`, stored on the diskette in drive A.

Using the $INCLUDE Metacommand

After you create and save the `PERIODIC.TXT` data file, do the following:

1. Choose **New Project** on the File menu. You will see a dialog box asking if you want to save the current project (`UNTITLED.FRM` with pasted set **DATA** statements).
2. Click the **No** button. Visual Basic will clear the code window.
3. Choose **Open Project** on the File menu and open the Periodic project.
4. Locate the window of declaration and **DATA** statements for the 109 elements (`PERIODIC.FRM`).
5. Select the statements for the DATA table (including comment lines), and delete those statements (**Delete** command on the Edit menu). Do not delete the **$FORM** metacommand (`'$FORM DataForm`) or the **DEFINT** and **CONST** declarations.
6. Replace the deleted **DATA** statements with the following **$INCLUDE** metacommand (shown in bold):

```
'$FORM DataForm
'Declarations
DEFINT A-Z
CONST TRUE = -1
CONST FALSE = 0

'$INCLUDE: 'PERIODIC.TXT'
```

7. Run the application.

You should see the Periodic application's table of elements, as shown in Figure 9-1.

When you run the application, Visual Basic's **$INCLUDE** metacommand automatically opens the `PERIODIC.TXT` data file, retrieves the stored lines of code (comments and **DATA** statements), and includes those lines of code as part of the application. **$INCLUDE** helps you manage large blocks of code (like the large DATA table). You can create and store code in separate, external files and, at run-time, retrieve the code with **$INCLUDE** metacommand statements.

```
                         Periodic Table
1
H                                                               2
                                                                He
3   4                                       5   6   7   8   9   10
Li  Be                                      B   C   N   O   F   Ne
11  12                                      13  14  15  16  17  18
Na  Mg                                      Al  Si  P   S   Cl  Ar
19  20  21  22  23  24  25  26  27  28  29  30  31  32  33  34  35  36
K   Ca  Sc  Ti  V   Cr  Mn  Fe  Co  Ni  Cu  Zn  Ga  Ge  As  Se  Br  Kr
37  38  39  40  41  42  43  44  45  46  47  48  49  50  51  52  53  54
Rb  Sr  Y   Zr  Nb  Mo  Tc  Ru  Rh  Pd  Ag  Cd  In  Sn  Sb  Te  I   Xe
55  56      72  73  74  75  76  77  78  79  80  81  82  83  84  85  86
Cs  Ba  Lan Hf  Ta  W   Re  Os  Ir  Pt  Au  Hg  Tl  Pb  Bi  Po  At  Rn
87  88      104 105 106 107 108 109
Fr  Ra  Act Unq Unp Unh Uns Uno Une

        57  58  59  60  61  62  63  64  65  66  67  68  69  70  71
        La  Ce  Pr  Nd  Pm  Sm  Eu  Gd  Tb  Dy  Ho  Er  Tm  Yb  Lu
        89  90  91  92  93  94  95  96  97  98  99  100 101 102 103
        Ac  Th  Pa  U   Np  Pu  Am  Cm  Bk  Cf  Es  Fm  Md  No  Lr
```

Figure 9-1 Periodic application display.

Viewing the Included Lines

You can view the lines of included code. The **Included Lines** command on the View menu displays any included lines that are retrieved by the **$INCLUDE** metacommand. Figure 9-2 shows the PERIODIC.FRM Code window where the **Included Lines** command has been toggled to **On.**

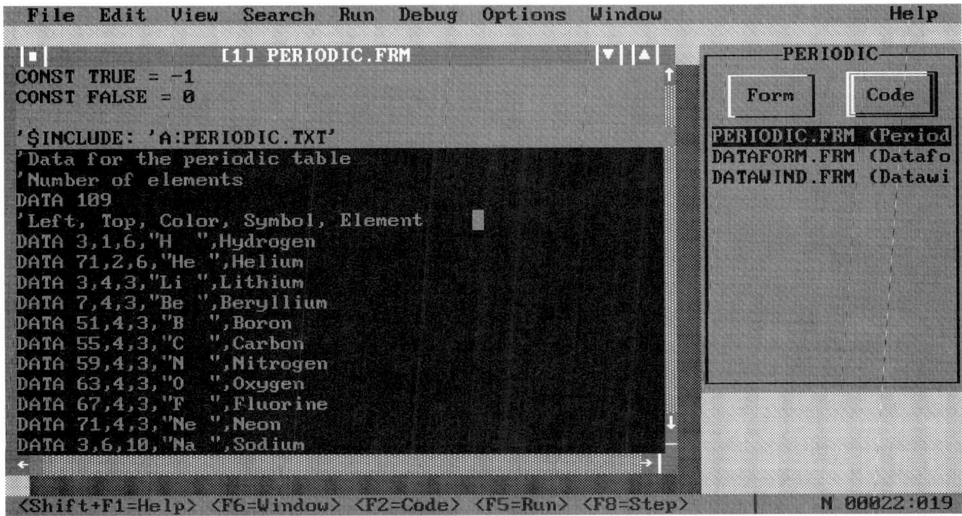

Figure 9-2 Showing included lines.

To hide included lines, choose the **Included Lines** command again. When you toggle that command to **Off,** the included lines disappear from the display.

Saving the Changes

If you wish to save this version of the application, choose the **Save** command on the File menu. The changes you have made to `PERIODIC.FRM` will be recorded, and the application will now use the **$INCLUDE** metacommand and the sequential data file `PERIODIC.TXT`.

If you do not want to save your changes, exit Visual Basic and click the **No** button when you are asked about saving changes.

Using INPUT to Read a Data File

Visual Basic has a set of keywords that give you control over the reading and writing of disk files. In the following example, you will modify the Periodic application so that it inputs data from a file on disk.

Set Up the Data File

To use the Visual Basic **INPUT** statement, you will need to adjust the Periodic application's file of data (`PERIODIC.TXT`). The following steps help you set up the Periodic data file so that it can be read with **INPUT** statements:

1. Start a new Visual Basic project. (Choose **New Project** on the File menu.)

2. Choose the **Add File** command on the File menu, and add the `PERIODIC.TXT` file. You will see the list of comments and **DATA** statements that you created and saved as `PERIODIC.TXT`.

```
'Data for the periodic table
'Number of elements
DATA 109
'Left, Top, Color, Symbol, Element
DATA 3,1,8, "H  ",Hydrogen
DATA 71,2,8, "He ",Helium
DATA 3,4,9, "Li ",Lithium
DATA 7,4,9, "Be ",Beryllium
DATA 51,4,9, "B  ",Boron
```

```
DATA 55,4,9, "C  ",Carbon
DATA 59,4,9, "N  ",Nitrogen
DATA 63,4,9, "O  ",Oxygen
•
•
• (rest of DATA table for 109 elements)
```

3. Delete the three comment lines.

4. Choose the **Change** command on the search menu. When the **Change** dialog box appears, enter the word DATA and a space character into the **Find What** text box:

   Type DATA_ (_ represents a space character that you must type).

5. Leave the **Change To** text box empty, and click the **Change All** button. The data file will be changed, and you will see a **Change Complete** dialog box. Click **OK** to dismiss the dialog box and accept the changes. The first few lines of the data file will now look like the following listing:

```
109
3,1,8, "H  ",Hydrogen
71,2,8, "He ",Helium
3,4,9, "Li ",Lithium
7,4,9, "Be ",Beryllium
51,4,9, "B  ",Boron
55,4,9, "C  ",Carbon
59,4,9, "N  ",Nitrogen
63,4,9, "O  ",Oxygen
•
•
• (rest of DATA table for 109 elements)
```

6. Choose the **Save Text** command on the File menu, and save the data in the following file:

```
A:PERIDATA.TXT
```

7. Choose the **New Project** command. A dialog box will appear asking if you want to save the changes to the project. Click the **No** button.

You now have two data files saved on the diskette: PERIODIC.TXT and PERIDATA.TXT. PERIODIC.TXT is a set of comments and **DATA** statements that can be brought into the application with the **$INCLUDE** metacommand.

`PERIDATA.TXT` is a data file that contains only the raw data. You will add code to the application that tells the program to read the data from this file using **INPUT** statements.

Modifying the Periodic Application to Use INPUT

To change Periodic to use **INPUT** statements, you only have to make a few minor adjustments to Periodic's existing code. The following steps tell you what you need to do to modify Periodic to use **INPUT** statements:

1. Open the Periodic project within Visual Basic.
2. Delete the **$INCLUDE** metacommand (or the set of comments and **DATA** statements) from the `PERIODIC.FRM` code window. Leave the **$FORM** metacommand and declaration statements as the only lines of code on this window:

```
'$FORM DataForm
'Declarations
DEFINT A-Z
CONST TRUE = -1
CONST FALSE = 0
```

3. Modify the **Form_Load** event procedure code to match the following set of statements. The new or changed lines of code are displayed in bold.

```
SUB Form_Load ()
 Num$ = SPACE$(3)         'element number variable
 CR$ = CHR$(13)           'Carriage return
 READ NumElem             'Get number of elements

 'Open the data file for input
 OPEN "A:PERIDATA.TXT" FOR INPUT AS #1

 INPUT #1, InDat$         'Get number of elements
 NumElem = VAL(InDat$) 'Convert string to number

 'Begin loop that reads element data
 'and generates the periodic table
```

```
    FOR index = 1 TO NumElem
       'Get data for an element
       INPUT #1, InDat$    'Left
       L = VAL(InDat$)
       INPUT #1, InDat$    'Top
       T = VAL(InDat$)
       INPUT #1, InDat$    'BackColor
       Bcolor = VAL(InDat$)
       INPUT #1, Sym$      'Symbol
       INPUT #1, Ename$    'Element name

       'Create picture box in control array
       LOAD Picture1(index)

       'Set picture box properties
       Picture1(index).BackColor = Bcolor
       Picture1(index).Visible = TRUE
       Picture1(index).AutoReDraw = TRUE

       'Create display text
       'Trim initial space and left justify in Num$
       LSET Num$ = LTRIM$(STR$(index))
       'Display element number and symbol
       Picture1(index).PRINT Num$ + CR$ + Sym$

       'Store data as Tag property value
       Picture1(index).Tag = Sym$ + Num$ + Ename$

       'Position the picture box
       Picture1(index).MOVE L, T, 4, 2
    NEXT index

    CLOSE                  'Close all open data files

       'Hide original picture box
       Picture1(0).Visible = FALSE
   END SUB
```

The Visual Basic **OPEN** statement is used first to open the data file (PERIDATA.TXT) as INPUT file #1. Then **INPUT #1** statements are used to input each data item as a string of characters. Items that are to be used as numbers are first read into the `InDat$` string variable and then converted to numbers with the **VAL** function.

Once all the data are read, a **CLOSE** statement with no arguments is used to close all open data files. If you wish to close a specific data file, you would use the **CLOSE #n** statement, where the argument, *n*, is set to the number of the file you wish to close. For example, in this block of code, you could use the following statement to close the input data file: **CLOSE #1.**

Try running this changed version of Periodic. Aside from these changes, the rest of the code for the application remains the same. Once you make the indicated changes to the existing Periodic code, the application should run and produce the same results as the original version of the program.

When you exit Visual Basic, you will be asked if you want to save the changes you have made. If the application is running correctly, go ahead and save the changes. Your saved version of Periodic will now use the `PERIDATA.TXT` data file when it starts up and generates the Periodic Table of Elements display.

For More About Files

The preceding discussions have provided you with an introduction to some of the standard file handling procedures for Visual Basic. For more information about using standard file operations within Visual Basic, you are referred to Chapter 12 of the *Visual Basic Programmer's Guide*, "Interacting with Files and Devices," which provides detailed examples of how to read, write, and interact with all of Visual Basic's file types.

The rest of this chapter introduces you to the Visual Basic Common Dialog Toolkit. This toolkit contains a form, controls, and code for seven of the most common types of dialog boxes that you might use in your applications. Included in the toolkit are examples of specific dialog boxes that handle file operations. Understanding how these dialog boxes work can save you lots of effort in building applications and in developing file handling interface procedures.

Visual Basic File Controls

Visual Basic has three objects that let you control the use of files from a form. The three control objects are *directory list boxes, drive list boxes,* and *file list boxes.* These controls can be used to build dialog boxes that let users open, print, browse, and save files.

Before you examine these file control objects and build a form that uses the controls, let's investigate Visual Basic's Common Dialog Toolkit. This toolkit contains running versions of dialog boxes that utilize the file control objects.

Visual Basic's Common Dialog Toolkit

Visual Basic includes a number of example projects. These projects demonstrate Visual Basic features and provide you with event procedure code that you can study and use in your own applications.

One example project is the Visual Basic Common Dialog Toolkit. This project provides the code and displays for seven frequently used dialog boxes. The project, `CMNDLG.MAK`, contains the following example, but operational, dialog boxes: **File Open, File Save, File Print, Find Text, Change Text, Color Palette,** and **About.**

To view these dialog boxes, do the following:

1. Start Visual Basic. If Visual Basic is already running, choose the **New Project** command on the File menu to clear the code windows.
2. Choose the **Open Project** command on the File menu, and open the `CMNDLG.MAK` project. This project is stored in the VBDOS subdirectory on your hard disk.

   The project has two files: `CMNDLG.BAS` and `CMNDLGF.FRM`. `CMNDLG.BAS` is the start-up file. It contains a set of subroutines that control the displays for each of the toolkit's dialog boxes. `CMNDLGF.FRM` is a form file that contains all of the controls for all of the toolkit's dialog boxes. The toolkit selectively hides, shows, and positions controls to create each separate dialog box.
3. After you open `CMNDLG.MAK` (the Common Dialog Toolkit), run the application. `CMNDLG.BAS` must be the start-up file for the application to run properly.

The Toolkit's File Open Dialog Box

When you run the toolkit, the application displays the series of dialog boxes, one after the other. The **File Open** dialog box appears first, as shown in Figure 9-3.

This example dialog box contains operational directory, drive, and file list boxes. You can change drives with the drive list box, and information

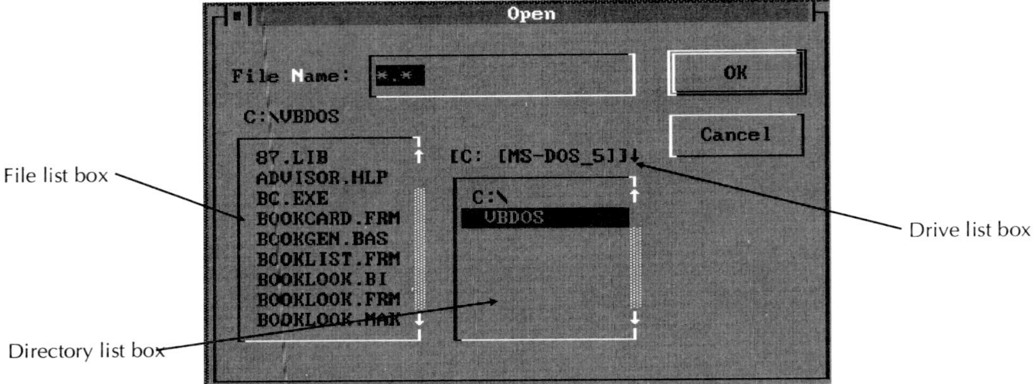

Figure 9-3 File Open dialog box.

about directories and files on the new drive appears in the other list boxes. You open subdirectories with the directory list box and display the files in that subdirectory in the files list box.

As you will see in a few moments, most of the file operations just described take place automatically. The Visual Basic file control objects have been preprogrammed to handle routine file operations and tasks. All you have to do is put the object on a form, add a small amount of code, and the object becomes fully operational.

The Toolkit's File Save Dialog Box

Click the **Cancel** button on the **File Open** dialog box. The toolkit's **File Save** dialog box appears. Figure 9-4 shows the File Save dialog box.

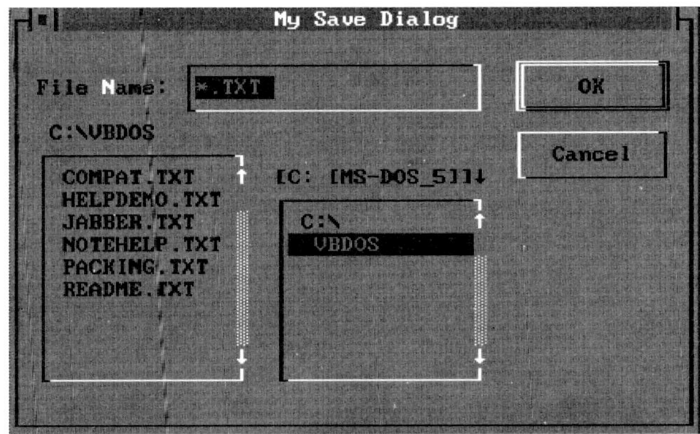

Figure 9-4 File Save dialog box.

This dialog box looks exactly like the **File Open** dialog box, except for the caption in the title bar. The main difference between a **File Open** and a **File Save** dialog box would be what the program does when you click the **OK** button. In the first case, the button's code would direct the program to open the designated file. In the second case, the code would save the file using the file name shown in the **File Name** text box.

The Toolkit's File Print Dialog Box

Click the **Cancel** button on the **File Save** dialog box. The **File Print** dialog box, shown in Figure 9-5, appears.

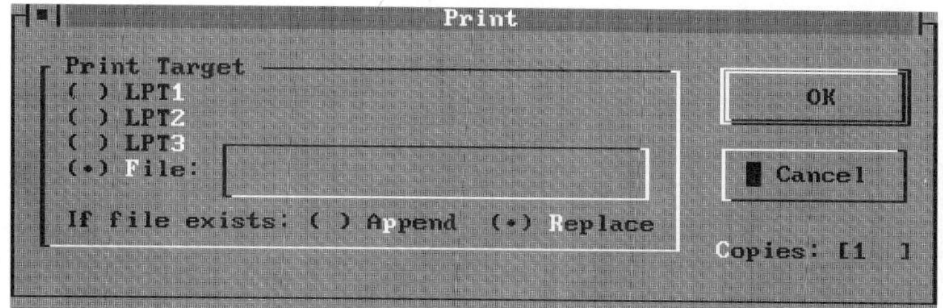

Figure 9-5 File Print dialog box.

This dialog box lays out a set of options that the user can select. The controls determine where information gets printed (to a device or to a file), whether the data are appended to an existing file or completely replace a current file, and how many copies will be produced. This dialog box utilizes any of the three file control objects. The dialog box uses option buttons, text boxes, and command buttons to set up the file printing tasks.

The Remaining Toolkit Dialog Boxes

To see the rest of the Common Dialog Toolkit dialog boxes, click the **Cancel** button on each new dialog box (except for the final **About** dialog box where you click **OK**). Visual Basic will display the four remaining dialog boxes: **Find Text, Change Text, Color Palette,** and **About.**

When you click **OK** on the **About** dialog box, the application hides the **About** dialog box and asks you to press a key. When you press a key at that point, you will be returned to the programming environment.

You are encouraged to browse through the toolkit's subprograms and event procedures. You can borrow and use any of this application's code and displays for use in your own applications. If you only need one or two of the seven dialog boxes, you can make a copy of the files in this project and delete all the objects and code modules that you do not plan to use.

The FileTest Application

In this application, you will put the three file control objects (directory, drive, and file list boxes) on a form. Then you will create two simple event procedures that will let you use and test the interactions of the three file controls.

Figure 9-6 shows the FileTest form with the three controls in place.

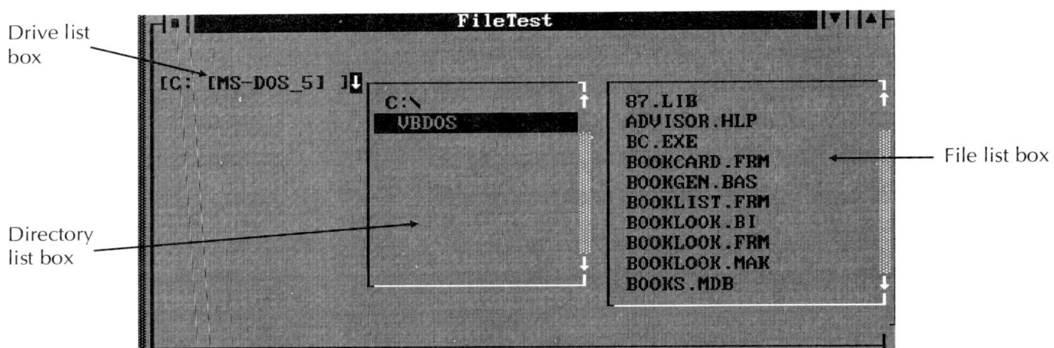

Figure 9-6 FileTest application.

FileTest Specifications

FileTest will be a single form with three controls. The form itself will not respond to any events. The controls will be the only active objects on the form, except for the standard controls built into the form's title bar (see page 241).

FileTest Application Control Specifications

FileTest uses a drive list box, directory list box, and file list box. Figure 9-6 shows FileTest and how its three controls appear on the form.

<u>Specification #9-1 (Form)</u>

FileTest Application

Controls	Event(s) to be detected		Response(s)
FileTest	None		None
Properties:	Location	15,3	
	Size	63 × 17 (default)	
	Caption	`FileTest`	

Notes/Comments: Form only used to house controls.

The following specification indicates where you place these three controls and the two controls that will require event procedure code.

<u>Specification #9-2 (File Controls)</u>

FileTest Application

Controls	Event(s) to be detected			Response(s)
Drive1	Change			Update directory list box, **Dir1**
Properties:	Location	0,2		
	Size	17 × 1		
Dir1	Change			Update the file list box, **File1**
Properties:	Location	17,2		
	Size	19 × 11		
	File1	None		None
	Properties:	Location	37,2	
	Size	24 × 12		

Notes/Comments: **Drive1** is *a drive list box* control. **Dir1** is *a directory list box* control. **File1** is *a file list box* control.

Build FileTest

You build FileTest just as you have built earlier applications. To begin, review the application's specifications and then do the following:

1. Start Visual Basic and create a new project. (If required, choose **New Project** on the File menu to create a new, untitled project.)
2. Open the File menu and choose the **New Form** command. When you see the **New Form** dialog box:

   Type `A:FILETEST.FRM` and press **Enter.**

   You will be placed in the Form Designer area with a form captioned `Filetest`. Change the caption to `FileTest`.
3. Based on the file controls' specification (#9-2), add the three file control objects to the form.
4. Save the project.

After you add the file controls to the FileTest form, your display will look like the one shown in Figure 9-7.

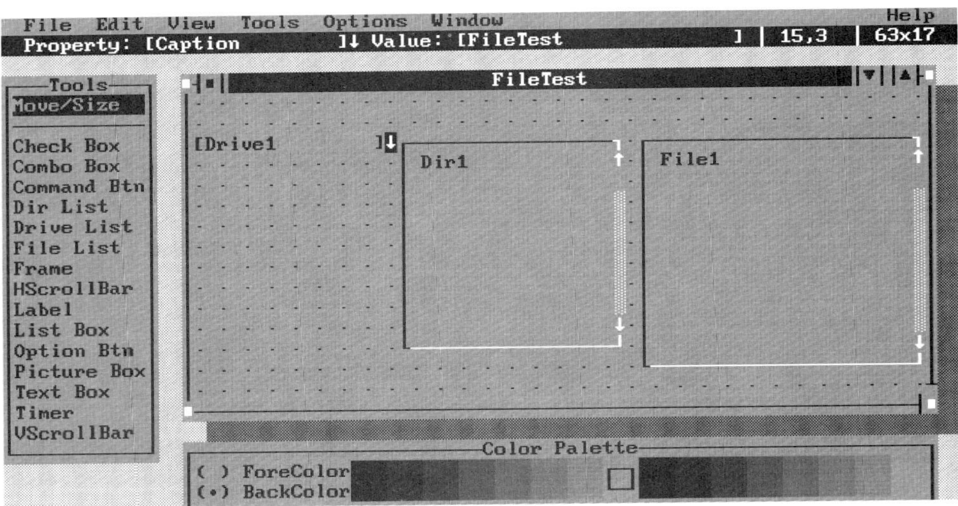

Figure 9-7 FileTest form with file controls.

The FileTest Event Procedures

FileTest has two event procedures, **Drive1_Change** and **Dir1_Change.** These two procedures perform the following tasks:

Event Procedure	Task
Drive1_Change	Updates the Dir1 object's **Path** property when a new drive is selected with the Drive1 object.
Dir1_Change	Updates the File1 object's **Path** property when a new directory is selected with the Dir1 object or when Dir1 gets updated by a change in Drive1.

The code for these two procedures is listed below (what you type is shown in bold). Choose the **Event Procedures** command on the Edit menu to set up these procedures.

```
SUB Drive1_Change ()
    'Update directory list box
    'when new drive is selected
    Dir1.Path = Drive1.Drive
END SUB

SUB Dir1_Change ()
    'Update file list box
    'when new directory is selected
    File1.Path = Dir1.Path
END SUB
```

In **Drive1_Change,** the **Dir1 Path** property is adjusted each time a new drive is selected. The **Path** property is assigned the value of the **Drive1** list box **Drive** property.

In **Dir1_Change,** the **File** list box **Path** property is adjusted each time the **Dir1 Path** property changes. The **Dir1 Path** property can be changed by either a user selecting a directory on the **Dir1** list box or by a change being made to the **Drive1** list box control.

These two event procedures give you the minimum amount of code required to activate the file controls on the FileTest form. To see fully completed code modules for using these controls, look at the Visual Basic Common Dialog Toolkit. This toolkit was discussed earlier in this chapter.

Run FileTest

After you enter the code for the two event procedures, save the project and run the FileTest application. FileTest's first display will look something like the one shown in Figure 9-8.

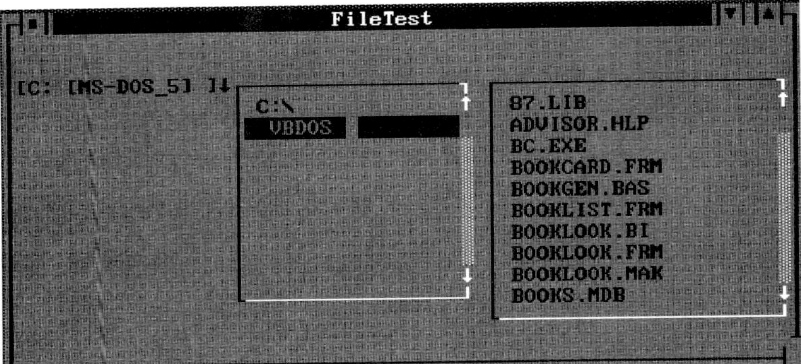

Figure 9-8 FileTest application at start up.

If you click the arrow on the right end of the directory list box, Visual Basic displays a list of available disk drives for your computer. Figure 9-9 shows FileTest with the contents of the **Drive1** list box displayed.

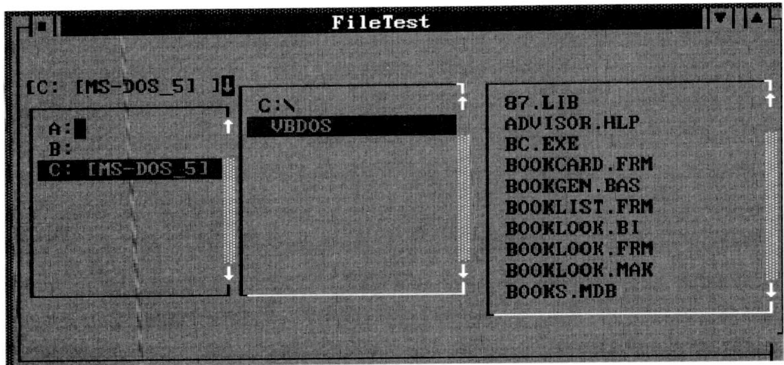

Figure 9-9 Contents of Drive list box displayed.

If you click the drive designation for your floppy disk drive (`A:`), the **Drive1** list box changes to that drive. The change to **Drive1** triggers a change to the **Dir1** list box, which in turn causes a change to the **File1** list box. Figure 9-10 shows FileTest after the user selects the floppy disk drive (`A:`) in the **Drive1** list box.

Experiment with this form and its controls. Display the directory for the hard disk drive again. Double click the `C:\` entry in the **Dir1** list box (the object in the middle of the screen). You will see a list of the directories on your hard disk. If you double-click one of the directory names, the **File1** list box will show the names of the files in that directory.

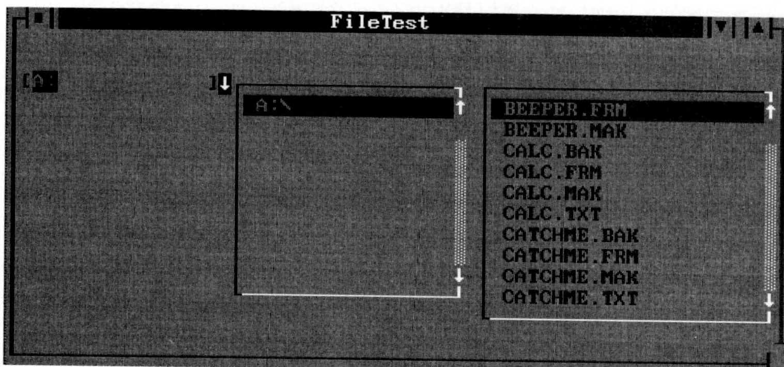

Figure 9-10 FileTest after drive changes.

Use the scroll bar to scroll through the list of files in the **File1** list box. In this example, no code exists that lets you access the files in the **File1** list box. As a challenge, you might try and add controls and code that let you use this dialog box to open a file shown in the file list box.

When you finish your explorations, double-click the control box in the upper left corner of the form. This action will close the form and display a message asking you to press a key. Press a key to return to the programming environment. Then save the project.

The purpose of having you build FileTest was to show you the fundamentals involved in using the file control objects, as well as the minimum code required to activate those controls. For more detailed code and information regarding the use of file controls, look at the Common Dialog Toolkit (`CMNDLG.MAK`) project code.

Summary

In the first part of this chapter, you learned how to store a block of comments and **DATA** statements in a data file and how to load that code block at run-time with a **$INCLUDE** metacommand. You also learned how to open, read, and close a data file by using the **OPEN, INPUT,** and **CLOSE** file statements.

In the last part of this chapter, you examined the Visual Basic Common Dialog Toolkit and built a simple application, FileTest, that used Visual Basic file controls. FileTest gave you a chance to see how the drive, directory, and file list boxes work together to display file information on a form.

You have now built applications that have used nearly all of the major Visual Basic control objects. The key remaining control object that you have not yet explored is a menu. The next chapter shows you how to build and use these objects. When you are ready, proceed to Chapter 10, "Menus," and learn how to create and activate menus on your forms.

10 Menu Controls

Visual Basic lets you build and attach *menus* to your application's forms. Menus are pull-down lists of commands that users can access to direct the actions of an application. You create menus on a form with Visual Basic control objects called *menu controls*. You specify properties and build code for menu controls just like you do with other Visual Basic controls.

In this chapter, you will learn how to put a set of menus on the Calc application form. The menu commands will replace the functions of the command buttons that you installed on the Calc form. You built Calc in Chapter 5, "Exploring Visual Basic with Small Applications."

Creating the MenuCalc Application

To create MenuCalc, a version of the Calc application that uses menu controls, you basically edit the existing Calc form and its event procedures.

Concepts and Terminology

menus	(247)
menu controls	(247)
MenuCalc application	(247)
Ctrl-click selections	(248)
Menu Design Window	(250)
separators	(254)
indentation of menu items	(252)
editing event procedures	(259)
keyboard equivalent codes	(262)
cascading menu controls	(262)
disabling menu controls	(262)
menu control arrays	(262)

QBasic/QuickBasic Keywords

REM	(259)
SUB	(259)
END SUB	(259)
VAL	(259)
STR$	(259)
CHR$	(259)

New Visual Basic Keywords

Visual Basic Event Procedures

mnuSquare_Click	(259)
mnuSqRoot_Click	(259)
mnuClear_Click	(260)
mnuExit_Click	(260)

To begin this editing process, you will save a copy of Calc's form under a new name.

Copy CALC.FRM to MENUCALC.FRM

Make a copy of `CALC.FRM` and save that copy as `MENUCALC.FRM`. To perform this operation, type the following at the MS-DOS prompt for your system:

Type `copy a:\calc.frm a:\menucalc.frm` and press **Enter.**

You will now have a copy of `CALC.FRM` on the diskette in drive A. The copy will be in a file called `MENUCALC.FRM`.

Edit MENUCALC.FRM

To edit `MENUCALC.FRM`, start Visual Basic and add `MENUCALC.FRM` as follows:

1. Start Visual Basic and begin with a new, untitled project.
2. Choose the **Add File** command on the File menu, and add `MENUCALC.FRM` to the project. When you add this form, you will see an empty code window with the following title:

   ```
   [1] MENUCALC.FRM
   ```

3. Click the **Form** button and switch to the Form Designer area. Figure 10-1 shows the form for this application before you start editing its controls and features.
4. Select all four of the command buttons (**Square, Sq. Root, Clear,** and **Exit**). You make this group selection by clicking the **Square** button and then **Ctrl-clicking** the remaining buttons. You perform a **Ctrl-click** by holding down the **Ctrl** key and clicking each object to be added to the group. Figure 10-2 shows the form, with the four command buttons selected as a group.
5. Press the **Delete** key to delete the selected group of command buttons. **Note:** All the control objects on the form may seem to disappear when you press **Delete.** If this situation happens, the

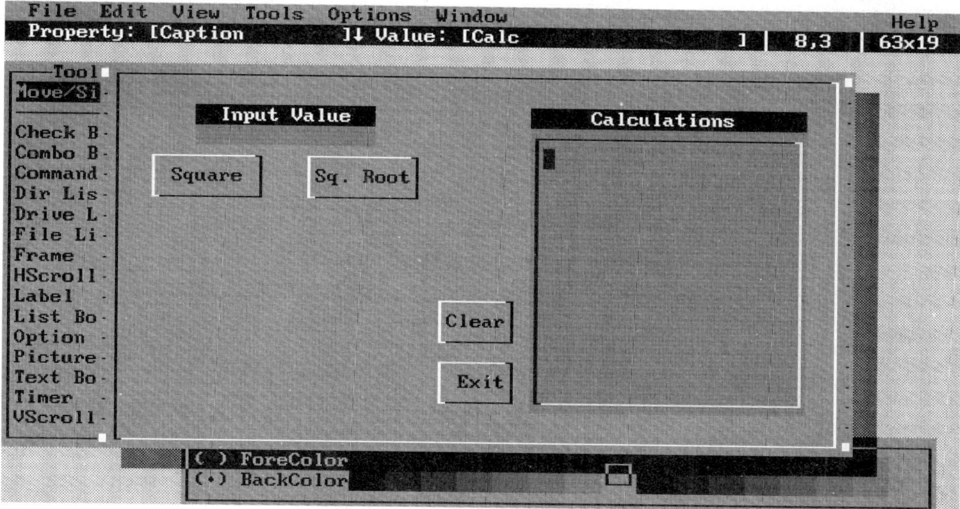

Figure 10-1 Form before editing begins.

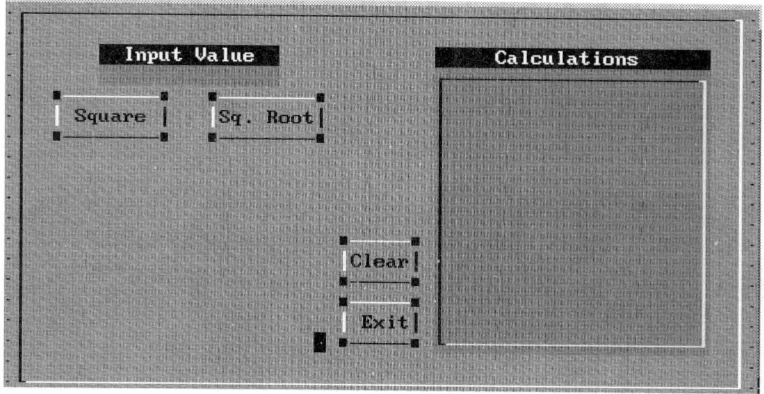

Figure 10-2 Four command buttons selected.

other controls (labels, text boxes) have been hidden behind the frame object. To reveal those hidden objects, press the **Tab** key repeatedly until all of the hidden objects reappear. Figure 10-3 shows the form after the command buttons have been deleted, and any hidden controls have been displayed by pressing the **Tab** key.

6. Save the project at this point. Save the project under the name `A:MENUCALC.MAK`.

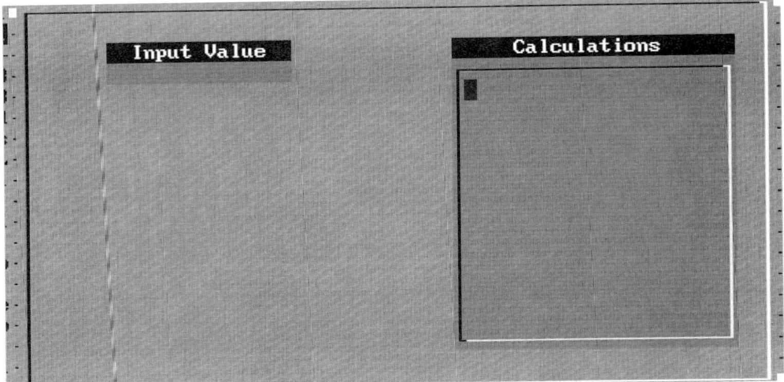

Figure 10-3 Form with command buttons deleted.

Adding a Menu to the Form

You will now add menu controls to the form to take the place of the four command buttons that were deleted. You create and specify Visual Basic menu controls with the Menu Design window. You activate this window as follows:

1. Pull down the Window menu on the Form Designer screen. The menu shows a list of the windows that you can activate. Figure 10-4 displays the Window menu and its list of commands.

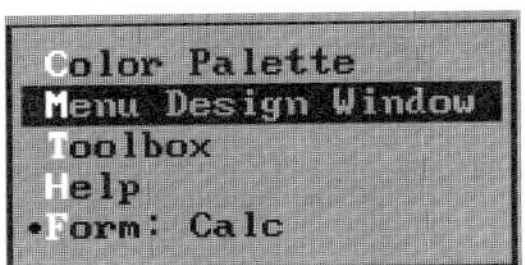

Figure 10-4 Window menu.

2. Choose the **Menu Design Window** command. The Menu Design Window overlays both the form and Form Designer screen elements. Figure 10-5 shows what this window looks like before you add any menu controls.

   You will use the Menu Design Window to accomplish two tasks:

   a. Identify menu controls and specify the controls' properties.
   b. Tell Visual Basic where you want the controls to appear on the form's menus.

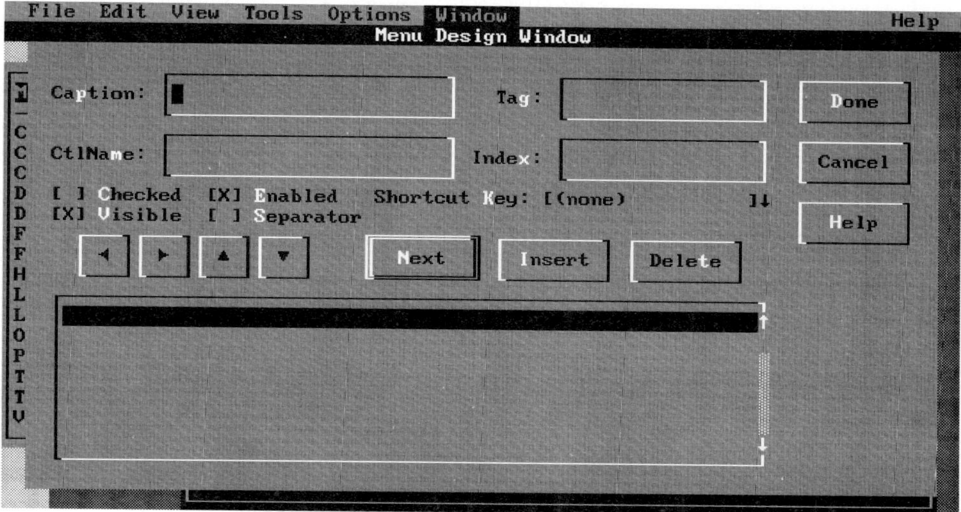

Figure 10-5 Menu Design window.

The set of four text boxes, four check boxes, and the **Shortcut Key** combo box let you identify each menu control (**Caption, CtlName**) and set that control's properties (**Tag, Index, Checked, Enabled, Visible, Separator,** and **Shortcut Key**).

The row of command buttons below the property controls has four buttons (four arrow icons) that let you tell Visual Basic where you want to place each menu control. The other three buttons on this row (**Next, Insert, Delete**) let you direct menu editing operations as you build menus for a form.

The list box below the row of seven command buttons will display an outline of the menus you create. The three buttons on the right side of the window let you signal when you complete the building of a menu (**Done**), want to exit the menu building window but not record any changes (**Cancel**), and need help (**Help**).

3. Create your first menu control by doing the following:

   a. Type `CalcMenu` in the **Caption** text box.
   b. Type `mnuCalcMenu` in the **CtlName** list box.

   When you complete these two entries, the Window Design window appears as shown in Figure 10-6.

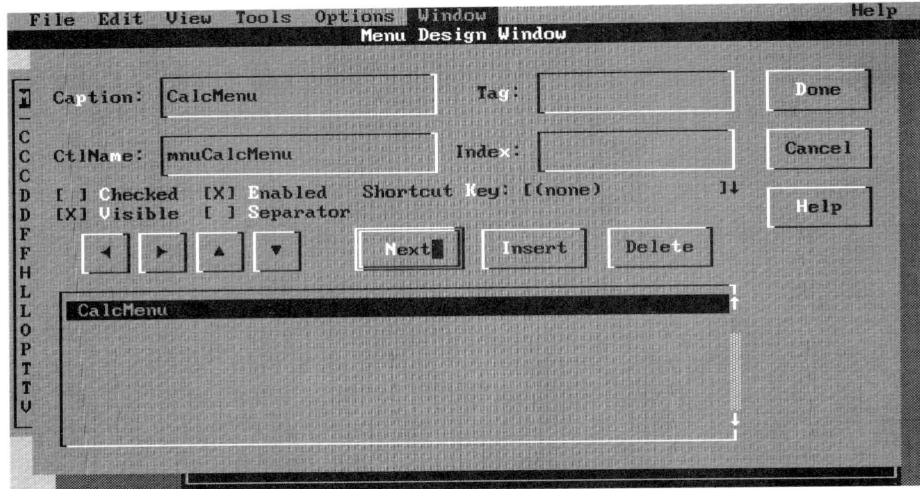

Figure 10-6 First menu control being created.

When you entered this first menu control's **Caption,** that caption value appeared in the list box at the bottom of the window. The caption for this control will be used as a title for one of the two menus that you will create.

4. Click **Next** to record the settings for this first menu control. You can now enter the data for the second menu control. Enter the following information:

   a. Type `Square` in the **Caption** text box.
   b. Type `mnuSquare` in the **CtlName** list box.
   c. Click the second button (right arrow icon) on the row of buttons across the middle of the window.

   Figure 10-7 shows what the screen looks like after you make these entries.

   The list box shows the following:

```
CalcMenu
..Square
```

   When you clicked the button with the right arrow icon, the entry for the second menu control moved to the right in the list box. Two periods (.) appeared in front of the entry. Clicking the button with the right arrow icon indented the second menu control entry. The indentation indicates that you want the caption for this menu control to appear on the CalcMenu pull-down menu as a command.

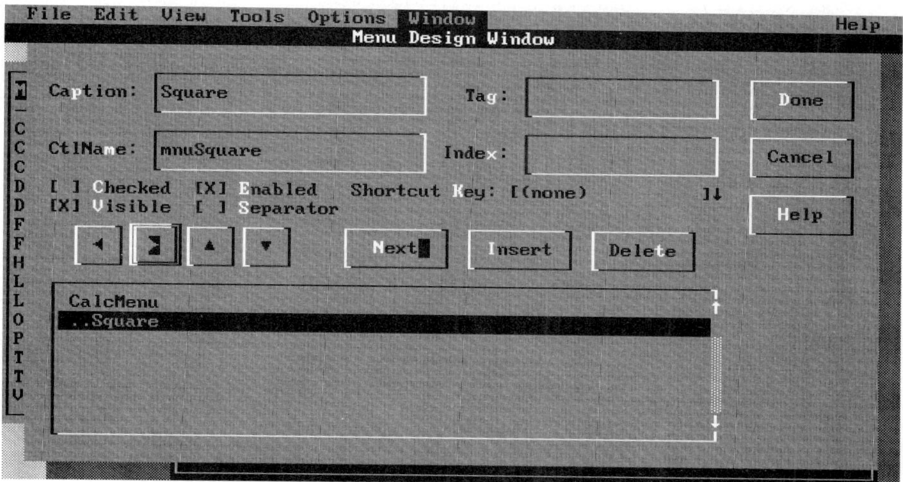

Figure 10-7 Second menu control being created.

5. Click **Next** to record the settings for the second menu control.

6. Enter the following data to complete the creation of the CalcMenu controls items:

   a. Type `Sq. Root` in the **Caption** text box.
   b. Type `mnuSqRoot` in the **CtlName** list box.
   c. Click the **Next** button.
   d. Type `-` in the **Caption** text box.
   e. Type `mnuSeparator` in the **CtlName** list box.
   f. Click the **Next** button.
   g. Type `Exit` in the **Caption** text box.
   e. Type `mnuExit` in the **CtlName** list box.
   f. Click the **Next** button.

Figure 10-8 shows the Menu Design window after you make these entries.

The list box on the design window shows the following outline for the CalcMenu pull-down menu:

```
CalcMenu
..Square
..Sq. Root
..-
..Exit
..
```

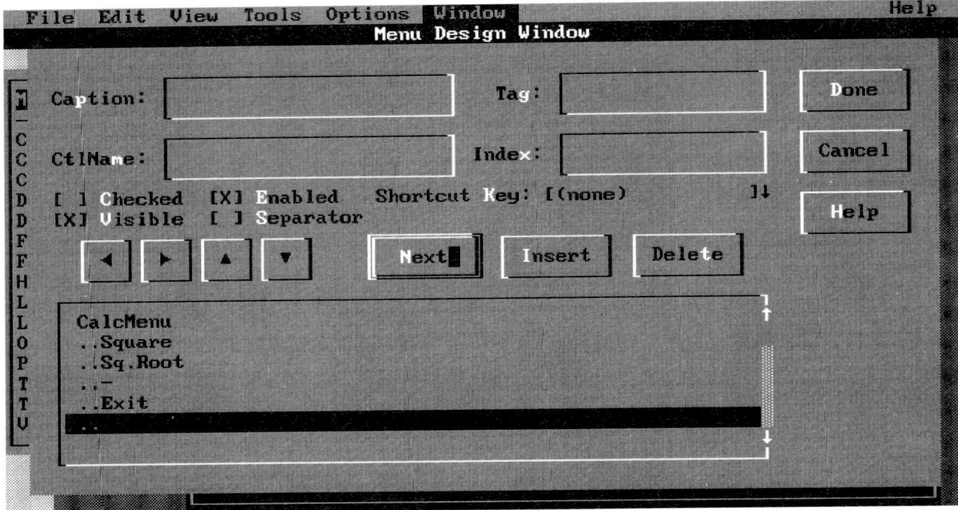

Figure 10-8 CalcMenu entries completed.

The first pull-down menu description is complete. The name of the menu will be CalcMenu. The menu will list three commands (**Square, Sq. Root,** and **Exit**). The first two commands will be separated from the **Exit** command by a control object that acts as a separator. When you entered the hypen (-) as the caption for the **mnuSeparator** control, Visual Basic automatically turned the **Separator** check box to **On** and recorded the control as a separator on the menu.

7. Click **Done** to record your menu specifications. The Menu Design window will disappear, and you will see the form (Figure 10-9). The form will show the name of the menu you just created (CalcMenu) in the menu bar across the top of the form.

8. Save the project.

Examine the Menu

You can view the menu you created without leaving the Form Designer. Simply click the menu title, CalcMenu. The pull-down menu you specified will appear, as shown in Figure 10-10.

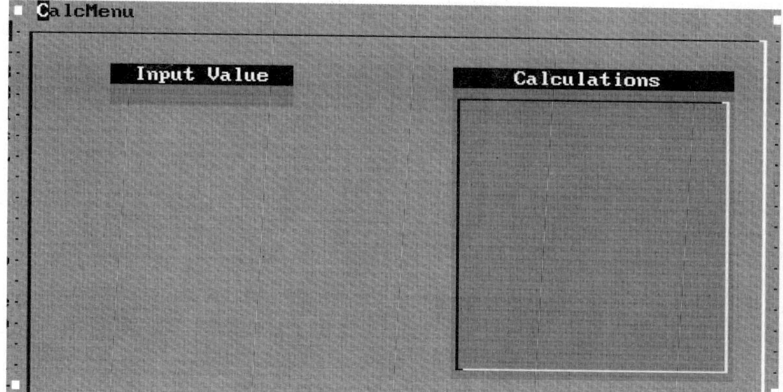

Figure 10-9 Form with CalcMenu menu.

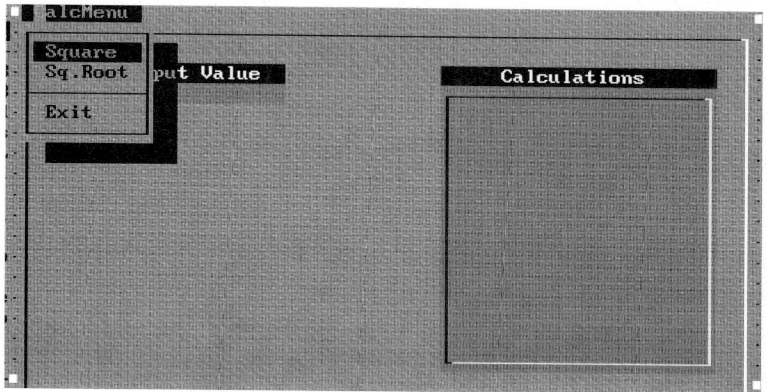

Figure 10-10 Pull-down menu displayed.

The captions you entered for each command appear on the menu list. The separator appears as a line across the menu list, separating the top two commands from the **Exit** command.

Add a Second Menu

You have replaced three of the original four command buttons with menu commands (**Square, Sq. Root,** and **Exit**). Let's replace the fourth command button (**Clear**) with a second form menu called Edit. Here is what you do to create this second menu:

1. Choose the **Menu Design Window** command on the Window menu (Form Designer screen). The Menu Design window will appear (Figure 10-11).

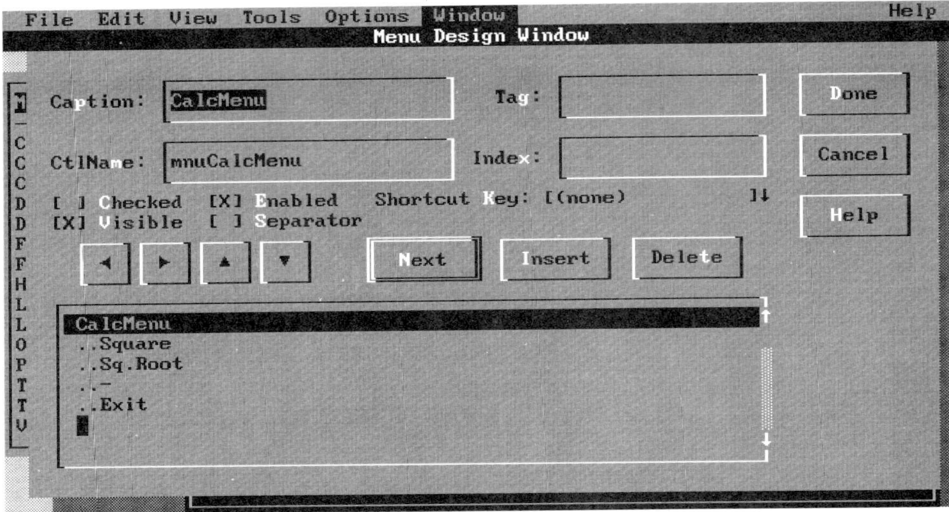

Figure 10-11 Menu Design window.

2. Click the space below `..Exit` to move the highlight to the blank line below this last menu entry. The **Caption** and **CtlName** text boxes will be empty. The design window is ready to accept your specifications for a second menu. Figure 10-12 shows what the screen looks like after you open the Menu Design window and position the highlight.

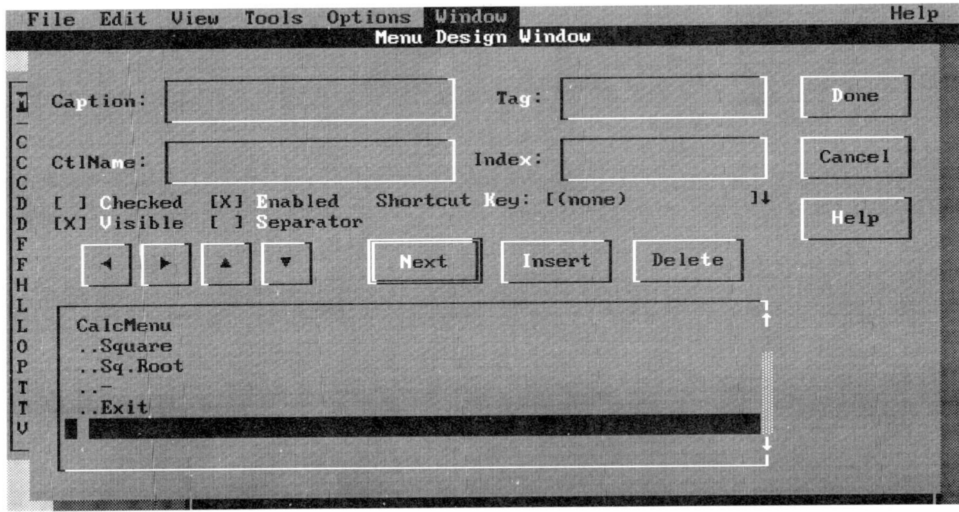

Figure 10-12 Window before entering data for second menu.

3. Enter the following information to create a second menu on the MenuCalc form:

   a. Type `Edit` in the **Caption** text box.
   b. Type `mnuEdit` in the **CtlName** list box.
   c. Click the **Next** button.
   d. Type `Clear` in the **Caption** text box.
   e. Type `mnuClear` in the **CtlName** list box.
   f. Click the button with the right arrow icon to indent this menu entry.
   g. Click the **Next** button.

   After you make these entries, the window looks like the one shown in Figure 10-13.

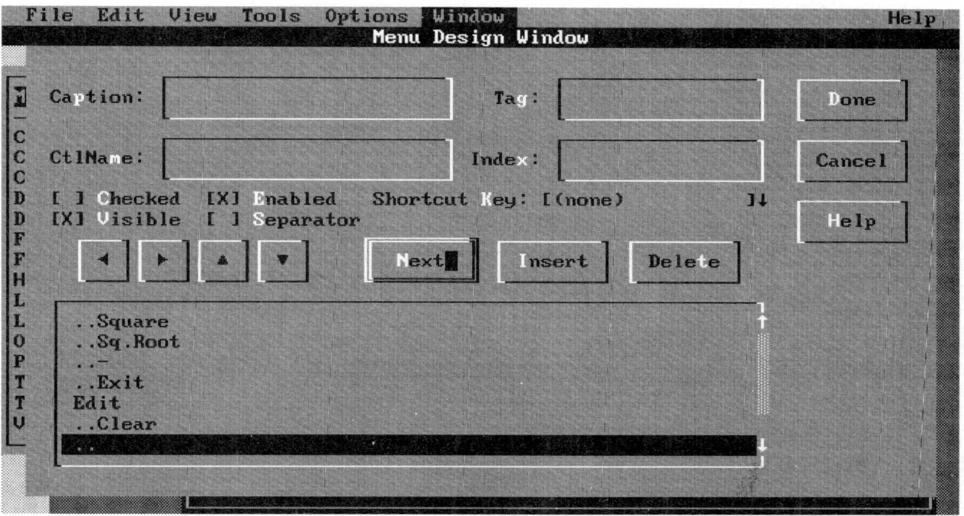

Figure 10-13 Second menu specification completed.

   The new menu, Edit, will have one command, **Clear,** on its menu list.

4. Click **Done** to record you new menu entries and return to the Form Designer screen. Your second menu title, Edit, now appears next to CalcMenu on the form's title bar.

5. Save the project.

Click **Edit** to verify that the second menu is active and defined correctly. Pull down CalcMenu and make sure it still displays as it did before you added the Edit menu. You are now ready to edit the form's existing event procedures and activate the menu controls that you have placed on the form.

Creating Code for the Menu Controls

The code required to activate the new menu controls already exists. The event procedures for the four command buttons are still attached to the form and available for editing. You removed the four command buttons from the form, but Visual Basic only removed the objects themselves and not any related code.

To access the existing code, do the following:

1. Exit the Form Designer and return to the programming environment. If you are asked if you want to save changes to the project, click **Yes** on the dialog box that appears.
2. When you reach the programming environment, click the **Code** button on the Project window. The **Code** dialog box will appear. This dialog box lists the five event procedures that are still attached to the form (Figure 10-14).

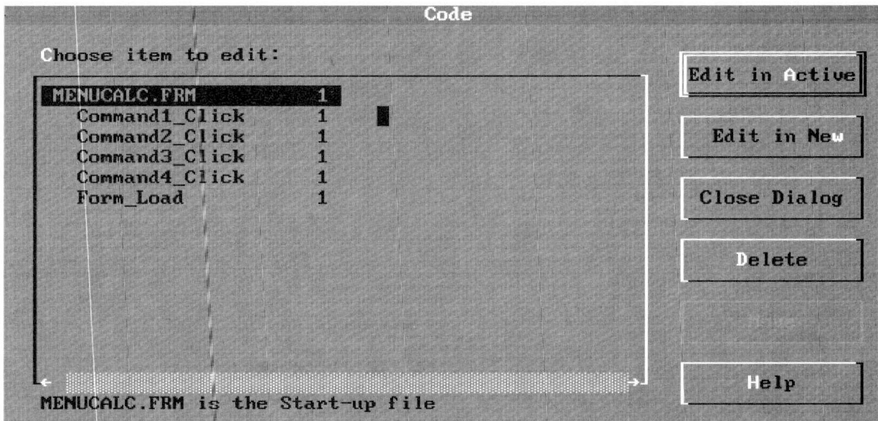

Figure 10-14 Code dialog box.

The first four procedures handle a **Click** event for the original four command buttons. The code in each of these procedures is exactly the code you need to activate your new menu controls. All you have to do is edit the name of the subprocedures to correspond to the control name values (**CtlName**) for the new menu objects.

3. Select **Command1_Click** in the list, and click the **Edit in Active** button. Visual Basic displays a code window with the code for the **Command1_Click** event procedure.

```
SUB Command1_Click ()
  'Convert input text to numeric value
  Number = VAL(Text1.Text)
  'Square the number
  Answer = Number ^ 2
  'Build the result string
  CalcText$ = " " +STR$(Number) 'pl "^2="
  CalcText$ = CalcText$ + STR$(Answer) + CHR$(13)
  'Append result to the display list
  Text2.Text = Text2.Text + CalcText$
END SUB
```

This block of code will work for the Square menu command if the code is attached to the correct menu object, **mnuSquare.**

5. Edit the first line of the procedure so that it reads as follows:

SUB mnuSquare_Click ()

You change the object name in the procedure from **Command1** to **mnuSquare.**

6. Click the **Code** button on the Project window. The **Code** dialog box appears again, but notice the difference. The **Command1_Click** procedure name is gone, and a new procedure name, **mnuSquare_Click,** appears in the list (Figure 10-15).

7. Select and edit the remaining three event procedures (**Command2, Command3,** and **Command4**) as follows:

   a. Select Command2_Click and click the Edit in Active button.
   b. Change Command2 in the first line of the procedure to mnuSqRoot. The result will appear as follows:

      SUB mnuSqRoot_Click ()

   c. Click the **Code** button on the Project window.
   d. Select **Command3_Click** and click the **Edit in Active** button.

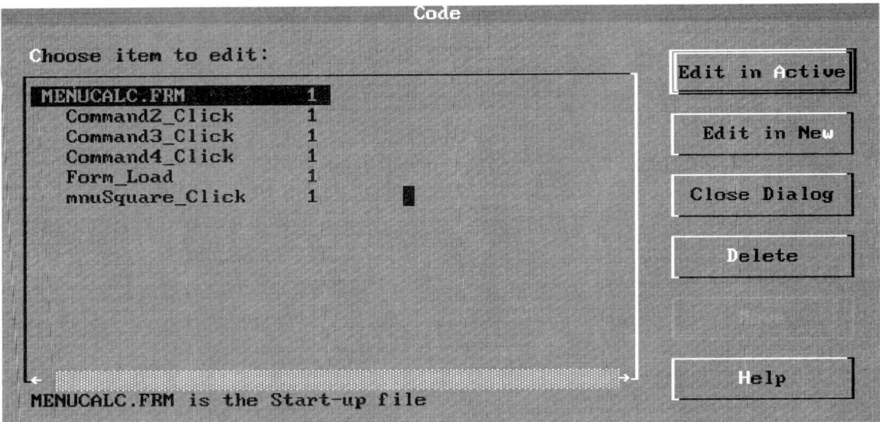

Figure 10-15 Code dialog box with procedure name changed.

e. Change **Command3** in the first line of the procedure to **mnuClear.** The result will appear as follows:

SUB mnuClear_Click ()

f. Click the **Code** button on the Project window.
g. Select **Command4_Click** and click the **Edit in Active** button.
h. Change **Command4** in the first line of the procedure to **mnuExit.** The result will appear as follows:

SUB mnuExit_Click ()

8. Save the project.

With these simple editing changes, you have completed the mapping of the original Calc application into the MenuCalc application, which uses menu controls to activate commands.

Run MenuCalc

Run the MenuCalc application. The form with its new menus should appear as shown in Figure 10-16.

Enter a data value into the **Input Value** text box region. Then pull down the CalcMenu menu and choose the **Square** command. Figure 10-17 shows the screen after an input value of `1234` has been entered and the **Square** command has been activated from the CalcMenu menu.

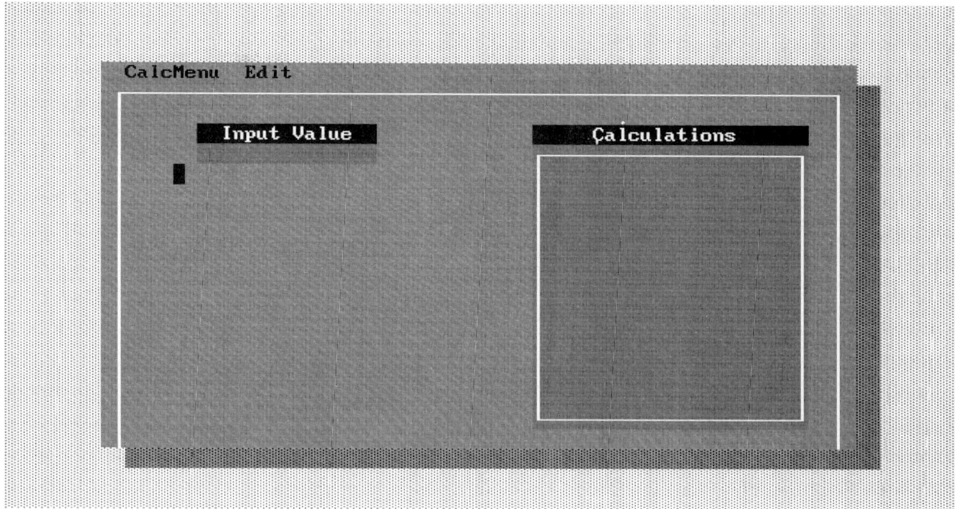

Figure 10-16 MenuCalc application screen.

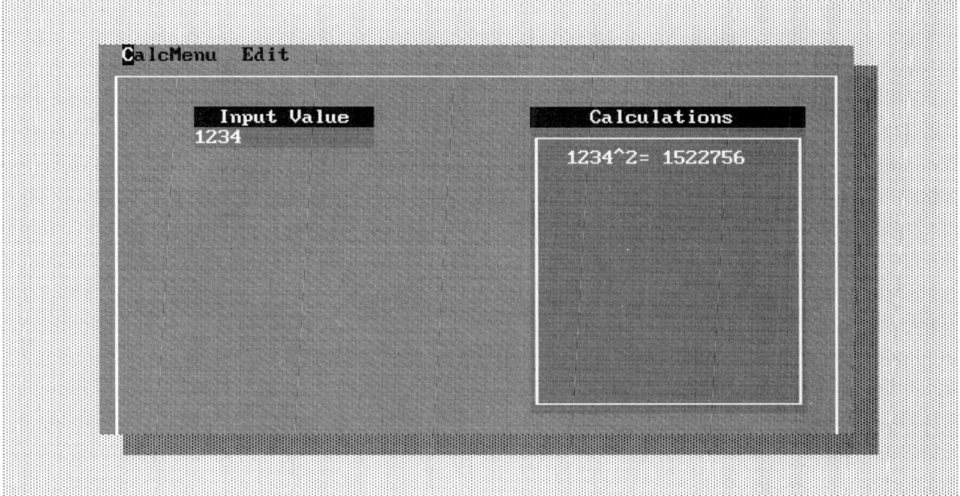

Figure 10-17 Screen after Square command is activated.

Try the other menu commands. Verify that the **Sq. Root** command produces the square root of the **Input Value.** Try the **Clear** command on the Edit menu. The **Input Value** and **Calculations** text boxes should clear. After you have tested the **Square, Sq. Root,** and **Clear** commands, try the **Exit** command. The **Exit** command should send you out of the application back to the programming environment.

After you experiment with MenuCalc, save the project and exit from Visual Basic.

More on Menus

The MenuCalc application demonstrates the basics of how you build menus and attach code to menu objects. The Visual Basic Menu Design window lets you set up other menu features, such as:

- Assigning a keyboard equivalent code to any menu item so that menu options can be invoked from the keyboard.
- Creating a cascading menu structure that can display up to five levels of menu options.
- Disabling menu controls that can be enabled later, based on the user's interactions with the application.
- Making a control invisible until a user's actions require that control become visible.
- Attaching unique information to a menu control by using the **Tag** property.
- Creating a control array of menu objects with the **Index** property.

As you may have noticed with the MenuCalc application, moving commands up into the menu bar freed up space on the form. If your forms start looking crowded or complex, consider shifting commands and actions into a simple, organized menu bar structure.

Summary

You created an application in this chapter that utilizes Visual Basic menu control objects. You created this application, MenuCalc, by editing a previously generated application, Calc.

To specify the menu controls for MenuCalc, you activated the Visual Basic Menu Design window. Using this window, you specified two menus, CalcMenu and Edit, and attached several commands to those menus. You then returned to the programming environment and edited existing event procedures, changing the code for those procedures into the new menu control procedures.

You have now used all of the major types of Visual Basic control objects. With these controls, you have built a number of applications to perform a variety of tasks. At this stage, you are ready to go on and develop your own Visual Basic applications. The last two chapters in this book provide you with helpful hints as you proceed to design, develop, and build custom applications.

Chapter 11, "Error Handling," shows you how to identify and handle run-time errors—errors that occur only when you run an application.

11 Error Handling

Visual Basic provides a set of standard keywords that can be used to develop *error handling* routines. Error handling routines are blocks of code that you create to intercept, identify, and deal with program errors that occur when users run an application. Error handling routines are built to let users know when errors occur and what actions they can take to correct problems, if the problems are correctable.

You have already utilized several Visual Basic error handling keywords and routines in Chapter 8, "Sound and Graphics." The Shapes application calls upon an external module, `SHAPEDRW.BAS`, which contains a subroutine, **VidConfig. VidConfig** determines the best graphics screen mode for the computer system running Shapes. **VidConfig** relies upon several error handling operations to determine and set the appropriate screen mode.

Concepts and Terminology

QBasic/QuickBasic Keywords

Visual Basic External Modules

VidConfig Subroutine

The code for the **VidConfig** subroutine appears in the following listing. **VidConfig** determines which screen modes are available on the current computer system, and installs the codes for those modes in the **Shapes** combo box (**cboScrnMode**). This block of code customizes the application to match the hardware on which the application is running.

As you saw in Chapter 8, the **VidConfig** code and the structure of this code was modeled on the routines found in the TORUS.MAK project code that comes with Visual Basic. In Chapter 8, you modified the code in this project to produce `SHAPEDRW.BAS` and the **VidConfig** subroutine.

In the following listing of **VidConfig,** statements and routines that deal with the handling of errors appear in bold. The constants VGA, MCGA, EGA256, EGA64, MONO, HERC, and CGA are defined in the declarations section of `SHAPEDRW.BAS`, and correspond to seven screen mode settings. The values of these constants are 12, 13, 9, 8, 10, 3, and 1, respectively.

```
DEFINT A-Z
'============================ VidConfig ============
' Determine best video mode for this system.
'===================================================
'
SUB VidConfig ()
   ' Assume best possible screen mode
   BestMode = VGA
   Available$ = "12789BCD"

   ON LOCAL ERROR GOTO VideoErr
   ' Fall through error trap until a mode works
   SCREEN BestMode
   ' If EGA, then check pages to see whether more than 64K
   ON LOCAL ERROR GOTO EGAErr
   IF BestMode = EGA256 THEN SCREEN 8, , 1

   ON ERROR GOTO 0
   ' Reset text mode
   SCREEN 0, , 0
   WIDTH 80, 25

   FOR tmp% = 1 TO LEN(Available$)
        scrnVal = VAL("&H" + MID$(Available$, tmp%, 1))
        Shapes.cboScrnMode.ADDITEM FORMAT$(scrnVal)
         IF scrnVal = BestMode THEN
            Shapes.cboScrnMode.ListIndex = tmp% - 1
```

```
        END IF
    NEXT
    EXIT SUB

' Error trap to make screen independent
VideoErr:
    SELECT CASE BestMode 'Fall thru until something works
        CASE VGA
            BestMode = MCGA
            Available$ = "12BD"
        CASE MCGA
            BestMode = EGA256
            Available$ = "12789"
        CASE EGA256
            BestMode = CGA
            Available$ = "12"
        CASE CGA
            BestMode = MONO
            Available$ = "A"
        CASE MONO
            BestMode = HERC
            Available$ = "3"
        CASE ELSE
            PRINT "Graphics support not available. Cannot
                    run Shapes program."
            END
    END SELECT
    RESUME
' Trap to detect 64K EGA
EGAErr:
    BestMode = EGA64
    Available$ = "12789"
    RESUME NEXT

END SUB
```

As you can see, most of **VidConfig**'s code seems to be part of the routine's error handling activities. Let's examine the subprogram and how its error handling features work.

Examining VidConfig's Error Handlers

The first section of **VidConfig** assigns the parameters for a VGA screen, enables Visual Basic's error handling features, and tries setting the screen to high-resolution graphics mode, VGA (12). That portion of the code looks like this:

```
SUB VidConfig ()
   ' Assume best possible screen mode
   BestMode = VGA
   Available$ = "12789BCD"

   ON LOCAL ERROR GOTO VideoErr
   ' Fall through error trap until a mode works
   SCREEN BestMode
```

The statement that enables error handling is shown in bold:

```
ON LOCAL ERROR GOTO VideoErr
```

This statement tells Visual Basic to activate error handling and, on the detection of a local error, to go to the code that begins with the label `VideoErr`. The formal syntax for this **ON ERROR** statement is:

```
ON [LOCAL] ERROR GOTO label
```

where `LOCAL` is an optional keyword that restricts the range of the `GOTO` keyword to the current procedure.

The Path of No Errors

If the **SCREEN** statement works, the screen mode is set to the VGA graphics mode and no error occurs. In this case, the program continues executing the following code:

```
' If EGA, then check pages to see whether more than 64K
ON LOCAL ERROR GOTO EGAErr
IF BestMode = EGA256 THEN SCREEN 8, , 1
```

This section of code redirects the program to a different error handling routine labeled `EGAErr`. This adjustment relates to the case where the system is using a 64K EGA screen mode. You will examine this branch in the program flow in just a moment. For a VGA system, the program falls through these statements and executes the following code:

```
ON ERROR GOTO 0

  ' Reset text mode
  SCREEN 0, , 0
  WIDTH 80, 25
```

```
FOR tmp% = 1 TO LEN(Available$)
     scrnVal = VAL("&H" + MID$ (Available$, tmp%, 1))
     Shapes.cboScrnMode.ADDITEM FORMAT$(scrnVal)
      IF scrnVal = BestMode THEN
          Shape.cboScrnMode.ListIndex = tmp% - 1
      END IF
NEXT
```

EXIT SUB

The **ON ERROR GOTO 0** statement tells Visual Basic to disable any currently enabled module-level error handling routine. If you wanted to restrict the disabling activity to the current procedure, you would add the `LOCAL` keyword to the statement. The full syntax for this version of the **ON ERROR** statement is as follows:

```
ON [LOCAL] ERROR GOTO 0
```

The remaining code in this section resets the screen to text mode (`SCREEN` keyword with parameters 0, ,0), reestablishes the screen width (`WIDTH`), and assigns the available screen mode codes to the **Shapes** application combo box control (`cboScrnMode`).

EXIT SUB is shown in bold as part of the error handling code, since local error handling routines are disabled when Visual Basic encounters this statement.

The Path of Errors

Look again at the initial code for **VidConfig.** That part of the subprogram is reproduced as follows:

```
SUB VidConfig ()
   ' Assume best possible screen mode
   BestMode = VGA
   Available$ = "12789BCD"

   ON LOCAL ERROR GOTO VideoErr
   ' Fall through error trap until a mode works
   SCREEN BestMode
```

If the **SCREEN** statement produces an error, the program will branch to the block of code that begins with the label `VideoErr`. That section of code appears as follows:

```
' Error trap to make screen independent
VideoErr:
   SELECT CASE BestMode 'Fall thru until something works
      CASE VGA
         BestMode = MCGA
         Available$ = "12BD"
      CASE MCGA
         BestMode = EGA256
         Available$ = "12789"
      CASE EGA256
         BestMode = CGA
         Available$ = "12"
      CASE CGA
         BestMode = MONO
         Available$ = "A"
      CASE MONO
         BestMode = HERC
         Available$ = "3"
      CASE ELSE
         PRINT "Graphics support not available. Cannot
               run Shapes program."
         END
   END SELECT
   RESUME
```

Each time the **SCREEN** statement at the beginning of the **VidConfig** subprogram produces an error, the program branches to this error handling routine, labeled `VideoErr`. The core of this routine is the **SELECT CASE** structure.

In the **SELECT CASE** structure, if the screen mode (`BestMode`) that caused the error was VGA, then the mode is switched to MCGA. If MCGA caused the error, the mode switches to EGA. If EGA created the error condition, the mode switches to MONO. If MONO does not work, the routine switches to HERC. If HERC also creates an error, then the program prints a message telling the user that the application will not run, and stops the program (`END`).

The **SELECT CASE** structure handles the cascade of different screen assignments. The key statement in this error handling routine is the last keyword, `RESUME`.

`RESUME` tells Visual Basic to branch back to the statement that produced the error (`SCREEN BestMode`) and to execute that statement again. If **SCREEN** works, the program has found an operational screen mode for the application and the program executes the statements following the **SCREEN** statement.

If **SCREEN** fails, the program branches back to the routine labeled `VideoErr`, and sets up the new screen mode. The process continues until the program either finds an operational screen mode or fails to do so completely and stops running (END).

The EGA Special Error Case

Let's look at one other error condition that **VidConfig** is set up to handle: a 64K EGA screen mode. When the program successfully sets the system's screen mode to EGA, the following section of code does two things:

- Enables an error handling routine labeled EGAErr.
- Checks the system for a 256K EGA screen mode.

```
' If EGA, then check pages to see whether more than 64K
ON LOCAL ERROR GOTO EGAErr
IF BestMode = EGA256 THEN SCREEN 8, , 1
```

If the **SCREEN** statement in this section of code produces an error, the system is not a 256K EGA system. If an error occurs, the program branches to the error handling routine labeled EGAErr. That section of code appears as follows:

```
' Trap to detect 64K EGA
EGAErr:
   BestMode = EGA64
   Available$ = "12789"
   RESUME NEXT
```

The assignment statements set up the parameters that describe a 64K EGA system. The **RESUME NEXT** statement directs the program to the next statement immediately following the one that produced the error. **RESUME NEXT** bypasses the statement that causes the error.

Other Visual Basic Error Handling Features

The preceding tour of the **VidConfig** subroutine in the Shapes application gives you a preliminary view of some of Visual Basic's error handling features. Visual Basic supports several keywords, functions, and statements that allow you to:

- Intercept, identify, and handle errors and events while an application is running.

- Obtain status information concerning error and event conditions.
- Define and create your own error codes and event procedures that isolate error conditions.

The following keywords, functions, and statements are used in Visual Basic to perform error handling and associated event handling tasks. Since Visual Basic is an event-oriented language, you often have to combine event procedures and error trapping code to identify specific error conditions. All of these Visual Basic items can be used with object-specific events except for ON KEY and KEY ON.

Error-/Event-Handling Feature	Brief Description
COM Statement	Controls trapping of COM port events
ERDEV Function	Returns error code from device
ERDEV$ Function	Returns device name that generated error
ERL Function	Returns line number where error occurred
ERR Function	Returns the most recent run-time error code
ERR Statement	Assigns integer value to ERR
ERROR Statement	Stimulates occurrence of an error
ERROR$ Function	Returns error message for specified error code
EVENT Statement	Enables/disables event trapping
GOSUB...RETURN	Statement branches to and returns from a subroutine
KEY Statement	Controls trapping of defined KEY events
LOCAL Keyword	Indicates local error handling routine
OFF Keyword	Disables event trapping with event statements
ON Keyword	Enables event trapping/specifies events to trap
ON COM Statement	Branches to routine on defined COM event
ON ERROR Statement	Enables error handling during program execution
ON KEY Statement	Branches to routine on defined KEY event
ON PEN Statement	Branches to routine on defined PEN event
ON PLAY Statement	Branches to routine when there are less than a specified number of notes in the background queue
ON STRIG Statement	Branches to routine on defined STRIG event

ON TIMER Statement	Branches to routine on defined TIMER event
ON UEVENT Statement	Defines event handler for user-defined event
PEN Statement	Controls trapping of defined PEN events
PLAY Statement	Controls trapping of defined PLAY events
RESUME Statement	Resumes program execution after error handling
SetUEvent Routine	Sets entry point for user-defined event
STRIG Statement	Controls trapping of defined STRIG events
TIMER Statement	Controls trapping of defined TIMER events
UEVENT Statement	Controls trapping of user-defined events

For more information regarding these error- and event-handling features, you are referred to the *Microsoft Visual Basic Reference* book and to Visual Basic's on-line help features.

Run-Time Error Codes

Visual Basic can provide status information on nearly 100 run-time errors—errors that occur while an application is running. You can test for, detect, and respond to these errors by using combinations of the Visual Basic **ERR, ERROR, ERROR$,** and **ON ERROR** statements and functions. For more information regarding run-time error codes and messages, refer to the *Microsoft Visual Basic Reference* book and to Visual Basic's on-line help features.

Summary

In this chapter, you have examined a few of the key Visual Basic error handling keywords, statements, and functions. You have seen how these code elements can be combined to create error handling routines. The routines you looked at sought to detect, identify, and fix problems that might otherwise have caused the Shapes application to stop running.

For more information regarding the design and development of error handling routines, look at Chapter 9, "Error Handling," in the *Microsoft*

Visual Basic Programming book. This chapter covers various strategies and techniques for inserting error handling code into your applications.

You have nearly completed your hands-on exploration of Visual Basic for MS-DOS. The following final chapter, Chapter 12, "Where Do You Go From Here?," outlines some steps you can take to continue exploring Visual Basic, and discusses some of Visual Basic's more advanced features and capabilities.

12 Where Do You Go From Here?

You are now ready to start designing and building your own Visual Basic applications. In this book you have learned to use most of the key Visual Basic tools and features. Your next step is to use what you have learned to continue to explore Visual Basic and to build interesting and useful applications.

Concepts and Terminolgy

Alarm Clock application	(276)
Address File application	(277)
Checkers application	(278)
Visual Basic Standard Edition	(280)
Visual Basic Professional Edition	(280)
custom controls	(281)
overlays	(281)
mixed-language programing	(281)
ISAM	(282)
Visual Basic toolkits	(282)
Presentation graphics toolkit	(282)
Financial toolkit	(283)
Matrix mathematics toolkit	(283)
Custom Help tools	(283)
Custom setup tools	(283)
code optimization	(283)
The Microsoft Profiler	(283)
Code View	(284)

In the first part of this final chapter, you will be shown the forms for a few simple applications that you can build. Creating these applications will reinforce your Visual Basic design and programming skills. In addition to these simple applications, you will find a list of other projects you may want to try to develop. Finally, you may now have your own set of ideas and projects to pursue.

The last part of this chapter provides you with an overview of Visual Basic professional-level tools and features. Visual Basic is available in two editions: *standard* and *professional*. The Standard Edition provides you with all of the design and programming tools you need to build operational, personal applications. The Professional Edition provides additional tools for the professional programmer who wants to build and distribute applications.

Try These Applications

You have already designed and built several applications as you made your way through this book. In all of these previous activities, you were given detailed specifications for each application, as well as the code required to make the application work. In the three proposed applications that follow, you will only be shown images of the forms to be developed. Your challenge is to build the proposed applications using just the descriptions provided, as well as the images of the forms and controls.

Build an Alarm Clock

Figure 12-1 shows the form and controls for an application that simulates a user-controlled alarm clock. The completed alarm clock might be used as part of a larger application where users are required to react to events that occur when the alarm sounds.

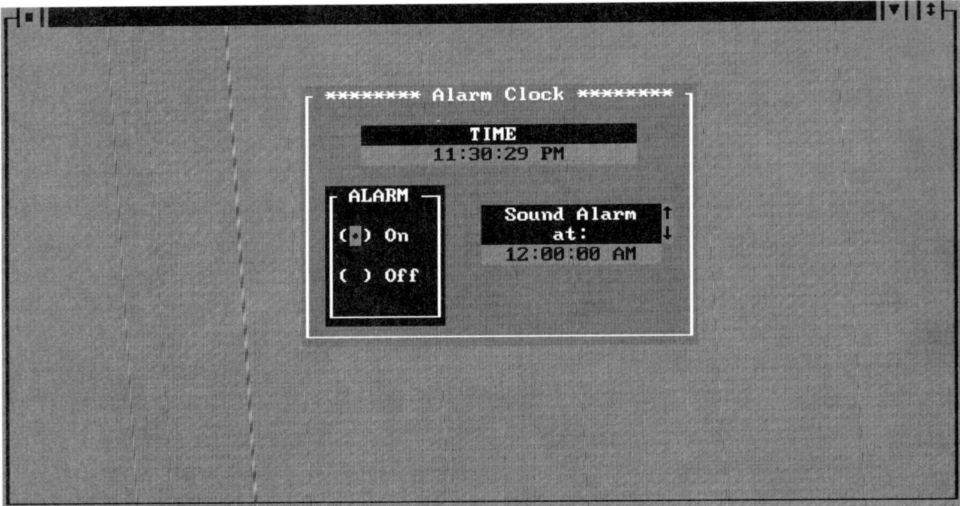

Figure 12-1 The Alarm Clock application.

The Alarm Clock application displays the current time in the text box at the top of the form. This text box carries the label `TIME`. On the left side of the form, there are two option buttons in the section labeled `ALARM`. These buttons let the user turn the alarm **On** and **Off.**

The user sets the time the alarm will sound in the text box on the right side of the form. The text box is below the `Sound Alarm at:` label. The user can either enter an alarm time into the text box directly or can use the vertical scroll bar to set the time for the alarm. For this application, when the current time equals the time set to sound the alarm (and the **On** option button has been selected), the application sounds an alarm and flashes the current time text box.

Based on the image of the form and controls shown in Figure 12-1 and the preceding description, design and build the proposed Alarm Clock application on your own.

Build an Address File Application

Nearly everyone keeps a list of names, addresses, and telephone numbers of people that they know. You can easily build a Visual Basic application that lets you create, edit, and retrieve information stored in an address file. Figure 12-2 shows the preliminary form and controls for an Address File application.

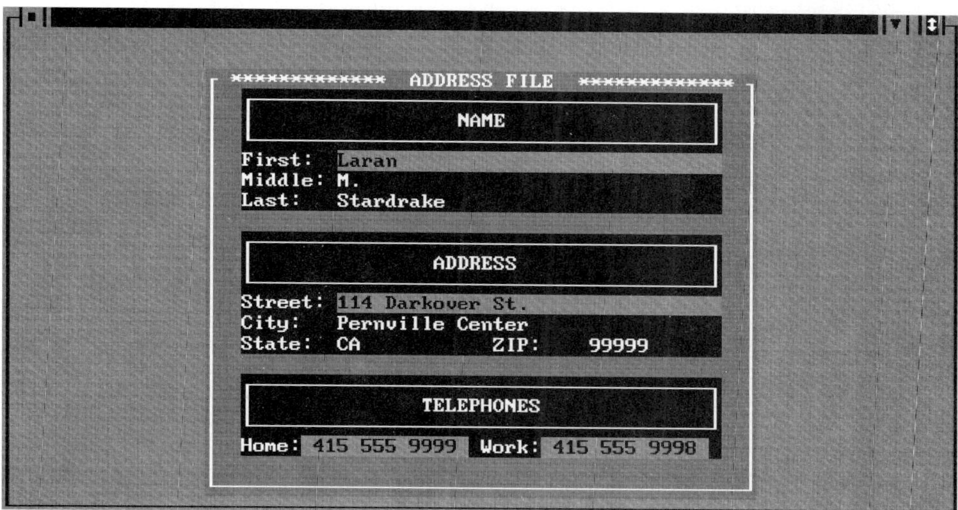

Figure 12-2 The Address File application.

This application has three main data display areas on the form: **NAME, ADDRESS,** and **TELEPHONES.** Each display area consists of sets of labels and text box controls. The labels identify the data fields on the form. The text boxes serve as both display and text editing regions on the form. The form, as shown, displays a single record of data for one individual.

Look over the form and its set of controls. How will you go about creating the application? Will you create each control in the Form Designer explicitly? Or will you create some of the controls during the **Load** event, by using control arrays and Visual Basic code to locate the controls on the form? Either approach will work. You decide which way works best for you.

Is the form and application complete? Will a user need other controls to help him or her browse through a complete set of address file entries, create new records, and edit existing data?

What about adding other fields, such as the name and address of the company each person works for, their fax number, and their electronic mail (e-mail) addresses? A modern address file would be incomplete without these additional fields.

You decide what other controls and fields you want this application to support. As you design and build the application, add those items to the form and develop the required event procedures to implement the functions you want the application to perform.

Build a Checkers Application

What about a fun application? How about a game? Figure 12-3 shows the rough layout and design for a checkerboard and a Checkers application.

Figure 12-3 The Checkers application.

How will you go about creating the checkerboard and the checkers for this application? In this case, you will probably want to use control arrays. If you do use control arrays, you will only need to create one checkerboard location (picture box) and one checker (text box). You can then use Visual Basic code to create the other control objects, position those objects on the screen, and set the objects to an appropriate color.

The actual screen colors for the objects shown in Figure 12-3 are as follows:

- Checkerboard frame (blue).
- Checkerboard locations (alternating red and black).
- Checkers (one set light blue, the other set white).

A much bigger question involves how much code you plan to write for this application. You can generate and display the board and the checkers by writing only a small amount of code.

You will have to write a bit more code to actually let two users play a game of checkers. If the controls that you use for the board locations and the checkers are control arrays, your code can still be relatively compact and efficient. Any code you create to let users actually play checkers will have to deal with what happens when "kings" get created and are moved around the board.

You may want to add a few menu controls to the application that let users start a new game and exit the application. Of course, if you are ambitious, you could add menu controls that let them save a game, backtrack through previous moves, and point out possible jumps. The ultimate challenge might involve writing code where you can play against the computer. Warning: to create such code is not a trivial coding task. This last statement is particularly true if you want the computer to play well.

Other Visual Basic Applications

Nearly every calculation task can be thought of as a possible candidate for a Visual Basic application. Tasks you currently perform that involve computations, the manipulation of data, and the presentation of results might be easier to do and might produce more effective results as a Visual Basic module.

Here is a list of home, school, and business tasks and activities that could be developed into Visual Basic applications:

Home	School	Business
Personal finances	Keeping grades	Accounting
Inventories	Attendance records	Project tracking
Address files	Learning games	Financial analysis
Automobile records	Learning aids	Reports
Health records	Experiments	Models
Reminders	Information systems	Prototypes

This list is by no means exhaustive. Try adding your own items to the list. Perhaps you keep records of your sports activities, such as golf scores or jogging statistics. Maybe you need to track your telephone conversations at work, including the time you talked with a client along with notes regarding the communication. How can Visual Basic help you with these tasks? What types of applications would you build to help in these situations?

Visual Basic Professional Features

The Standard Edition of Visual Basic contains the tools and features that you used in this book to develop your first applications. The Standard Edition provides you with sufficient design and programming tools to build functional, personal applications. The Professional Edition of Visual Basic provides additional tools for the person who wants to build and distribute full-featured programs.

When compared with the Standard Edition, Visual Basic's Professional Edition offers the following extensions:

- Greater speed for specific code generation tasks and calculations.
- Development tools that let you specify and build custom controls.
- An overlay system that lets you create large-sized applications (up to 16 megabytes).
- Mixed-language programming features.
- An integrated high-speed database system, ISAM (Indexed Sequential Access Method).
- Toolkits for handling presentation graphics, financial calculations, matrix mathematics, and customizing an application's help and installation features.
- A facility that allows you to insert your own custom run-time routines into the Basic run-time module.
- A tool that helps you optimize the code in your applications.
- A debugging tool to help you isolate bugs in mixed-language applications.

The remainder of this chapter provides an overview of these Professional Edition tools and features. For more information on how to use these items, refer to the *Microsoft Visual Basic Professional Features* manual that accompanies the Professional Edition.

Custom Controls

Visual Basic Professional Edition allows you to build and install custom-control objects that you specify and create. Once installed, custom controls appear in the Toolbox and on the Tools menu in the Form Designer. While in the Form Designer, custom controls look like picture boxes and can be moved and resized like other controls.

You can write event procedures for a custom-control object, as well as access and set its properties at run-time. The code you install as part of the custom-control description will determine what the control looks like when you run an application that uses the control.

For custom controls, Visual Basic Professional Edition lets you access a specific set of methods where you define the code for each method as part of the custom-control description. Custom controls can detect and respond to most standard events, plus a set of special Visual Basic custom-control events.

To the user of an application, your custom controls look and behave like any of the standard controls. The custom code you use to create the controls and to direct a control's actions appears to be part of the Visual Basic system.

Overlays

If you ever build an application that is too large for your computer's memory, you will need to use Visual Basic's Professional Edition overlay feature. An overlay is a set of form and code modules that you group together and that only gets loaded into memory when needed. Otherwise, the overlay resides on disk.

Visual Basic provides several linking and compiling tools that help you specify, build, and manage overlays. Using Visual Basic's overlay feature, you can build and run programs that use as much as 16 megabytes of memory.

Mixed-language Programming

In many commercial products, developers often use two or more languages as they build different parts of the product. For example, the user interface might be coded using Visual Basic, custom data-handling routines might be coded in the C language, and communication modules might be coded in assembly language.

No matter how you mix and match languages in your applications, Visual Basic Professional Edition supports the use of mixed-language programming. The only major requirements are that you must follow Visual Basic's mixed-language conventions regarding naming and calling procedures and the passing of parameters.

ISAM

Visual Basic Professional Edition includes a complete set of statements and functions to support the Indexed Sequential Access Method (ISAM) database system. ISAM automatically handles a variety of database processing tasks, including such items as indexing operations (controlling the order of presentation of the data), moving and positioning data, seek operations, exchanging data, and transaction processing.

ISAM can be used with large databases. The ISAM approach lets you use and manipulate large databases that would normally be too big to handle in the computer's limited memory. ISAM preprogrammed routines and operations save you the effort of having to write your own database routines, and ISAM has been optimized to be both fast and efficient.

If you plan to build Visual Basic applications that involve large ISAM-style databases, you will find that an investment in the Visual Basic Professional Edition will be worthwhile.

Toolkits

In Chapter 9, "Using Data Files," you examined the Visual Basic Common Dialog toolkit. In the Professional Edition, you will find five additional toolkits to help you speed up your development of applications. These additional toolkits and a description of how they work follows.

Toolkit	Description
Presentation Graphics	A complete set of tools to help you create and display charts and graphs from your Visual Basic applications. This toolkit lets you transform data into pie charts, bar charts, line graphs, and scatter diagrams.

Toolkit	Description
Financial	A library of functions that will help you perform standard financial calculations, such as depreciation, present and future value, principal and interest payments, internal rate of return, and number of payments.
Matrix Mathematics	A set of six functions that can be used to perform matrix calculations. Most of these functions operate on five types of data: integer, single-precision floating point, currency, long integers, and double-precision floating point numbers. The six matrix calculations that can be performed on these data types are addition, subtraction, multiplication, determinant evaluation, multiplicative inverse, and solution of linear equations.
Custom Help	When you build an application, you can create and install a custom help system that looks and operates like the one you use in Visual Basic. Your custom help displays can include "hot" items that branch to other parts of the help system. Visual Basic includes a specific set of tools and run-time modules to help you create and install your own help files in your applications.
Custom Setup	When you installed Visual Basic on your computer, you used a setup program that came with the system. The Professional Edition provides a toolkit that lets you build custom setup programs so that users can easily install your applications on their computers.

Code Optimization

The Professional Edition of Visual Basic provides a program, called The Microsoft Profiler, that analyzes the run-time characteristics of your applications. The statistics produced by the profiler program can be used to identify the parts of your application that might work better if they were optimized in some way. For example, the profiler might identify old blocks of unused code that can be removed from the application.

The profiler lets you analyze your code in several different ways, and helps you decode the results by displaying summary reports. The profiler can even output results that can be read and displayed in other programs, such as Microsoft Excel.

CodeView

When you develop mixed-language applications (applications that use two or more languages for different parts of the program), you may encounter bugs that become difficult to isolate. The Professional Edition contains a copy of the Microsoft CodeView debugging tool to help with this problem. CodeView lets you step through the code in your applications, including mixed-language modules and display instructions as they are executed. CodeView lets you open up multiple windows that can show code in different parts of an application, and the program lets you print the contents of these windows to your printer.

Summary

This chapter concludes your initial tour through the Visual Basic for MS-DOS programming system. You were encouraged at the beginning of this chapter to go ahead and start building your own Visual Basic applications. You can either choose one of the suggested projects or can create a project of your own. No matter which route you take, keep experimenting with Visual Basic. Continue to learn more about how it works and how you might use it to help you at home, at school, or in the office.

If you get to the stage where you are developing an application you plan to distribute and support, consider obtaining the Professional Edition of Visual Basic. As discussed in this chapter, the Professional Edition contains tools and features that can help you with larger-scale development tasks.

We trust that you have enjoyed your preliminary exploration of Visual Basic for MS-DOS—one of the more exciting new types of languages that will influence how we all use computers in the future.

Appendices

A Visual Basic for MS-DOS/Windows

Visual Basic for MS-DOS, Visual Basic for Windows, QuickBasic, QBasic and Basic Compiler 7 form the Microsoft family of Basic programming languages. Many Visual Basic for MS-DOS users may have existing QBasic, QuickBasic, or Basic Compiler 7 applications that they would like to convert to Visual Basic for MS-DOS. Some users may have Visual Basic for Windows programs that they want to convert to Visual Basic for MS-DOS. Others may want to write Visual Basic for MS-DOS programs that can be converted to Visual Basic for Windows. In any of these situations, consult Appendices E through I of the *Microsoft Visual Basic for MS-DOS Programmer's Guide* which contain a compatibility summary, and methods for converting programs and building portable applications.

This appendix discusses compatibility and incompatibility between the Standard Edition of Visual Basic for MS-DOS and Visual Basic for Windows. Of primary concern is the ability to write Visual Basic for MS-DOS programs so that they can be ported (moved) to Visual Basic for Windows.

Compatibility will be high if the Visual Basic for MS-DOS application contains only keywords, objects, properties, events, and methods recognized by both languages. For more detailed information, see Appendix E, *Microsoft Visual Basic for MS-DOS Programmer's Guide*. Also look at the Visual Basic for MS-DOS file, COMPAT.TXT.

Keywords

There are some Visual Basic for MS-DOS keywords that cannot be used in a Visual Basic for Windows program. These keywords should be avoided whenever possible when you are writing a Visual Basic for MS-DOS program, if you want to port the program to Visual Basic for Windows. There are usually ways to modify an application containing these keywords so that the application will port and run under Visual Basic for Windows. If your Visual Basic for MS-DOS program does contain some incompatibilities, you may also wish to port the program to Visual Basic for Windows first, and then modify the program in that environment.

The following tables contain lists of Visual Basic for MS-DOS keywords that are only partially compatible, or that are incompatible, with Visual Basic for Windows.

Partially Compatible Keywords

CALL (Basic procedure)
CALL (Non-Basic)
CONST
DECLARE (Non-basic)
DEFtype
DIM
EXIT
HIDE method
INPUT #
LEN
MKDIR
ON ERROR
OPEN (File I/O)
PRINTER object
REDIM
RETURN
SCREEN object
STATIC statement
TAB
TIMER statements
TYPE

Incompatible Keywords

ABSOLUTE routine BLOAD
BSAVE
CALLS (Non-Basic)
CDECL (in DECLARE statement)
CHAIN
CIRCLE statement
CLEAR statement
CLS statement
COLOR COM
COMMON
CSRLN
CVI, CVL, CVS, CVD, CVC
CVSMBF, CVDMBF
DATA
DECLARE (Basic procedures)
DEF FN
DEF SEG
DRAW
$DYNAMIC metacommand
EQV
ERDEV, ERDEV$
EVENT
FIELD
FILES
$FORM metacommand
FRE
GET (graphics)
$INCLUDE metacommand
INKEY$
INP
INPUT
INTERRUPT routine
INTERRUPTX routine
IOCTL
IOCTL$
KEY (assignments)
KEY (event trap)

Incompatible Keywords

LINE statement LINE INPUT
LIST
LOCATE
LPOS
LPRINT, LPRINT USING
LSET
MKI$, MKL$, MKS$, MKD$, MKC$
MKSMBF$, MKDBMF$
ON event statements
OPEN COM
OUT
PAINT statement
PALETTE, PALETTE USING
PCOPY
PEEK
PEN function
PEN statement
PLAY function
PLAY (event trap)
PLAY (music)
PMAP
POINT function
POKE
POS
PRESERVE (in REDIM statement)
PRESET
PRINT statement
PRINT USING
PSET statement
PUT (graphics)
READ
RESTORE
RUN statement
SADD
SCREEN function
SCREEN statement
SEG (in CALL, DECLARE statements)
SETMEM
SHARED statement
SHELL statement
SLEEP statement
SOUND statement
SSEG
SSEGADD
STACK function
STACK statement
$STATIC metacommand
STICK
STRIG function
STRIG statements
STRINGADDRESS routine
STRINGASSIGN routine
STRINGLENGTH routine
STRINGRELEASE routine
SWAP
SYSTEM
TRON/TROFF
UEVENT
USING
VARPTR$
VARPTR, VARSEG
VIEW (graphics)
VIEW PRINT
WAIT
WIDTH statement
WINDOW
WRITE statement

Objects

Most objects used in Visual Basic for MS-DOS are also available in Visual Basic for Windows. The following table contains a list of Visual Basic for MS-DOS objects that are only partially compatible with Visual Basic for Windows.

Partially Compatible Objects
CLIPBOARD special object
Directory List Box
Form
Picture Box
PRINTER special object
SCREEN special object

Properties

Many properties used in Visual Basic for MS-DOS are compatible with Visual Basic for Windows. The following table contains a list of Visual Basic for MS-DOS properties that are incompatible or only partially compatible with Visual Basic for Windows.

Partially Compatible Properties	Incompatible Properties
BackColor, Forecolor	Attached
Border Style	Columns
CurrentX, CurrentY	Control Panel()
Height, Width, Left, Top	FormType
Min	PrintTarget
Mouse Pointer	
ScaleHeight, ScaleWidth	
SelLength, SelStart, SelText, Tag, Text	

Events

Most events used in Visual Basic for MS-DOS are compatible with Visual Basic for Windows. The following table contains a list of Visual Basic for MS-DOS events that are only partially compatible with Visual Basic for Windows.

Partially Compatible Events
KeyDown
KeyUp
MouseDown
MouseMove
MouseUp

Methods

Most methods used in Visual Basic for MS-DOS are compatible with Visual Basic for Windows. The following table contains a list of Visual Basic for MS-DOS methods that are only partially compatible with Visual Basic for Windows.

Partially Compatible Methods
HIDE
PSET
SHOW

Hints for Building Portable Applications

This section contains hints for creating Visual Basic for MS-DOS applications that are portable to Visual Basic for Windows. For more detailed information see Appendix I, *Microsoft Visual Basic for MS-DOS Programmer's Guide.*

- Create your application in Visual Basic for MS-DOS then use the TRNSLATE.EXE file to port the application to Visual Basic for Windows.
- Restrict code as much as possible to language elements common to both languages.
- Put all executable code in procedures. Visual Basic for Windows allows no executable code at the module level.
- Visual Basic for Windows does not recognize variables differentiated only by type-declaration characters (such as A%, A!, A$). Use unique

variable names and use the AS data type clause with your variable descriptions.

- Visual Basic for MS-DOS allows only standard ASCII characters (codes less than 128) while Visual Basic for Windows allows the extended ANSI set — use only standard ASCII characters.

- Visual Basic for Windows does not allow the dot character in variable names. Use the dot character only when referring to object properties and elements of user-defined types.

- Global variables (including arrays) are declared differently in the two languages.

- Visual Basic for MS-DOS allows variables that are recognized at the module level; Visual Basic for Windows does not — do not use such module level variables.

- Visual Basic for MS-DOS allows DEFtype statements at either the module or procedure level. Visual Basic for Windows only allows such statements at the module level.

- Differences exist in the insertion of DECLARE statements. Visual Basic for Windows uses a Global Module for declarations. For portability, remove all DECLARE statements inserted at the beginning of each Visual Basic for MS-DOS module and place them in an INCLUDE file.

- Graphics are allowed only on forms in Visual Basic for Windows. Graphics cannot be displayed on a form in Visual Basic for MS-DOS. Put your Visual Basic for MS-DOS graphics in a code module.

- When forms are converted from Visual Basic for MS-DOS to Visual Basic for Windows, the size and spatial relationships of controls change. Make adjustments after the conversion.

- Differences exist in the BorderStyle property. If you need Minimize/Maximize buttons and a control box, use only BorderStyle 1 or 2. Otherwise, use BorderStyle 0 through 3 since Visual Basic for Windows only supports these four property settings.

- Visual Basic for Windows allows only form-based user input and output. Use a forms-based approach for your Visual Basic for MS-DOS application.

- File and Device I/O are virtually identical, but avoid using the PrintTarget property of Visual Basic for MS-DOS. It is not supported by Visual Basic for Windows.
- External procedures written in languages other than Basic contain major differences in the way they are created and used by the Visual Basic languages. Refer to the mixed-language discussions found in *Microsoft Visual Basic for MS-DOS Professional Features* manual for more details.

B Visual Basic for MS-DOS Keywords

This appendix contains the Visual Basic for MS-DOS keywords that are used in this book. Each keyword that has been used is listed, followed by the chapters in which it appears.

Keyword	Chapters
$FORM	6,7,8,9
$INCLUDE	9
ADDITEM	8
AS	3,4,9
AutoReDraw	5
BEEP	2,5
CASE	8,11
CHR$	2,5,6,7,9,10
CIRCLE	8
CLOSE	9
CLS	3,4,5
COMMON	3,4
CONST	3,4,6,7,8,9
DATA	3,4,6,7,8,9
DECLARE	4,8
DEFINT	3,4,6,7,8,9
DIM	3,7,8
ELSE	4,7,8,11
END IF	4,7,8
END	2,3,5,8,11
END SELECT	8,11
END SUB	2,3,4,5,6,7,8,9,10,11
ERR	11
EXIT SUB	8,11
FOR-NEXT	3,4,6,7,8,9,11
FORMAT$	8,11
GOTO	8,11
IF-THEN	3,4,7,8,11
INPUT	9
INPUT #	9
INT	5
INTEGER	3,4
HIDE	3,7,8
LEFT$	6,7
LEN	7,8,9,11
LINE	8
LOAD	6,7,9
LOCAL	11
LOCATE	8
LSET	6,7
LTRIM$	6,7,9
MID$	6,7,8,11
MOVE	5,6,7,9
MSGBOX	2,5
ON ERROR	8,11
ON LOCAL ERROR	8,11
OPEN	9
PAINT	8
PRINT	5,6,7,8,9,11
RANDOMIZE	5,8
READ	3,4,6,7,8

Keyword	Chapters
REDIM	4,7
REM	3,4,5,6,7,8,9,10,11
RESTORE	7,8
RESUME	8,11
RESUME NEXT	8,11
RIGHT$	6,7
RND	5,8
SCREEN	3,4,5,7,8,11
SELECT CASE	8,11
SETFOCUS	3,5,6,7
SHARED	3,4
SHOW	6,7,8
SLEEP	8
SOUND	2,8
SPACE$	6,7,8,9
SQR	5
STR$	5,6,7,9,10
SUB	2,3,4,5,6,7,8,9,10,11
UNLOAD	6,7,8
VAL	5,7,8,9,10,11
WIDTH	8,11

C Visual Basic for MS-DOS Event Procedures

This appendix contains a list of Visual Basic for MS-DOS event procedures that are used in this book. The event procedures are listed by the chapter in the order in which they were created and used. A brief description of each procedure is given.

CHAPTER 2: BEEPER Application

Command1_Click	Beeps the speaker.
Command2_Click	Ends the program.
Command1_Click (Altered)	Beeps the speaker and displays message box.

CHAPTER 3: FLASHCARD Application

Form-Level Code	Makes declarations and supplies data.
Form_Load	Sets up the screen, loads data into array, and controls visibility of command buttons.
Command1_Click	Clears text boxes, sets contents of first text box, and selects visible button.
Command2_Click	Removes form from screen and ends program.
Command3_Click	Sets contents of second text box, selects visible button, increments index, and checks for end of data.

CHAPTER 4: FLASHCARD Application (Altered)

Form-Level Code (altered)	Second data set added.
Form_Load (altered)	Adds code to read second data set.
Command1_Click (altered)	Adds code to determine which of two data sets is used.
Command3_Click (altered)	Adds code to select one of two data sets.
Check1_Click (new)	Resets program and data set.
Check2_Click (new)	Resets program and data set.

CHAPTER 5: CALC Application

Form_Load	Clears screen and sets attributes.
Command1_Click	Converts text to number, squares the number, converts result to text, and displays it.
Command2_Click	Converts text to number, takes the square root of the number, converts result to text, and displays it.
Command3_Click	Clears text boxes and sets focus to input text box.
Command4_Click	Hides the form and ends program.

CHAPTER 5: CATCH ME Application

Form_Load	Seeds random number generator, sets picture box position, activates. **AutoReDraw** property of picture box, and inserts text in picture box.
Form_MouseMove	Moves picture box to random location and activates when it detects user moving mouse.
Picture1_Click	Beeps speaker and displays message.
Picture1_MouseDown	Moves picture box to random location and reacts to mouse down event.

**CHAPTER 6:
PERIODIC TABLE Application**

Form-Level	Contains data.
Form_Load	Reads data, creates picture box controls, displays chemical data.
Picture1_Click	Shows data for selected chemical (name, symbol, and atomic number).
Command1_Click	Unloads data form.

**CHAPTER 7:
PERIODIC TABLE Application (altered)**

Label1_Click (new)	Checks if lanthanides are visible and hides or shows lanthanides.
Label2_Click (new)	Checks if actinides are visible and hides or shows actinides.

Form_Load (altered)	Adds captions to lanthanides and actinides.
Picture1_Click (altered)	Sets focus for new command buttons.
Form-Level Code	New data added for detailed description of selected chemicals.
Command2_Click	Code to display detailed information of selected chemicals.
Command1_Click	Code for **Cancel** button on DataWind form.

Chapter 8: MUSIC Application

Form-Level	Contains frequency data.
Command1_Click	Dimensions array, reads frequencies, displays the name of the selected note, and sounds the note.
Command2_Click	Hides the form and ends the program.

CHAPTER 8: SHAPES Application

Form-Level Code	Declares external SUBs and constants.
Form_Load	Calls subprogram that determines screen modes available, sets scroll bar limits, and initializes text box.
txtNumShapes_KeyDown	Traps **up arrow** and **down arrow** keys to increase or decrease number of shapes, and checks for out-of-range error.
vsbNumShapes_Change	Updates text box (triggered by **txtNum Shapes_KeyDown**).
cmdDrawShape_Click	Hides the form, calls the external routine to draw shapes, and waits for a keypress; then resets screen and restores form.
cmdExit_Click	Unloads shapes.

Chapter 8: SHAPEDRAW.BAS (External Module)

Form-Level code	Declares $FORM shapes and constants.
VidConfig (SUB)	Contains code to determine best video mode for user's system.
DrawShapes (SUB)	Contains code to draw shapes.

CHAPTER 9:
PERIODIC TABLE Application (Altered)
First Altered Program

PERIODIC.TXT (external file)	Holds data for modified PERIODIC TABLE program.
Form-Level Code	**$INCLUDE** metacommand replaces **DATA** statements.

Second Altered Program

PERIDATA.TXT (External file)	Data table to be read by new program.
Form_Load	Modified to OPEN PERIDATA.TXT file and INPUT chemical data, then close the file.

CHAPTER 9: FILE TEST Application

Drive1_Change	Updates Dir1 object's **Path** property when a new drive is selected with the Drive1 object.
Dir1_Change	Updates the File1 object's **Path** property when a new directory is selected with the Dir1 object or when Dir1 gets updated by a change in Drive1.

CHAPTER 10: MENUCALC Application
(CALC Application modified)

mnuSquare_Click	This name replaces **Command1_Click** of the original CALC Program.
mnuSqRoot_Click	This name replaces **Command2_Click** of the original CALC Program.
mnuClear_Click	This name replaces **Command3_Click** of the original CALC Program.
mnuExit_Click	This name replaces {IBCommand4_Click of the original CALC Program.

CHAPTER 11: VidConfig Subroutine

VidConfig (SUB)	Error handling to determine best screen mode available on current system (see Chapter 8).

Index

Visual Basic® for MS-DOS® CONVENIENCE DISK

In order to save you time and trouble you can order this disk which includes:

- All the *project files* described in this book.
- Variations of *projects* described in the book.
- Additional *projects* not described in the book.
- A README.DOC file that contains a listing of all the project files on the disk and information about contacting the authors for questions, comments and criticisms of *Visual Basic for MS-DOS*.
- An ORDER.DOC file which contains a list of products available from K & T and how to order them.
- A GO.EXE program which provides a nice interface for reading the README.DOC and ORDER.DOC files as well as printing them on your printer.

Disk sizes and prices are as follows:

5¼″ DS/DD	$9.00
3½″ DS/DD	$9.00

These prices include shipping and handling. Disks are shipped first class postpaid. Please allow approximately 1 week for delivery. Send check or money order to:

K & T
P.O. Box 1635
Sebastopol, CA 95473-1635

California residents please add the applicable sales tax.

Disk format (circle one): 5¼″ 3½″

Name: ____

Address: ____

____

City: ______________________ State: ________ Zip: __________